£2-50

GW00382000

WOMEN'S WORKING LIVES
Patterns and strategies

SUSAN YEANDLE

Tavistock Publications
London and New York

First published in 1984 by
Tavistock Publications Ltd
11 New Fetter Lane, London EC4P 4EE

Published in the USA by
Tavistock Publications
in association with Methuen, Inc.
733 Third Avenue, New York, NY 10017

Typeset by Folio Photosetting, Bristol
Printed in Great Britain by
J. W. Arrowsmith (Bristol) Ltd

British Library Cataloguing in Publication Data
Yeandle, Susan
Women's working lives: patterns and strategies.
1. Women—Employment—Great Britain
I. Title
331.4'0941   HD6135

ISBN 0–422–78960–7

Library of Congress Cataloging in Publication Data
Yeandle, Susan.
Women's working lives.
Rev. and shortened version of author's thesis.
Bibliography: p.
Includes index.
1. Women–Employment–England–Kent.   2.Women–Employment.
I. Title.
HD6136.Z6K48 1984   331.4'09422'3   84–16250
ISBN 0–422–78960–7 (pbk.)

Table of contents

Introduction and acknowledgements

My intention in writing this book has been both to present the findings of my study of some employed women in Kent, and to make some theoretical observations about the nature of female labour in an advanced industrial society. In particular, I have tried to use the evidence from my small-scale, qualitative study to shed some light upon some of the questions surrounding the supply of female wage labour, and to investigate the relationship between the two principal forms of women's labour: domestic labour and wage labour.

The kind of study which I could undertake was restricted by the limited resources available to me as a graduate student, and by the need to produce data which could be written up as a doctoral thesis. This book is a revised and shortened version of that thesis, and some of the methodological detail which is of interest only to specialist readers has been excluded.

The book begins with two chapters which set the scene for the presentation of the study's findings. In the first, I make some observations based on historical evidence about women's labour in the past, and introduce some of the theoretical issues which are discussed throughout the book. The second chapter contains a brief critical account of existing analyses of female labour, both empirical and theoretical, and a discussion of the methods used in collecting my own data.

The third, fourth, and fifth chapters are all devoted to detailed presentation of the research findings and to discussion of the issues raised by the data. They contain information about the patterns of the women's 'employment careers', and about the strategies for employment adopted by the women interviewed. These strategies are discussed as aspects both of the social arrangements surrounding employment and the labour market, and of the social relations of household work.

One of the principal advantages of qualitative research methods is that the subjects of the research can be seen as rounded individuals rather than as numbers in boxes. In conducting the research, it has been impossible for me to forget that the women who participated in the study are real people with real feelings, aspirations, difficulties, relationships, and personal histories. I hope that readers can share some of this awareness of the women I have talked with. It is not feasible, of course, to introduce detailed background information about each of the sixty-four women in the book. I have therefore chosen to conclude each of the three detailed empirical chapters with a 'coda': an account of one woman's working life. These stories will both illustrate some of the points made in the chapter, and serve as a reminder that each of the women in the study had her individual characteristics, some of which she shared with, and others of which distinguished her from, each of the other women.

Two objectives are pursued in the final chapter, which opens with a discussion of the material presented in the three individual portraits. First, using material from the previous chapters, I consider the inter-relationship of the structures of capitalism and patriarchy, and its impact on women's labour. The implications of recent changes in economic conditions are subsequently drawn out, and in a final section I debate the implications of the study for social policy.

My thanks to all the women interviewed, whose patience and co-operation made the study possible, and to those trade unionists, managers, and others who helped me to find them. I am grateful to the Social Science Research Council (which financed my post-graduate studies) and to the University of Kent at Canterbury where I was a graduate student between 1979 and 1982. I am especially indebted to Mary Evans, without whose advice and support this book could not have been written, and to Simon Perryman, who read the manuscripts and endured interminable conversations about the research. I should also like to thank Veronica Beechey for her helpful comments on an earlier version. Those shortcomings which remain are, of course, my own.

Durham, February 1984

1 Observations from the history of women's labour

In this opening chapter, I want to draw attention to certain historical features of women's labour in Britain, and to point to their significance for the study of women in Kent which follows. There is now a substantial, albeit incomplete, literature on the work which women have done since pre-industrial times, and this provides an important context for my study of the patterns of women's labour and of the social arrangements which surround their employment and family lives. In making these observations I shall confine my discussion to a number of key points which seem to me especially salient, and will not attempt to present an overview of the historical literature on the subject. I shall then go on to outline a number of theoretical issues on which the study sheds some light and which are referred to, using data from the interviews, in subsequent chapters of the book.

DOMESTIC LABOUR AND ECONOMIC DEPENDENCE

The first point I wish to emphasize is that, within the family, women have continued to be economically dependent upon men, and have consistently been assigned the principal tasks of domestic labour.[1] These social arrangements have been buttressed by an ideology of family life which has maintained women's subordinate position within the family household, and has permitted their participation in the public sphere, including the wage labour market, only on certain, unequal terms.

A reading of the literature on women's labour in the pre-industrial period reveals that the lives of many women at this time were characterized by hard physical work (notably in agriculture and household production), and that what earnings they obtained were often essential for household survival, particularly in those cases where insufficient land was owned to supply the household's needs. It is clear from contemporary accounts, artistic representations, and historical records that most of the tasks of domestic labour (and in particular the preparation of food and the care of infants) were assigned to women, although frequently women also had other important responsibilities — in textile production, farm work, and in the craft trades. These latter tasks, however, were mostly undertaken in or around the household, and it was not until industrialization and the emergence of factory employment on a large scale that this unifying feature of women's work began to disappear. Then a sharp division developed between women's domestic work in the family household and their waged work away from home. This change in social arrangements has been noted by Rowbotham (1973), who explains that factory labour undermined the unity of the family as a productive unit, and altered the basis of the social relations between family members. For although some factory owners at first recruited whole families to work as teams for a single wage, this form of employment was short-lived and never widespread, and individual wage labour soon became the norm.

The textile factories were at first the most important source of industrial employment for women, and in the mid-nineteenth century women and children represented approximately three-quarters of the labour force in textiles.[2] Within these factories, however, there was a marked sexual division of labour and sharp irregularity in rates of pay (Baines 1970; Pinchbeck 1981). Women's labour was also widely used in other trades: in nail and pin factories, for example; in the potteries; in the clothing and footwear trades; and in the commercial and service sectors of the economy which grew up and expanded as industrialization progressed.

Throughout the whole range of women's employment, two important features remained constant. Tasks were almost always allocated on the basis of gender, and men's wages were consistently and significantly higher than those paid to women. The details of these historical sexual divisions have been documented elsewhere by writers on employment and industrialization (e.g. Alexander 1976; Baines 1970; Collet 1902; Pinchbeck 1981), and need not be repeated here. What is significant, however, is that the lower wages paid for female labour rendered most women incapable of supporting themselves and their children. This ensured their at least partial dependence on men to provide for them, although the significance of their wages for maintaining and raising household standards of living should not be underestimated. Their confinement to 'women's' trades and occupations both denied women access to male rates of pay, and played a significant part in reinforcing gender roles and in restricting women's expectations and ambitions.

Alongside these forms of employment, the other important area of paid work for women was as domestic servants, where the tasks women performed for wages mirrored those which other women performed unpaid at home. There was an established tradition of domestic service: it was 'the typical form of female employment outside of agriculture before industrialization' (Tilly and Scott 1978:68). Other, mostly married, women could frequently earn meagre wages charring and laundering, especially in the cities. This latter work was the exclusive preserve of women, and while a minority of domestic servants were male, their tasks were not interchangeable with those of women and girls. Higher status and wages accompanied men's domestic work, which included butling, valeting, and (later) chauffeuring.[3]

WOMEN'S PARTICIPATION IN THE WAGE LABOUR FORCE

As I have already suggested, women's participation in the wage labour force has been subject to wide variation, both regionally and over time, and this is the second point which I wish to stress. In the literature much attention has been paid to the growth in the employment of married women in the post 1945 period, but it is also important to note other significant changes in the way female labour is and was employed, such as changes related to major occupational shifts in the formal labour market, the use made of women workers in time of war, and the rise and decline of private domestic employment. These historical developments were all important in shaping the labour market in which the women studied here have participated, on and off, for two decades.

Major occupational shifts

The structural changes in the labour market which occurred during the initial period of industrialization had important effects upon the lives of working women. Gradually, opportunities for labouring in agriculture declined while new industries and occupations emerged. The regional distribution of the new industries yielded wide variations in employment opportunities for women. In the textile districts of Lancashire and Yorkshire, for example, there was widespread demand for female labour in the factories, and this touched married women as well as single girls. In the emerging great cities, on the other hand, there was a whole range of new occupations for women — in retail, garment and shoe manufacture, in domestic service and in other service work such as laundering — and in many of these cases women were employed in small workshops or in private households (see, for example, Alexander (1976) who describes the evidence relating to nineteenth-century London). Other regions, of course, had their own dominant forms of employment, and this meant that at any one time women in different parts of the country were engaged upon many different tasks. But this diversity in women's experience should not be allowed to mask the impact of those major occupational shifts which have changed the overall character of the labour market in the past century or so. As already indicated, agriculture declined over many decades and became far less important as a source of employment for women in Britain. As this change took place domestic service grew in its significance as an outlet for female labour, and this was especially so in the latter half of the nineteenth century. During the present century, however, domestic employment became increasingly unpopular, especially after the First World War, and after 1945 not only the supply but also the demand for such labour declined sharply. Throughout the early period of industrialization, the expanding textile industry provided large numbers of women with paid work in mills and factories, but, because of competition from abroad and changes in the manufacturing process, by the early twentieth century, this industry was also to decline and to employ a decreasing proportion of the female labour force. Alongside the changes brought about by production technology, changes in the administration of business, trade, and public services were to have very important consequences for women, and some of these are outlined below in a brief discussion of the service sector of the economy. It is sufficient for present purposes to emphasize that the feminization of clerical work gradually led to the extensive employment of female workers in banking, insurance, business and government administration. Further, the emergence of the welfare state after 1945 led to a very significant expansion of employment opportunities for women in public health, education and social services. The similarities between women's domestic labour and the tasks involved in these latter occupations have been noted by many observers.

Domestic employment

Throughout the nineteenth century, large numbers of women and girls were engaged as domestic servants in the homes of families better off than their own. As the century progressed their numbers increased, rising from some 670,000 in 1831 (Thompson 1968) to almost three times this figure at the outbreak of the First World War (Braybon 1981). Young girls were sent into service by their parents because places were plentiful — 'The expanding middle-class populations of cities created more demand for household servants' (Tilly and Scott 1978:108) — because their families were unable to support them until marriage, and, very frequently, because their wages were needed to supplement the family income (Thompson 1973:156-65). While they remained in domestic service, women were usually required to 'live in' and to remain unmarried. This stipulation contributed to a tendency towards late marriage among servants. However, at the end of the century the extension of formal education and changes in the demand for domestic servants meant that fewer young girls and more older women were being recruited. Gradually, living in became less common and during the last two decades of the century the number of servants under 15 years old fell by 34 per cent while the number aged between 25 and 44 rose by 33 per cent (Tilly and Scott 1978). This shift did not reduce overall numbers however, and the domestic labour force continued to expand despite the growing unpopularity of this type of work. As is well known, the First World War diverted many female domestic servants into alternative employment in support of the war effort, but after its end, and in the face of acute employment difficulties, steps were taken to halt the shift away from this type of work.

> 'Between the wars ... governments ... pursued a policy of what amounted to compulsory domestic service for women. Unemployed women who refused this work when it was offered them at Labour Exchanges had their unemployment benefit stopped. The result was that domestic service accounted for nearly a quarter of all women at work in Britain, and remained the largest single occupation for women.'
>
> (Lewenhak 1980:207)

By this time, however, domestic service had become one of the least attractive employment possibilities for many women, and when the Second World War again diverted large numbers of women into war production it served only to accelerate an already established trend. After 1945 labour shortages and an expanding economy ensured that there would be no wholesale return to this form of employment for women, and large households of living-in servants rapidly became a thing of the past. Nevertheless, women continued to find paid work in cleaning, cooking, childcare, laundering, and waiting at table. Increasingly this work took place outside of private homes — in offices, restaurants, public houses, laundries, hospitals, and schools — although 'charring' and childminding have both remained tasks performed within private houses, the latter of course most often in the home of the worker, not the employer.

War-time employment

During the First World War, very large numbers of women workers were brought into occupations from which they had previously been excluded; in particular, women's labour was required in the engineering and munitions industries, especially between 1915 and 1917. Braybon (1981) demonstrates that many women came to these (better paid) jobs from domestic service and the garment-making trades, but also records that many married women (whose place as employed workers had been seriously questioned in public debate in the preceding decades) were drawn into the labour force. Indeed, the government encouraged the setting up of nurseries with the aim of bringing mothers of young children into war production (Boston 1980).

Although many women were brought into types of work which were new to them during the war, at its end those whose labour had been diverted from other occupations found that they were no longer required. The expectation (on the part of the government and the men's unions) appears to have been that women would return to their previous working lives — a belief which took no account of women's newly acquired skills, their changed personal and family circumstances (e.g. many women were widowed during the war), and the fact that often the jobs which they had held before the war had been taken over by others. It was, however, a belief which was supported by the prevailing ideology concerning both family life and the sexual division of labour. The lack of planning for women's needs in this changed situation led to extensive female unemployment in the post-war period until women's labour was redirected back into domestic service and into the new, expanding clerical occupations.

Two decades later, female labour was again needed for war production in the Second World War. Women were once more drawn into the engineering industry and into munitions production, and they were used to replace male workers in the civil service and in agriculture. In 1941, conscription was introduced for single women in their twenties. Thus for a second time women were required in time of war to labour in ways which were not socially acceptable, and which were officially discouraged in peacetime.

It is important to recognize that the effect of the Second World War on women's employment was largely short-term and specific to the war economy. As other writers have observed, 'Postwar changes in patterns of women's employment stemmed largely from changes in economy, demography, and family already under way by 1939. The war may have hastened the impact of these changes, but it did not cause them' (Tilly and Scott 1978:215). Thus domestic service as a form of female employment was becoming increasingly unpopular before 1939, and its rapid decline after 1945 should not surprise us. The feminization of clerical work in the early twentieth century has already been noted, and while the more extensive use of female labour in the civil service during the war undoubtedly left its mark, the trend had already been set in motion.

Post 1945: married women's employment

The post-war period was to see very significant and rapid developments in women's employment. As the 1950s and 1960s progressed, not only were almost all single women in employment, so too were increasing numbers of married women. Most of the demand for female labour now came from the rapidly developing service sector, but there were also new opportunities for women in manufacturing industry and in electrical engineering. Some employers even began to introduce special conditions of work, such as flexi-time, part-time work, and 'mum's shifts' (to fit in with school hours) to attract married women's labour. By 1951, 43 per cent of employed women were married, and this figure was to continue rising in the succeeding decades.

The 1960s and 1970s were the years during which the women who took part in the present study were moving in and out of the labour force.[4] These decades saw a marked increase in the participation rates of married women, from 29.7 per cent in 1961 to 49.7 per cent in 1979, many of these women being employed on a part-time basis. The most dramatic increase in participation rates occurred amongst women aged 25 to 44 years old (33.1 per cent in 1961 to 58.8 per cent in 1979) and those aged 45 to 59 (32.6 per cent in 1961 to 60.9 per cent in 1979).[5] It appears that in the boom years of the 1960s and early 1970s an increasing proportion of married women returned to or sought paid work in the years following childrearing and that many of these women, usually in their mid-thirties, then continued in employment until retirement. There was a marked tendency for women who were mothers of dependent children to take part-time jobs, working 30 or fewer hours each week (Department of Employment 1973-80). Much of the increase in part-time employment was attributable to the expansion of the service sector and to the concentration of women within it: approximately four-fifths of part-time women workers were employed in this sector (Mallier and Rosser 1979).

During the post-war period, women have continued to be disproportionately represented in certain occupations and industrial sectors. The trends during this time have been towards increased feminization of the clerical occupations and of selling, and towards a greater concentration of women workers in the unskilled and semi-skilled manual occupations. Thus while there have been changes in the occupational distribution of women workers, these have taken place within a continuing sex segregation of the workforce (more attention is given to this point below).

Just as segregation of occupations has persisted, so have disproportionate rates of pay for women. Comparison of hourly rates of pay for male and female manual workers, for example, reveals that between 1948 and 1968 women in manual jobs were consistently paid at much lower rates than their male counterparts: women's average hourly earnings were approximately 60 per cent of men's throughout this period (Department of Employment and Productivity 1971). Some improvement in women's pay took place during the 1970s, following the 1970 Equal Pay Act which came into force in 1975, and by 1977 women's earnings were approximately 75 per cent of men's (Equal Opportunities Commission 1981a). There has been some subsequent deterioration, however, revealing the long-term ineffectiveness of the legislation.

OCCUPATIONAL SEGREGATION

The third point which I wish to stress is that an understanding of the nature and characteristics of female labour must be informed by an awareness of the sharp and persistent segregation of most occupations along the gender divide. Historically, it has been rare for a sex 'label' not to be attached to any given job by both workers and employers, and this has remained substantially true despite some significant changes in which label is attached to which jobs, some important changes in the occupational composition of the labour force, and, most recently, legislative changes intended to remove sexual barriers to employment.

Before industrialization the tasks performed by all but the youngest children were clearly differentiated by sex, and young girls were taught the domestic, agricultural, and other skills considered appropriate for them by their mothers or, when working away from their parents, their mistresses (Tilly and Scott 1978). As the country industrialized, this sexual division of tasks spread into the new workplaces and occupations. Detailed information reveals, for example, highly differentiated tasks within the textile trade, and that these tasks were allocated to workers according to both sex and age. Thus in a mid-nineteenth-century Yorkshire woollen factory, Baines (1970) found women employed as power-loom weavers, knotters and burlers, warpers, and as a wool weigher; men employed as overlookers, beamers, wool sorters, slubbers, and mule spinners; and children as billey piecers, fillers, and mule piecers. Indeed, a marked sexual division of labour prevailed throughout the eighteenth and nineteenth centuries in almost all areas of paid work. Industrial production, domestic service, agricultural work, trade and commerce — all had their 'women's' and 'men's' jobs which were rarely, if ever, undertaken by persons of the other sex.

Hakim (1979) has made a detailed study of trends in occupational segregation during the twentieth century, and has been able to demonstrate the extent to which women are, and have been, employed in predominantly female occupations. She found that between 1901 and 1971 occupations exclusive to one sex mostly disappeared, but that at the later date 'over half of all men were still in occupations where they outnumbered women by at least nine to one... [and] half of all working women were still in jobs where they were greatly overrepresented (at 70 per cent or more of the workforce)' (Hakim 1970:23). The author makes a useful distinction between 'horizontal' occupational segregation (where divisions are between different types of occupation, e.g. nursing and coalmining) and 'vertical' occupational segregation (where divisions are between grades of the same occupation, e.g. civil service clerical assistants and principals). She is able to show that while horizontal segregation declined between 1901 and 1971, vertical segregation increased, with the overall result that 'occupational concentration and occupational segregation have remained relatively unchanged in Britain over seven decades' (Hakim 1979:34).

Despite this overall situation, however, some occupations have witnessed important changes in the sex composition of their labour forces. Clerical work provides the most striking example, changing from an almost exclusively male area of work in the nineteenth century to a predominantly female one in the post-war period. A similar though less marked change also took place in the selling occupations. However, other changes have occurred too: for example, during the past two decades, women have ceased to be the majority of those appointed as both primary school head teachers and as children's officers (Mackie and Pattullo 1977). Looking at major occupational groups, Bain and Price (1972) found that while the proportion of manual workers who were women changed little between 1911 and 1971, nevertheless women lost ground in skilled jobs and were much more likely to be in those classed as unskilled at the later date.

Political pressure in the post-war period, and especially in the 1960s, resulted in new legislation which redefined the position of women in employment. This legislation made provision for some employed women to take maternity leave (Employment Protection Act 1975), laid down women's right to claim equal pay for equal work (Equal Pay Act 1970), and made it unlawful to discriminate against a job applicant or employee on the grounds of her (or his) sex, except in a very few specified occupations (Sex Discrimination Act 1975). Feminists, and others who fought for these legislative changes, hoped that they would open up wider opportunities for women and result in a significant improvement in women's position in the labour force. As others have demonstrated however (Rendel 1978; Snell 1979), although some important changes have taken place, women have not gained permanent entry into the main areas of male employment, except in fairly small numbers. This has been especially true of higher status occupations. In a recent article, Hakim has attempted to assess the precise impact of this legislation, and her analysis indicates a significant decline in occupational segregation in the immediate wake of the legal changes. She claims that between 1973 and 1977 change occurred almost four times as quickly as the evidence of the previous seven decades had led observers to expect, but notes that after 1977 'the situation was almost completely reversed' (Hakim 1981:526). In the face of this evidence her suggestion that 'the impact of the recession on job opportunities may have affected women's recent gains in the labour force' (Hakim 1981:529) certainly appears a plausible one.

SERVICE SECTOR EMPLOYMENT

The expansion of the service sector of the economy has been one of the most important developments in the structure of the formal labour market during the present century. Whilst it has been accompanied by, and is related to, other occupational shifts, it is of particular interest here because of its very significant impact on the labour of female workers, especially those large numbers of married women who have entered the paid labour force in the decades since the Second World War. Until relatively recently the major changes in women's participation in paid employment have taken place within the framework of a substantially unchanging sexual division of labour. The question of how effectively develop- ments in the decades since 1945 have challenged this situation is raised in the discussion at the end of this chapter and is a major focus of the empirical data in this book. I now want to consider briefly the nature of the occupational shifts within the service sector, and to look at how female labour has been affected by these changes.

While domestic service had long been a very important source of paid work for women (see above), during the late nineteenth and early twentieth centuries there was significant expansion of other sections of the service sector, especially retailing and commerce. Tilly and Scott (1978) present evidence concerning the increase in the number of shops and shopworkers over this period, and, together with other commentators, note that a more bureaucratic organization of all areas of employment required large numbers of workers in administration and distribution. As noted above, the feminization of clerical work is a striking feature of this period. An almost exclusively male occupation in the mid-nineteenth-century (less than 1 per cent of clerks were women in 1851), it was both to expand and to draw increasingly on female labour in the late Victorian period; by the end of the 1930s female clerical workers had begun to outnumber male. The expansion of employment opportunities for women with some education in teaching and nursing also began at this time. Between 1875 and 1914 women came to dominate elementary teaching, representing three- quarters of its workforce by the latter date. Nursing was slower to develop as a profession, but about 77,000 women were employed within its ranks by 1911.

The inter-war years saw a period of widespread and large-scale unemployment, and many women found opportunities for employ- ment restricted; as already indicated, some were forced to return to domestic service. Nevertheless, the 'new' occupations in the service sector — including retail, banking, public administration, and other forms of clerical work — continued to expand. Indeed, Rowbotham notes that 'the twenties saw the emergence of the office girl' (Rowbotham 1973:128). Women were now taking an increasing share of white-collar employment (29.8 per cent in 1911, 35.8 per cent in 1931) and by 1931 almost half of all clerical workers were female (Hakim 1979). Most of these workers were single, and indeed it was common for women to lose their positions on marriage (Rowbotham 1973).

The major trends in women's employment which were established in the inter-war period continued to be significant after 1945. By the 1960s women occupied almost half of all white-collar jobs, and within this category their share of clerical jobs rose from 46.0 per cent in 1931 to 69.3 per cent in 1966. The selling occupations were also progressively feminized during this time: women's share of sales jobs rose from 37.2 per cent in 1931 to 58.7 per cent in 1966.

The expansion of state bureaucracy and of public services has been a notable feature of the post-war years. This period has witnessed the establishment of the National Health Service (by 1979 the NHS had well over a million employees in Great Britain — measured as 984,000 'whole-time equivalents'[6] — approximately three-quarters of whom were women), the extension of compulsory education and very significant growth in further and higher education, and a large increase in central and local government employment (from around 8 per cent of the civilian labour force between the wars, to approximately 17 per cent in 1971 (Westergaard and Resler 1975). Indeed, the total numbers of those employed by central and local government and in publicly-administered education, welfare, and health grew dramatically right up until the end of the 1970s. Thus in the short period between 1977 and 1979 the number of women employed in the 'professional and scientific services' increased from just under 2 million to a little over 2.5 million.

The expanding service sector has been a particularly important source of part-time employment for women. As is well known, employment on this basis is especially attractive to women who have onerous family responsibilities — notably those with larger families or with young children. The rise of part-time employment was an important debating topic for the TUC women's conference in 1980, and a supplementary report on part-time women workers was presented to delegates. The report stated that in 1976:

'Over 80 per cent of these (part-time) women were employed in the service sector, that is: transport and communications; distributive trades; insurance, banking and finance, as well as professional, scientific, miscellaneous services (excluding private domestic services) and public administration (excluding HM Forces).'

(TUC 1980:32)

Others have made similar observations (e.g. Mallier and Rosser 1979), and, despite the inadequacies of data on part-time work, it is clear that the expansion of the service sector and the concentration of women in this area of the economy can account for much of the increase in part-time female employment in the post-war period. In addition, international comparisons demonstrate that the part-time employment of women has been more common in the United Kingdom than elsewhere in Western Europe. Manley and Sawbridge (1980) have made this point, showing that in 1977 41 per cent of employed women in the United Kingdom worked part-time, compared with 28 per cent in West Germany and the Netherlands, 18 per cent in France, and 12 per cent in Italy. The authors note that

> 'in the United Kingdom ... a clear and effective distinction has been drawn between part- and full-time work for the purposes of social security and employment legislation. . . . the climate for part-time employment has been a good deal more favourable in this country than in the others under review over much of the period.'
> (Manley and Sawbridge 1980:34-5)

I have indicated that historical accounts of women and their work enable us to draw certain important conclusions about the way female labour has been employed, and about what this has meant for women. To sum up, women have consistently been assigned the tasks of domestic labour, and despite significant variations in their partici- pation in the wage labour force, they have mostly been confined to 'women's' jobs offering relatively low pay, and little chance of individual economic independence. This historical legacy has shaped the experience of all women at work, including those who were the subject of this study. In the discussion below, which concludes this chapter, I introduce some of the themes which the study has sought to illuminate.

DISCUSSION

I have suggested above that industrial capitalism in Britain did not substantially transform the pre-existing sexual division of labour, but rather adapted itself to the arrangements which had become a standard feature of pre-industrial social organization. Essentially this means that the new relations which emerged as part of the industrial revolution were shaped by the nature of the existing division of labour, both within the home and between the sexes. Women's responsibility for the daily care of children, for the preparation of food, and for the performance of household tasks (albeit in conjunction with other forms of labour, such as agricultural work or the home production of textiles) was well established in the pre-industrial social structure. As other writers have shown (e.g. Clark 1920), the early capitalist development of the craft trades had already begun to deprive many craftsmen's wives of a chance to participate in their husband's trades. Unlike their menfolk, they were not free to leave home and children to work on another's premises. As more production took the form of wage labour, and came to involve working away from home in a factory, mine, or workshop, the existing sexual division of domestic labour made it inevitable that it would be women whose access to jobs in the labour market would be less secure. This was especially so as the continued exploitation of child labour became incompatible with the dominant ideology, and childhood emerged as an extended period of dependence (Aries 1962), involving longer periods of demanding domestic labour for women. However, as Barrett has pointed out, the separation of home and workplace under capitalism led to a gradual restriction of women's access to wage labour and their relative confinement to the home, *not* as a result of any biological imperatives associated with the care of children, but 'because the problem (of responsibility for childcare) was resolved according to an ideology of gender that pre-dated capitalism, in the interests of men' (Barrett 1980:165).

Historically, industrial capitalism has been characterized by a number of features which have been important in maintaining and reinforcing this sexual division of labour. Most significant among these are the struggles by (principally male) organized labour for the 'family wage', and direct and indirect intervention by the state, and it is to these aspects that I now wish to turn. I shall suggest that the relationship between the family wage and protective legislation is illustrative of the ideological accommodations which have characterized Britain's patriarchally-structured, industrial capitalist society. Both, in my view, were important in maintaining the pre-industrial sexual division of labour.

The idea of a 'family wage' — the idea that a man's wage should be adequate to support himself, his wife, and his children — 'was not a familiar one in the early decades of the nineteenth century' (Land 1980:56), and it is important to take note of this if we are to avoid making false assumptions about its relationship to capitalist relations of production. We know that in the early development of industrial capitalism, the labour of women (and children) was used extensively, above all in textiles. However, in the middle part of that century, following legislative steps to limit female and child labour (a matter to which I return below), male workers 'resisted the wholesale entrance of women and children into the labor force, and sought to exclude them from union membership and the labor force as well' (Hartmann 1981a:21). Others have noted that 'the relegation of women to the home cannot be explained solely with reference to the 'needs of capitalism' but was the object of struggle, and therefore choice of the working class' (Barrett and McIntosh 1980:53-4). The choice to which these writers refer lay between pushing women out of the labour market (as in fact happened 'with pressure from the bourgeoisie') and drawing women into the organized labour movement, so that male and female workers together might struggle more effectively against capitalist exploitation. That the latter option was not adopted can be explained only by reference to the dominance of patriarchal ideology, according to which a woman's place is in the home. In the event, the struggle for a family wage for men has been furthered by the adoption of restrictive practices, designed to exclude women from skilled employment and its relatively high pay, and by the continued sex structuring of the entire labour force whereby male and female labour is rarely interchangeable in a given occupation. It should be noted that the higher rates of pay for men which existed in the initial stages of industrial capitalism (and which had their origin in the family wage economy of pre-industrial times, when wages were not paid on an individual basis[7]) formed a kind of trap, in which the costs to married women of taking employment could often outweigh the benefits of the low wages which were all they could command.

State intervention has also played an important part in encouraging industrial capitalism to adapt to a pre-existing sexual division of labour. There are a number of ways in which the state has acted to shape the relations of capitalist production, including the passing and enforcing of protective legislation, and its actions in ensuring the restoration of the status quo ante following both world wars, with respect to employment practices.

In the mid-nineteenth-century legislation was introduced banning women from underground employment in mines. Whilst this step was progressive, in that it offered women protection from the appalling working conditions underground, it also acted to reinforce the sexual division of labour and played a part in structuring the labour force along the lines of gender. Shortly after the passing of the Mines Act in 1842, the 1844 Factory Act restricted women's working hours in the textile industry to a maximum of twelve per day, and banned women's night work. This legislation served to extend to women the protection embodied in the 1833 Factory Act, which had dealt only with the labour of children and young persons. Pinchbeck (1981) notes the significance of the 1844 Act, affirming that 'the principle of protection for women was [thus] definitely adopted'. Although the passing of the early protective legislation coincided with the emergence of organized trade unions, it was middle-class social reformers and not organized labour who were responsible for pushing the first Factory Acts into law. Men and women textile workers may have been the first to organize together: 'The textile unions became the pioneers of mixed unions . . . . Not only did they accept men and women into membership, they negotiated rates based on "the rate for the job" and not on a rate for "the sex of the worker doing the job" ' (Boston 1980:23). However, they only achieved wage-related gains through collective bargaining, and were not involved in promoting the early protective legislation. As Boston goes on to record, 'male trade unionists almost entirely washed their hands of the plight of women workers. It was the government which became the main body concerned with their protection.'

What motivated the state thus to intervene in the workings of *laissez-faire* capitalism? The protection of women workers from harsh conditions and long hours of employment is not self-evidently in the interests of the capitalist class. It has been suggested that the social reformers were concerned just as much with the 'possible effect of the working conditions upon women's behaviour and their social role' (Braybon 1981:20) as with the physical strain and danger to which all workers (not just women and children) were subject. Much was made by reformers of the alleged neglect of domestic responsibilities by working women, and of their inability to provide domestic comforts and services for their husbands. Thus the initial pressure for protective legislation regarding women formed part of an attempt to re-establish a sexual division of domestic labour which had been a feature of pre-industrial social organization and which was challenged by extensive use of female individual wage labour in the early factories and workshops.

In the later campaigns for legislation to ensure shorter working hours organized labour itself applied pressure and initiated campaigns. In the early 1870s, for example, the (mixed) textile unions formed a 'Factory Acts Reform Association' with the aim of securing a maximum working week of 54 hours. Cole notes that male trade unionists used the welfare of women and children as a weapon in this struggle:

> 'The trade unions . . . put forward their demand for shorter working hours for all workers in the industries concerned in the form of a demand for legislative protection for women and children. They knew well enough that, if women and children had their working day shortened by law, the men would share in the benefit, because most of the factories could not be kept open for the men alone.'

> (Cole 1948:221)

Thus, through its introduction of protective legislation, the state has played a part in various ways in structuring the labour force according to gender.

The state also performed an important role in re-establishing the sexual division of labour following both world wars. As indicated above, large numbers of women workers were called upon to labour in munitions factories and to undertake other work usually performed by men when male labour was required in the armed forces. For many women war work represented an opportunity to enter skilled jobs which would not otherwise have been open to them. However, in the First World War working conditions for women in factories were allowed to deteriorate out of line with the existing protective legislation: 'In many munitions factories, hours were long (often twelve hours, plus overtime) and conditions poor . . . . In addition, the Factory Acts were effectively put to one side, and women were employed on night work once more' (Braybon 1981:113). The government, employers, and trade unions alike were of the view that the war situation necessitated special arrangements, and a massive influx of women into factory work, but there was no systematic attempt to regulate developments, or to plan for the post-war period. Agreements were struck between employers and unions about rates of pay, the employment of women in skilled trades, and the need to restore work to the men on their return. Braybon documents these in detail, and indicates the extent of state intervention. The most interesting period for present purposes is the immediate post-war one, when men were de-mobilized and women factory workers dismissed in large numbers.

> 'There was talk of the state encouraging public works and con-tinuing to place contracts with engineering and munitions em-ployers after the war, in order to maintain employment, but in fact the government brought many war contracts to an end in 1918, regardless of the fact that women workers were laid off *en masse.*'
> (Braybon 1981:179)

She goes on to document the treatment of unemployed women workers, and the pressure placed upon them through agencies of the state to return to the traditional occupations such as domestic service. The state was able to apply such pressure because of its control over the availability of unemployment benefit, which was denied to women who had not been employed before 1914, or who refused any kind of work. 'Women were being pushed back towards the staple female trades of laundry and domestic service, where wages were poor and conditions bad, as even the Ministry of Labour admitted' (Braybon 1981:181).

By the Second World War some lessons had been learned from the experiences of twenty-five years before, and state intervention was more extensive. Under the 1941 National Service (No. 2) Act, all single women aged between 20 and 30 years were conscripted to serve in the armed forces, in auxiliary services, or in industry (Davies 1975). In 1942, following pressure from the trade unions, the Restoration of Pre-War Practices Act was passed. Its purpose was to ensure that 'practices abandoned by the unions would be restored if desired at the end of the war' (Pelling 1971:213-14). The main concern of the unions was to prevent the dilution of skilled labour from becoming a permanent arrangement, and to ensure that the men's skilled jobs would once more be available to them when the war ended. Boston notes that the Act 'guaranteed the enforcement of pre-war practices particularly in terms of job demarcation on sex grounds' (Boston 1980:219) and argues that it was important in ensuring that women returned to their homes or to unskilled work after the war. She reminds us that although it was faced with acute labour shortages in the post-war period, the government closed down nurseries, denied women equal pay and opportunities, and retained restrictive practices, thereby compounding the difficulties facing working women. She points out also that the 1945-50 Labour Government 'allotted an unequal place to women in the welfare state. The social security system was based on the concept of the family, with the male as breadwinner' (Boston 1980:220). Thus the actions of the British state surrounding the waging of the two major world wars ensured that the war-time sexual division of labour remained an aberration in social arrangements, and secured a rapid return to the status quo ante in the post-war periods.

The state is, and has been, an important employer of women, and this has given it further opportunities to influence the workings of the labour market. One illustration of the state's attitude towards its married women employees can be found in the history of the civil service. The marriage bar, applicable to all women in pensionable posts as civil servants until its removal in 1946, required the resignation of women civil servants on marriage, and served as a reminder to them and to others that in the eyes of the state the place of the married woman was not in paid employment, whatever her talents, but in her home, caring for her family and performing domestic labour. It is interesting to note Boston's evidence that following the removal of the bar, male members of the Civil Service Clerical Association proposed its restitution on a number of occasions throughout the 1950s, arguing that married women were occupying jobs needed by men and restricting men's opportunities for promotion.

Looking to the present, and indeed to the future, we may note that changed social conditions since the Second World War have offered a formidable challenge to pre-existing assumptions about the sexual division of labour. In the post 1945 period, women's lives have been substantially altered by the reduction in average family size (for which readily available and relatively reliable methods of birth control are responsible) and by the extension of employment in the clerical field and in other service occupations. It has become usual for women to take paid jobs both before and after marriage, and their education to secondary level has become an established feature of the social structure. In addition, material standards of living rose substantially throughout the 1950s and 1960s (although more recently in some sectors of the population these have begun to decline), raising individuals' material expectations and increasing the motivation for married women to seek employment, even where their husbands were in steady work. It has thus gradually become the norm for women both to have jobs for several years before raising a family, and to seek paid work outside the home after becoming mothers. The extension of female employment during the 1960s and 1970s has been extensively documented and commented upon (see Chapter 2). Above all, it is evident that women are expected to have paid jobs for an increasingly large part of their lives. Some women do not withdraw from the labour force at all, others spend perhaps five or ten years of their lives between 16 and 60 caring for children or other dependants. But this shift in patterns of female labour has not been accompanied by a corresponding shift in the sexual division of domestic labour. Women are still expected to take responsibility for the young, sick, and elderly in their families, and to perform the bulk of domestic chores. Their increased participation in the wage labour force has not been complemented by any significant and parallel shift towards male involvement in domestic labour. Further, women continue to earn only about two-thirds of men's wages — a situation which has hardly changed since the seventeenth century. How do such women cope? What arrangements do they make to accommodate the competing demands on their time and energy? What is the effect of these upon relationships within the home? Is there consensus within the household about how the tasks of domestic labour should be divided, or is this a matter which generates domestic conflict? These are some of the subjects which the present study has addressed. Empirical data about individual women's lives have been collected in order to consider some of these questions, and an attempt has been made to focus on the underlying theoretical issue of the relationship between capitalism and patriarchy as revealed by the concrete exercise of female labour.

2 The background to the study

The questions about women's labour which I raised at the end of the previous chapter have been the central concerns of my study of women's working lives. In this chapter I want to introduce the study, describing the research methods which have been employed, and suggesting ways in which it may have contributed to a fuller understanding of female labour. Before that, however, I present a brief review of the wide range of writings on women and work which have provided the framework for my own investigation.

THEMES IN THE LITERATURE ON WOMEN AND WORK

Writers on women and work since 1945 have concerned themselves with a large number of empirical, practical, and theoretical issues, which I want for present purposes to group under three headings. First, many writers in the 1950s and 1960s focused on rapidly rising female participation rates, and concerned themselves with women's social roles, and with the question of how the conflict or tension between the two principal roles of wife/mother and employee might be resolved. This literature is referred to here as 'two roles theory'. Others, especially those writing within the discipline of economics, developed what I have termed 'theories of the labour market'. They examined women's structural position in the labour market, and were able to document and offer explanations for their relative confinement to the low pay, insecurity and poor status of most 'women's work'. Finally, some writers attempted to unravel the specific nature of the relationship between female labour and capital. These 'theories of the sexual division of labour within capitalism' have been informed by the dual sources of Marxism and feminist theory, and have paid attention to women's unpaid domestic labour, as well as to their wage labour within market capitalism.

Two roles theory

'The technical and social developments of the last few decades have given women the opportunity to combine and to integrate their two interests in Home and Work... The best of both worlds has come within their grasp, if only they reach out for it.'
(Myrdal and Klein 1956:xii-xiii)

The work of Myrdal and Klein, and of the many others who adopted their 'two roles' perspective in writing about women workers, contained an implicit assumption that once the temporary phenomenon of 'tension' between the two 'feminine' roles could be resolved, the 'problem' of women and work would go away. As they put it, 'both feminine roles' might be fused into 'one harmonious whole'. The idea of a conflict between these two social roles also suggested that in attempting to combine them, women might fail to perform one or both successfully. A variety of social policy issues emerged and were debated in the literature. These concerned: the way in which mothers' employment might affect family life, and especially the relations both between mothers and their children (e.g. Yudkin and Holme 1963; Hoffman 1963), and between wives and their husbands (e.g. Young and Willmott 1973; Rapoport and Rapoport 1971); the relations between employers and their female workers, and the possibility that certain changes in employment practices might be appropriate; and the psychological effects of role-conflict on individual women.

Those who concerned themselves with identifying the particular difficulties which families and their members might experience when women took employment outside the home, mostly worked with an unspoken assumption that before opportunities for such employment arose, families were harmonious, functional units contributing to the stability of society.[1] It was felt that as women were presented with and took up employment opportunities, it became increasingly difficult for families to operate as before: the assumption of an additional role by women upset the domestic arrangements within the home. Researchers were keen to identify exactly how these domestic arrangements were disturbed, and to suggest to policy-makers ways of relieving the tensions in this situation. This meant looking into the welfare of children, the status and responsibilities of husbands, the relationship between spouses, and certain aspects of the domestic division of labour.

At a time when John Bowlby's work was influential, with its stress on the overwhelming importance of the mother-child relationship (*Maternal Care and Mental Health* was published in 1951, *Childcare and the Growth of Love* in 1953), it is not surprising that authors felt it disadvantageous for children to be away from the full-time care of their mothers before the age of 3 years: 'In *favourable circumstances* many children can do without their mothers' constant presence from about the age of three' (Yudkin and Holme 1963:123). Most writers, however, saw potential benefits for older children if their mothers had an 'interest' outside the home (i.e. employment). In the 1950s and 1960s the issue of 'working mothers' was a matter of heated public debate. Whilst contemporary discussions tend to be developed principally in the context of high rates of unemployment, in this earlier, quite different, context it was issues of juvenile delinquency, 'difficult' behaviour at school, etc., which assumed importance.[2] Most of the writers on women and employment, however, rejected the more extreme aspects of this argument, asserting, for example, that 'Some teachers are known to have observed that children of working mothers are intellectually more alert and socially more independent than others' (Myrdal and Klein 1956:134). Lois Hoffman was enthusiastic about part-time work for mothers 'because it interferes less with the mothering role'. She suggested that the employed mother provides 'a more positive role model for her daughter', and that employment may enable the 'mother of adolescents' to 'perform her maternal functions in a more wholesome manner' (Hoffman 1963:197).

Writers also considered the division of domestic labour and relationships between spouses. They noted that widespread ownership of labour-saving devices, a decline in the home preparation of certain foods, and smaller average family size had all gradually reduced time spent performing household tasks, but observed that, while some husbands were 'helping' more at home when their wives were employed, these tasks remained primarily a wife's responsibility (Blood 1963; Hedges and Barnett 1972; Vanek 1980; Young and Willmott 1973). Nevertheless, Young and Willmott argued on their evidence that there was a move towards greater 'symmetry' between the roles of the marital pair.

Adopting a slightly different approach, the Rapoports studied families in which 'both heads of household pursue careers and at the same time maintain a family life together' (Rapoport and Rapoport 1971:18). Putting forward policy recommendations in the second edition of their book, they pointed to the need for changes at four different levels — societal, institutional, interpersonal, and personal. Other studies of dual-career families emphasized the tensions which can arise within such families and how these tensions are managed or resolved (e.g. Poloma 1972; Epstein 1971). Lotte Bailyn, in a related piece of research, concluded that her data on 200 British women graduates and their husbands 'corroborates the hypothesis . . . that a husband's mode of integrating family and work in his own life is crucial for the success — at least in terms of marital satisfaction — of any attempt of his wife to include a career in her life' (Bailyn 1970:108).

The 'dual-career families' literature formed a strand within the whole 'two roles' approach. It was still based on empirical evidence, but, while useful within its own limitations, it did not look beyond its immediate perspective to examine the social and historical roots of women's subordination in the family and in society. Looking back, some of the predictions about new forms of the family seem premature and ill-founded: 'By the next century — with the pioneers of 1970 already at the head of the column — society will have moved . . . to . . . two demanding jobs for the wife and two for the husband. The symmetry will be complete' (Young and Willmott 1973:278). It is possible, with a decade's hindsight, to challenge such views and their emphasis on technological and ideological change on at least two counts: first, unemployment has been increasing in all industrialized countries, especially Britain; and second, there is little evidence to suggest that technological advances are likely to result in more rewarding and creative employment opportunities in any but a very few cases.

Writers also wanted to identify what motivated married women to take employment, what difficulties they experienced as employees, and what advantages and disadvantages their employment created for employers.[3] Viola Klein claimed that

'the taking up of employment by married women is not . . . part of the plans they make for the future, but is done under the impact of circumstances most of which were unforeseen . . . . Among these are economic stringency, preference of office or other paid work to household routine, desire to provide means for extra expenditure, loss of husband, interest in making use of earlier training, or the desire to escape from drudgery or loneliness.'
(Klein 1965:78)

Yudkin and Holme (1963) suggested similar complexity of motive, while Myrdal and Klein (1956) indicated that an increase in employment opportunities for married women had also been important: there was a 'wide range of suitable jobs' as well as more readily available 'back-up services'. There was also stress on women's increased 'leisure time', and on economic, social, and psychological motivations.

Investigating the impact of women's employment on the workplace, most writers identified employers as liable to receive less than the full commitment to employment responsibilities to which they felt they were entitled. Klein (1965) emphasized that employers could not be expected to bear the full burden of making the adjustments necessary to accommodate the special needs of married women workers. Myrdal and Klein (1956) believed it important to analyse resistance to employing women. They tried to introduce an historical perspective, but in emphasizing the separation of male labour from the family household and the 'man-made' nature of modern industrial organization, their analysis largely ignored the important part played by women in industrial production in the early stages of the industrial revolution. The authors made no mention of the gradual exclusion of women from much industrial employment by protective legislation and employers' and male trade unionists' requirements, or of the way they were frequently pushed back into the domestic sphere and dependence upon that new phenomenon, the male breadwinner responsible for the economic well-being of his entire family. This is especially interesting when one notes the convenient 'fit' between 'two roles' theory and the authors' version of history: an approach that prevented them from confronting some of the more challenging questions about the historical and social origins of women's position in post-war society.

In the literature, attention was also focused on 'employers' problems': absenteeism (among younger married women), high turnover of female labour, the productivity of women workers. Policy recommendations for dealing with these included labour market adjustments (part-time employment, training for re-entry to employment, maternity leave), personal adjustments (attitudes to and choice of work, maintaining skills, re-arranging domestic responsibilities), and social adjustments (nurseries, school meals, more appropriate housing and distribution of goods, etc.).

The attention paid to the needs and characteristics of individuals focused mainly upon women, but also touched upon the husbands of employed women. Myrdal and Klein discussed the three components of women's 'Career and Family' dilemma. On the first component, vocational choice, the authors recommend that 'young girls . . . should choose a career best suited to their interests and inclinations, and work on the assumption that they will have to live by it, for marriage is not a panacea' (Myrdal and Klein 1956:143).

A second aspect concerned whether or not it was possible for women to combine a career and marriage. The Rapoports also addressed this question, turning their attention to identity conflicts and to the educated, professional couple: 'for the men, domestic tasks were comfortable psychologically only if it was "help" for her. And for women, employment was comfortable psychologically only if it was temporary, secondary, non-essential' (Rapoport and Rapoport 1976:310). Thus the role-conflict which was seen by these authors as temporarily 'dysfunctional' for society both in the family and at work, was also seen as psychologically 'dysfunctional' for the individual. There was optimism, however, that once attitudes could be changed, women would be able to adopt the dual role with relative ease. The third aspect of the dilemma, 'the housewives' dilemma' concerned the financial dependence and low status which characterize housework. Myrdal and Klein addressed a theme which would be taken up and developed by later writers (Gavron 1968; Oakley 1974 a and b). They noted the social isolation, lack of intellectual stimulus, and economic dependence of the housewife role, and were scathing in their assessment of 'the sentimental cult of domestic virtues' (p.146-47). However they did not offer any analysis of how women's labour within the family acts as a crucial support for the entire economic structure of capitalism. Later, Gavron and Oakley each took up the theme of the 'captive wife'. Gavron (1968) interviewed samples of both working-class and middle-class mothers with the intention of assessing and analysing the 'conflicts of housebound mothers'. She found that such women were experiencing increasing social isolation 'in a way that previous generations may not have been', and was very much in sympathy with the 'two roles' approach. Her own view was that 'the "problem" of women represents a network of conflicting roles which interact with each other, thereby aggravating the situation' (Gavron 1968:145).

Ann Oakley has written extensively on the subject of housewives and housework, and has recently referred to the 'prison-house of home'. Recalling the findings of an earlier study, she noted 'the general sense of captivity' (Oakley 1981:175). Many other writers drew attention to the housewife's economic and financial dependence which results from the unpaid nature of her labour. They noted the paradox that, unpaid and isolated though it may be, housework does not offer women a genuine opportunity freely to organize their time. It may lack the formal regulation which characterizes much paid work, but 'The pressures of housework are . . . insidious: neighbours criticise and compare; grandmothers hand on standards; within you and without you is your mother's voice, criticising and directing' (Williams, Twort, and Bachelli

1972:32). Examination of the social bases of the conflict and dissatisfaction experienced by many housewives, by turning to the meanings which individual women attached to their feelings and behaviour, provided an important account of the subjective conditions of housewives' lives. But an adequate analysis of the objective circumstances which shape this aspect of women's labour was still lacking. This was to begin to emerge later in the 'domestic labour debate' (see below).

Of course some of the conclusions drawn by authors writing on the basis of studies from the 1950s and 1960s would be inappropriate in today's changed circumstances. As already suggested, the recent rise in unemployment and the higher economic activity rates of married women put the issue in a rather different light. Nevertheless, the 'two roles' approach prompted some important empirical research and provided a valuable descriptive survey of women's employment. Unfortunately its functionalist analysis and the absence of the necessary socio-historical foundation have meant that it is weak and sometimes misleading as an analytical framework. The analysis focused primarily upon 'problems' which the family and its members were experiencing as a result of married women's employment. Policies were sought to accommodate mothers' employment within existing family structures, and there was an assumption that those families which were being disturbed by this phenomenon would otherwise be harmonious units promoting the well-being of all their members. There was no adequate examination of structural inequalities within the family, and of the power relations between family members.

Theories of the labour market

Important contributions to the analysis of female labour have emerged from various attempts to uncover and explain women's position in the labour market. I wish to raise here two main areas of debate: that of the structure of the labour market, and the position of female labour within it; and that of the related issue of the segregation of (most) occupations by sex.

Concern with the ways in which labour markets are structured is not new. However, recent theoretical explanations have broken with an older tradition, in which the economic system was seen as reflecting structural inequalities external to it, by introducing the idea that structural features within the economic system can be responsible for creating segmented labour markets. Rubery (1980) has identified two sets of theories within this more recent tradition:

those which accord much significance to the effects of technological change, and those which focus primarily on the ways in which the changing needs of capitalists have promoted increasing segmentation of labour markets. For the sake of convenience, the former will be referred to as 'dual labour market theories' and the latter as 'radical economic theories', following Rubery and others.

Dual labour market theories recognize the existence of a primary and a secondary sector within the labour market. The primary sector is characterized by relatively high wages, job security, and opportunities for promotion. Often, the primary labour market operates as a firm's 'internal labour market', especially where firms devote substantial resources to the training of their workforce, and where skills have become 'firm-specific'. The secondary sector, by way of contrast, is characterized by low wages, insecure employment, and a dearth of opportunities for advancement. Female workers and workers belonging to ethnic and other minority groups are typically found in this secondary labour market. It has also been observed that 'the primary/secondary division cuts through manual and non-manual work — a phenomenon which is reflected in the extensive mobility of women workers between lower grade clerical and office jobs and the semi- and unskilled manual sector' (Barron and Norris 1976:51).

Technological change, interacting with the economic structure, acts as a pivot for this theory. Thus as technology develops workers require more sophisticated skills involving greater investment in training, and the worker's experience (often defined in terms of length of service) becomes increasingly valuable to the employer. This is then rewarded with higher pay, greater security, and other 'benefits'. Meanwhile the relatively dispensable secondary sector 'provides that degree of flexibility still required by the system' (Rubery 1980:246).

In seeking to suggest causes for the segmentation of labour markets,[4] Edwards (1979) allocates importance both to systems of control of labour processes, and to discrimination by sex and race, whether of a 'deliberate' or an 'institutionalized' nature. In introducing the notion of control of the labour process, he links the theories of dual labour market theorists with those of radical economic theorists. For the latter, issues of control by capitalists over their workforce outweigh in importance the impact of technological developments. Thus employers have sought to control an increasingly organized labour force by means of 'divide and rule', 'so that the actual experiences of workers would be different and the basis of their common opposition would be undermined' (Edwards, Reich, and Gordon 1975:xiii). Thus, in this account, employers' behaviour led to the formation of internal labour markets. The authors go on to note: 'Employers quite consciously exploited race, ethnic, and sex antagonisms in order to undercut unionism and break strikes' (p.xiv). Once formed, this dual labour market went on to 'interact' with racial and sex differences already in existence in such a way as to 'produce persistent objective difference along these dimensions' (p.xvi).

Rubery, however, has noted the functionalist nature of such an explanation: 'Labour market segmentation arose and is per-petuated because . . . it facilitates the operation of capitalist institutions' (Rubery 1980:239). For her, the most important missing element in the dual labour market and radical economic analyses is the role of organized labour in creating structured labour markets. She argues that organized labour aims 'to control the competition in the labour market that the capitalist system generates, and, further, adapts and restructures itself in response to developments in the economic structure' (Rubery 1980:266). Citing Braverman's work, she suggests that the claims made by dual labour market theorists for the role of technology in creating primary sector employment may be over-stated. Technological developments and changes in the organization of work under capitalism increasingly *reduce* the worker's control over the labour process through de-skilling (Braverman 1974), in contradiction to what is proposed by dual labour market theory where techno-logical developments *increase* skill levels among the primary workforce.

Introducing her argument about the role of worker organization in structuring the labour market, Rubery states:

> 'Expansion of trade union organization tends to extend primary-sector type employment, improving job security and wages. . . . It is possible that the expansion of trade union organization may increase the difficulties of developing organization for those still excluded . . . . The barriers to the extension of primary sector employment throughout the job structure may be strong, both for the reasons suggested by radical and dual labour market theorists, and because of the resilient barriers to mobility, or competition set up by trade union organization.'
>
> (Rubery 1980:267)

Following her analysis, then, explanations of women's position in the labour market require an understanding of low levels of unionization of, and male trade unionists' resistance to, female workers. This argument finds some support in the work of Hartmann (1979a). On the basis of historical evidence, Hartmann concludes that the experiences of female workers cannot adequately be explained solely in terms of the operations of capitalists' interests. In her view, male workers, particularly when in organized trade unions, have had an important effect:

> 'That male workers viewed the employment of women as a threat to their jobs is not surprising, given an economic system where competition among workers was characteristic. That women were paid lower wages exacerbated the threat. But why their response was to exclude women rather than to organize them is explained not by capitalism but by patriarchal relations between men and women.'
>
> (Hartmann 1979a:219)

As suggested in Chapter 1, men and women tend to be occupationally segregated, that is, concentrated in different types of work. Similarly, particular jobs are frequently thought of as 'men's jobs' or 'women's jobs', both by employers and by those in or seeking work. Many jobs can thus be said to be 'sex-labelled'. As a result, and despite legislation banning discrimination on the grounds of sex in the field of employment,[5] many individuals believe certain jobs are closed to them or would not be suitable for them because of their sex. A number of writers have attempted to document changes in patterns of occupational segregation, and to discover what the causes of and explanation for the phenomenon might be.

Oppenheimer (1970) locates her discussion of occupational segregation in the USA within the framework of a theory of structured and multiple labour markets, and argues that it is appropriate to speak of 'a demand for female labor'. Using statistical evidence, she demonstrates the extent to which women are concentrated in 'disproportionately female occupations', and identifies a range of factors which she believes have promoted the use of women in certain types of work. These include combinations of cheapness with other factors such as availability and skill, and tradition. Certain other characteristics, such as career-continuity, motivation, and geographical mobility, tend to make jobs male-labelled. Oppenheimer suggests ways in which these sex-labels on jobs affect both demand for and supply of labour, noting that in some cases 'the supply of one type of labor at one point in the history of the occupation affects the whole future course of the sex composition of that occupation' (Oppenheimer 1970:120).

Hakim (1978), writing on Britain, looked at the degree of change over time in occupational segregation. As noted in Chapter 1, she explains that segregation can be both vertical (men and women in different grades) and horizontal (men and women in different types of occupation). Her research shows that horizontal segregation has declined gradually during the twentieth century, though change has been slower than might have been expected. At the same time, vertical segregation has increased, and is observable in both white-collar and blue-collar occupations. Some of Hakim's observations contradicted what had come to be the received wisdom on the changes in women's position in society. For example, she records: 'women were more evenly represented among managers and administrators in 1911 than at any time since then' (Hakim 1978:1,267). Her distinction between horizontal and vertical occupational segregation enables us to perceive 'continuity within change': change in one type of segregation can cancel out change in another type. The distinction is helpful in revealing why legislation has been so ineffective in removing inequalities between male and female workers.

Chiplin and Sloane (1976) also note the prevalence of occupational segregation by sex and of lower wage rates for women. However, they stress the importance of 'underlying economic forces' and of the 'application of rational free choice by women' in their explanation of these phenomena. Although they advocate the elimination of what they call 'pure' discrimination, they are less sure that the removal of other forms of sex discrimination in the labour market can or should be achieved on the grounds of either efficiency or equity: 'an optimum distribution of labour may imply an unequal distribution of the sexes by occupation largely because of differences in labour force attachment' (Chiplin and Sloane 1976:140). They refer to women's reluctance to 'offer themselves' for some types of job, and although they base their arguments concerning the relationship between sex discrimination and sex inequality on the institution of the family and the division of labour within it (making particular reference to women's role in childbirth and the rearing of children), they offer no satisfactory explanation of this division of labour. Nor do they clearly spell out for whom a sexually unequal distribution of labour might be 'optimum'.

Zellner looked at the relationship between occupational segregation and sex discrimination, emphasizing that 'it is discrimination against women in "masculine" (male dominated) occupations that plays the central role in explaining... occupational segregation and [the] low relative wage' (Zellner 1972:157). Discrimination, she maintains, has the direct effect of lowering women's wages in male-dominated occupations (the demand for female labour is low), and the indirect effect of lowering women's wages in female-dominated occupations (because it increases the supply of women). She also differentiates between what she calls 'deliberate' discrimination, 'based on a subjective preference for males' and 'erroneous' discrimination, 'based on an underestimation of female capacities'. However, Zellner does not offer any convincing account of the causes and origins of the discrimination which she describes, although her description of its outcome in the form of occupational segregation seems to be a fruitful one.

Goldberg (1970), writing on the USA, focused on women's 'marginal' position in the labour force. In her analysis, ideological factors play an important role, and she stresses the effects of the way girls are socialized, linking these with women's willingness to take on part-time or temporary work. In her rather polemical discussion of the economic exploitation of women, Goldberg makes a link between these ideological factors and the requirements of capitalism, but nevertheless fails to provide a satisfactory explanation of their development.

Work on occupational segregation by sex has thus provided ample evidence to show that the phenomenon both exists and persists. Some writers have identified factors which promote such segregation, others have fruitfully made the distinction between horizontal and vertical segregation. However, there is little in the way of consensus on the origins of the phenomenon. Some (Oppenheimer 1970; Zellner 1972) attribute it to discrimination or the perceived characteristics of male and female workers; others emphasize the role of ideology (Goldberg 1970) or claim that, in some respects, occupational segregation by sex represents a rational free choice on the part of individual women workers (Chiplin and Sloane 1976).

Theories of the sexual division of labour within capitalism

In the preceding sections reference has been made to various inadequacies in the attempts to explain the specificity of female labour through the use of descriptive techniques, the application of functionalist social theory, and reference to labour market economics. The analyses of female labour discussed below attempt to overcome such shortcomings by a location of theory not in the labour market as a separate entity, but in the relationships, both between female labour and capital and between women and men. Marxist theory thus represents one starting point for those adopting this perspective, feminist theory the other.[6] Marx himself offered no systematic and thorough explanation of the relation between female labour and capital, and it is partly in an attempt to remedy this omission that various writers have drawn on feminist theory to formulate a Marxist-feminist analysis. Such work has implied a recognition of the usefulness of Marx's analysis of the struggle between labour and capital and of the material and historical basis of that struggle, and especially of the usefulness of Marx's method. It adds to the growing body of literature on female labour offering new answers, and indeed new questions, concerning the position of women workers. Most importantly however, a progressive Marxist-feminist analysis, as Hartmann (1979b) has pointed out, involves refuting the idea that feminist theory is in some sense 'subordinate' to Marxist theory. Hartmann argues that it is in understanding the interaction of capitalism with patriarchy that Marxist-feminist theory can offer a promising new analysis of women's position and of female labour, and overcome the theoretical difficulties which both Marxism and radical feminism encounter when they confront the issue of female labour separately.[7]

In Hartmann's view, patriarchy, which she defines as 'the hierarchical relation between men and women in which men are dominant and women are subordinate' (Hartmann 1976:138) pre-dates capitalism, but has become transferred into capitalist structures. Her argument, which returns us to certain issues raised above in the discussion of structured labour markets, is that 'the hierarchical domestic division of labour is perpetuated by the labour market, and vice versa' (Hartmann 1970:139). Job segregation by sex cannot be explained by ideological factors, like sexist attitudes towards women workers (as neo-classical economics would have it), nor by the lone power and activities of capitalists (as per vulgar Marxist theory). She does not deny the role of capitalists, and indeed refers to labour market segmentation theory to suggest that, historically, capitalists' actions have acted 'to exacerbate existing divisions among workers in order to further divide them' (Hartmann 1979a:228). However, she is unequivocal about the pervasive role of patriarchy in determining women's role in society (and thus in employment) in all stages of capitalist development, though on the question of male workers' opposition to much female employment she suggests 'the actions of capitalists may have been crucial in calling forth those responses from male workers' (Hartmann 1979a:229). The role of patriarchal social relations interacting with capitalist economic structures is thus crucial to her analysis. Occupational segregation by sex cannot be eliminated unless 'socially imposed gender differences . . . and . . . the very sexual division of labour itself' (Hartmann 1979a:232) are eradicated.

What kind of questions must an analysis of female labour under patriarchal capitalism[8] confront? Marxist-feminist writers have proposed a number of possible approaches. First, they argue that it is important to understand how patriarchal relations have shaped the kind of use capital can make of female labour. In what ways have patriarchal relations aided capital in exercising control over female wage labourers? How has the subordinate position of women affected the way labour-power is exchanged with capital? How has capital's control of the labour process been affected, in the case of female workers, by patriarchal relations, and further, is it only the patriarchal nature of capitalism which has enabled occupations to remain sharply sex-segregated, both vertically and horizontally? Second, given that patriarchal relations pre-date capitalism, how have such relations been adapted under capitalism? In what ways has the exercise of patriarchal power within the family been changed as modern capitalism has developed? In particular, what has been the effect of capital on women's domestic labour and the way it is exploited by men within the family? Crucial, too, is a grasp of the implications of the acknowledgement that capitalism is patriarchal. What, specifically, is the response women can be expected to make when they become fully conscious of the dual nature of their exploitation? As capitalism evokes in the working class a consciousness of and opposition to its exploitation (albeit beset with periodic reversals), will patriarchal capitalism similarly evoke increasing awareness of and resistance to both men's exploitation of women as women and capital's exploitation of women as wage workers?

Two themes in the developing Marxist-feminist literature can illustrate the explanatory potential and unresolved problems of this approach: the question of whether women constitute a reserve army of labour for capitalism, and, if so, why; and the issue of women's domestic labour under patriarchal capitalism, its role in reproducing society, and its relationship to female wage labour.

Thus we return to the two aspects of women's lives identified as crucial social roles by bourgeois social theorists such as Myrdal and Klein (1956) (women as employees/workers and women as wives/mothers). In substituting the terms 'female wage labour' and 'women's domestic labour' for Myrdal and Klein's 'work' and 'home' it is possible to focus analytically on the relations between female labour and capital, and on the sexual division of labour within the family household. These concerns, which are central to the present empirical study, can promote understanding of female labour and how it is exercised in ways which a focus on women's *roles* as mothers and employees cannot adequately achieve. The recognition that the two types of labour are frequently combined in the same individuals, and that each form of labour depends to some extent on the other for its existence, is also of central importance.

The concept of an industrial reserve army, of a reserve force of unemployed workers, originates with Marx, although its specific formulation in his theory has not always been strictly adhered to in subsequent analysis.[9] Women workers and other groups have been characterized by Marx and others as forming part of this 'reserve army', upon which capitalism can draw as and when it requires additional labour. Once the workers employed in this way become surplus to the requirements of capital, they can once again be expelled from the workforce and rejoin the ranks of the reserve army.

In the twentieth century, the two world wars provide the most striking examples of the use of female labour to cover labour shortages. In both cases, women were drawn into the labour force (or into different areas of it) to bolster production during wartime, and were expelled from it when their labour was no longer required. However, other less dramatic examples of such uses of female labour can be found. It is well known, for example, that companies respond to fluctuations in demand for their products or services by making use of female labour in this way. Some of the women whose experiences are described in the present study had been employed on this basis (see Chapter 4).

Braverman (1974) employs Marx's concept of a reserve army of labour in his discussion of the structure of the working class and how it is affected by changes in production technology. He notes that, in accordance with Marx's theory, there is a progressive tendency for labour to accumulate in those occupations where productivity can least easily be improved by technological or mechanical developments (since more and more labour is rendered unnecessary by such developments in those occupations where they are possible). As he points out, 'the purpose of machinery is not to increase but to decrease the number of workers attached to it' (Braverman 1974:384). Braverman notes that the post-1945 period was one of rapid capital accumulation, that supplementary sources of labour were required by capitalist production, in accordance with Marx's theory, and that women became 'the prime supplementary reservoir of labour'. He draws attention to the increase in the size of the female labour force, and the (much smaller) decrease in the size of the male labour force.[10] He also discusses the tendency for women to be concentrated in lower-paid jobs, and suggests that there has been a polarization of incomes 'among job-holders'. In particular, in the USA employment has increased in those sectors where below-average wages are paid. In these sectors, wages 'do not approach the income required to support a family at the levels of spending necessary in modern society' (Braverman 1974:395-96), and Braverman doubts whether multiple job-holding within households compensates adequately for this situation.

How have analysts of specifically female wage labour employed the concept of a reserve army of labour? Veronica Beechey has suggested that 'those categories of labour which are partially dependent upon sources of income other than the wage to meet some of the costs of the reproduction of labour power' (Beechey 1977:56) will form 'preferred sources' of the industrial reserve army. Married women form one such category of labour, and unlike other such groups, they 'have a world of their very own, the family, into which they can disappear when discarded from production' (Beechey 1977:57). Beechey has also suggested that because of their position within the family, married women 'constitute a specific form of industrial reserve army which is different from the forms described by Marx' (Beechey 1978:190). She examines the various ways in which women become flexible and disposable members of the labour force, noting the central importance of their family position, and the dominant ideological assumption that this represents women's primary role. Not only do women 'return to the family', but they are also 'horizontally mobile and willing to take on part-time work' (Beechey 1978:190). The possibility of such a return to 'invisibility' within the family depends upon the continuing existence of a patriarchally structured family. Beechey notes that the state 'refuses to recognise married women as individuals in their own right' (Beechey 1977:57).

Irene Bruegel adopts a slightly different approach to Marx's concept, and is concerned to identify 'whether or not women bear, to a disproportionate extent, the burden of unemployment in times of crisis, whether they are *more* "disposable" ' (Bruegel 1979:13). She identifies factors which would tend to make female labour more vulnerable. (Briefly, these include women's lower levels of skill, their tendency to work for small, less unionized firms, the lower mobility of married women, the practice of 'last in, first out', the current practice of 'freezing' employments, and ideology about 'a woman's place'.) Factors which might operate against this include the cheapness of female labour, and the sexual division of wage labour. On the basis of evidence from the period 1974-78 in Britain, when 'the official rate of unemployment amongst women increased more than three times as fast as that of men' (Bruegel 1970:15), Bruegel proposes a 'disposability model', with two forms. In the first, 'women's employment opportunities, taken as a whole, deteriorate relative to men's in times of recession', while in the second, 'any individual woman is more susceptible to redundancy and unemployment than a man in an equivalent situation would be' (Bruegel 1979:16). This has not always been especially evident, because women are distributed differently amongst occupations than men. Bruegel anticipates the end of 'the long-term shift towards women in the workforce', and predicts that 'the fight for jobs will increasingly be a fight for women's jobs' (Bruegel 1979:20).

The special vulnerability of female labour to redundancy and unemployment is thus partially but not fully explained by reference to Marxist theoretical categories. However, Barrett maintains that the concept of a reserve army 'cannot explain why it should be women who *necessarily* occupy a particular place in (wage labour)' (Barrett 1980:159). She rejects the radical feminist position which accords complete explanatory power to the concept of patriarchy, and urges 'a more precise and specific use of the concept'. She outlines the principal theoretical inadequacies of the 'reserve army thesis' as an explanation of the nature of female labour. In the first place, she argues, it provides no convincing analysis of women's lower rates of pay; and second, it does not account for occupational segregation by sex. Since both of these are important characteristics of female labour, the omissions are significant ones.

The 'reserve army thesis' then, is useful as a partial account of the relationship between capital and women workers, helping to explain how some women have been absorbed into and expelled from the paid labour force at certain historical points; but, as Barrett makes clear, the gender ideology which reinforces the sexual division of labour (and which is not incompatible with women's lower pay and with occupational segregation) 'cuts across' the reserve army thesis. This means that the analytical usefulness of the theory as applied to female labour in general is restricted: women workers do represent a 'pool' of labour upon which capital can draw, but only under certain conditions. The problems posed for the thesis by the nature of relations between men and women are illustrative of the contradictions and tensions within patriarchal capitalism. The present study of women's labour provides an opportunity to explore some of these tensions, and to move towards an understanding of their impact on the lives of individual women.

Turning to analyses of domestic labour, I want now to examine the ways in which Marxist analysis and feminist analysis have been employed in the debate about this subject,[11] and the extent to which it has been possible to unite them. As Gardiner, Himmelweit, and Mackintosh (1975) have noted, there is general agreement that 'women's role in the home is crucial to her subordination under capitalism' (sic). This role comprises women's part in reproduction and childrearing, their part in producing and maintaining the material requirements of their families (food, clothes, housing, etc.) and their role in reproducing the ideology of the family and social relations within capitalism (mainly through the socialization of children). In Marxist terminology, then, the concern is with women's role in the reproduction of labour-power and in the reproduction of relations of production.[12] Secombe (1974) has argued that the former of these two 'reproductions' is an economic function, while the latter is 'ideological in nature'. Marxist analysis has concentrated on the economic function and has attempted to ascertain precisely how women's domestic labour contributes to the generation of surplus value within capitalism.[13] The question of whether or not domestic work is 'productive' has been a crucial element in the development of the debate. Its usefulness for capital is not in dispute: clearly, capitalist production requires a permanent supply of workers (and thus women to bear children) who are competent adult members of society (women's role in the initial socialization of children is crucial to this) and who are also relatively healthy, well-nourished, and adequately clothed. However, the issue of whether domestic labour is productive in the specifically Marxist sense of producing surplus value for capital remains unresolved.

Marxist-feminists view the impasse which the debate reached in employing Marxist theoretical categories in isolation as a good illustration of the need to take feminist theory 'to the heart' of Marxist analysis. The concern with strictly economic aspects of modern society masked the important role of sexual politics and more general ideological factors in its constitution.

Barrett has noted this point, maintaining that

'A functionalist Marxist approach has tended to argue that men as men benefit only incidentally from domestic labour since it functions ultimately to keep down the value of labour-power and reproduce the class relations of capitalism . . . . Radical feminists . . . have tended to stress the way in which men benefit from the daily services of their wives for their personal gratification and have seen this in terms of patriarchy or male dominance.'

(Barrett 1980:175)

She considers the arguments underlying these two positions, and argues persuasively that each contains implicit generalizations which are untenable. The former position, in which the organization of domestic labour within capitalism is seen as a response to and functional requirement of capitalism itself, idealizes and distorts what evidence there is about the pre-capitalist sexual division of labour. Radical feminism, on the other hand, accords no importance to the 'changing needs of capitalist production' in shaping the development of the family.

Those analyses of housework which have recognized the fact that many housewives currently also perform labour as wage workers have begun to escape the unfortunate consequences of this dichotomy of opinion. Gardiner, Himmelweit, and Mackintosh (1975) take pains to avoid characterizing domestic labour as typically performed by full-time housewives. They emphasize the structural factors which underlie the unequal division of resources between men and women within the family household, and go on to argue:

> 'the undervaluation of women's work and women's needs within the home both influences and is influenced by the undervaluation of women's work in the wider sphere, and by the process by which domestic labour is socialized and women are drawn into the sphere of wage labour.'
>
> (Gardiner, Himmelweit, and Mackintosh 1975:8)

Hartmann (1979b) focusing on women's relative powerlessness has noted that the 'mutual accommodation' of capitalism and patriarchy eventually led to the development of the family wage ideal.[14] She argues that wage differentials have a dual purpose: both defining the secondary nature of women's work, and securing women's economic dependence upon men. This is an important point, since it provides a striking example of how patriarchy has reacted on capital. An analysis of capitalism which fails to take account of pre-existing patriarchal structures cannot adequately explain the sex-specific wage differential.

In the 1980s, the issue of 'wages for housework' has receded in the face of growing ideological pressure on women (from both the Conservative Government and sections of the trade union movement) to define themselves as wives and mothers first, and wage workers second (so long as there is room for them in the labour market). This situation underlines the need for clarity in our understanding of how domestic labour fits into the social structure. Narrow economistic explanations have now been substantially rejected, and important links have been forged between Marxist and feminist analysis which have effectively furthered our understanding of domestic labour. It would, however, be premature to suggest that a genuinely unified approach has been achieved.

METHODOLOGY AND CONTRIBUTION OF STUDY

I now want to describe the methods used in collecting data for the present study, and to explain why they were chosen. The study was conceived as a specifically feminist sociological contribution to the existing literature on women's labour which has been outlined above. This meant that both the theoretical framework of the study and the conduct of the empirical research had from the outset to be informed by a critical awareness of that literature.

My critique of the policy-oriented empirical investigations discussed above centred around their failure to challenge the widely-held ideological assumptions about the role assigned to women within the family in our society, and their tendency, because of their 'objective' and functionalist theoretical perspective, to conceal the historical and material basis of women's 'position'. In the present study I have attempted, like those authors, to understand how women combine wage labour with domestic labour, or, to put it in their terms, how women can be employees as well as wives and mothers. However, such a superficial likeness, as I have already indicated above, conceals very real differences in both methodology and theory.

The empirical data collected for present purposes has involved the tracing with respondents of their 'employment careers', by which is meant the progress of their lives of wage labour. This was considered a useful concept as it offered the possibility of overcoming some of the shortcomings of existing empirical studies in this area, many of which have drawn on data which only give a 'snap-shot' picture of the phenomenon. Very frequently, studies of women's employment have been occupational studies. The work of Pollert (1981) — women in the tobacco industry, McNally (1979) — women office workers, Cavendish (1982) — women factory workers, and the many studies which have emerged from the United States, especially about women in 'the professions', are all examples of these. These studies have made useful and important contributions to the developing body of knowledge about female labour. But like all empirical research (and the present study is of course no exception), they offer only partial accounts of the social world. Inevitably, such accounts can be misleading; and I believe that occupational studies of women workers may sometimes give an inaccurate picture of the general experience of female wage labourers. Readers of these studies do not always gain an understanding of what in my view is the general experience of most working-class (and many middle-class) women. This experience is typically fragmented, including an experience of a variety of occupations and working conditions, and has to be accommodated to the frequently changing demands of domestic labour. I want to suggest that the decision to focus on women's employment careers has enabled my study to shed some light upon this. The concept of an 'employment career' has been used in the present study to uncover data about the variation and flexibility of women's employment experience, about the variable relationship between women's wage labour and bargaining between the sexes over the division of labour within the family household (and thus about some of the important ways in which female labour supply is structured), and about patterns of women's employment experience from the end of formal education through to the formation (and in many cases completion) of their own families. Of course some previous studies have concerned themselves with longitudinal data about female employment (e.g. Iglehart 1979). But the reliance in such studies upon official statistics, or upon data in which the broader social circumstances of individuals' lives cannot be investigated, has operated to inhibit full understanding of the phenomenon under study. The principal exception to this is Chaney's valuable study of women in Sunderland (1981) which is concerned with women 'who had returned to work since 1970', and thus excludes women who did not leave the labour force. Chaney notes the absence of adequate information on women's work history patterns in her conclusions.

In undertaking a small-scale, qualitative investigation of the social circumstances surrounding the employment careers of the women here described, I hoped to contribute some new information and understanding to the growing body of sociological knowledge about women's labour. This knowledge remains incomplete, and in the final chapter of the book, I discuss some of the reasons for this, and some possible new directions for future research.

I have already suggested that recent Marxist-feminist analysis of the relationship between female labour and capital has made a significant advance in our understanding of the social context of women's labour. Much of this theoretical work has been developed without reference to detailed empirical data. The absence of such data does not detract from the importance of this work, but it is of course a powerful challenge to any theoretical idea to test it against empirical material. Often, however, the authors of studies which are empirically based fail to locate their data within an adequate theoretical framework. This appears to have been the case with certain of the studies discussed earlier in this chapter. The weakness of the 'two roles' approach lay in its failure to identify the specific relationship between women's wage labour and women's domestic labour. The two were seen as 'separate spheres', in both of which, by chance, women in the 1950s and 1960s were invited to act. The precise developments which led to the (never complete)[15] separation of home and work under industrial capitalism were hinted at, but not fully analysed. Similarly, studies of the wage labour market have often given insufficient attention to the wider social factors which influence the way individuals and groups of individuals (e.g. women) are able to participate in it. In the present analysis, the two spheres are not perceived as separate, but rather as opposite sides of the same coin. Their nature and conditions are determined by the historical and material development of patriarchal capitalism, in which female labour has had a changing but indispensable part to play. Earlier phases of industrial capitalism have been characterized by their relative success in confining married women's labour to the private, domestic, sphere, and in exchanging wages with labour which has been predominantly male. In the current phase of modern capitalism, it is no longer possible for profits to be maintained in a high-wage economy. Real wages have been falling as a result of capital's attempts to maintain profitability, and patriarchal ideology has become a football to be kicked in different directions as different (and incoherent) economic and social imperatives demand. Historically, the lacunae in the 'logic' of capitalism have provided us with examples of how, when required, the sexual division of labour has been broken down (as, for example, in wartime) and, alternatively, reinforced. This has been echoed in a corresponding withdrawal and resurgence of patriarchal values.

The female labour which is discussed in the present study has been exercised in various ways over the past two decades. The second of these decades has witnessed a mounting attack on levels of paid employment, material prosperity, and standards of public welfare, coupled (more recently) with a re-assertion of 'traditional' family values. It is only when we take account of forms of labour (in this case wage and domestic labour) as parts of a single social and economic whole (patriarchal capitalism) that our understanding of the way labour is currently organized, reproduced and rewarded can be furthered. In the case of female labour, and from the point of view of the interests of the women who perform it, we are of course left with many unanswered questions, not least that of whether wage labour, as currently experienced by women, can provide a route to women's emancipation (through the opportunities it presents for collective action and participation in public society), or is merely an aspect of their subordination and exploitation which they would do better to escape.

THE ORGANIZATION OF THE INTERVIEWS

Sources of respondents

The main aim of the empirical research was to collect data about a group of employed mothers aged between 25 and 45 years old. It was hoped that in selecting this age group, the women interviewed would include both mothers of young children, and those whose children were teenagers or older. Interviews were conducted with sixty-four women in three areas in Kent: Canterbury, Whitstable/ Herne Bay, and Maidstone. All were within the chosen age group at the time of their first interview, and had a mean average age of 35 years and 5 months. Most of the women were in their thirties, with just ten of the sixty-four aged under 30, and twelve aged 40 or over.

From the information available about women and the local labour market (see Appendix 1), it was clear that a high proportion of the respondents could be expected to work in the service sector of the economy, especially in Canterbury. As random sampling of the entire female population in Kent aged between 25 and 45 was impractical, I decided to seek suitable respondents from a number of sources where such women could be found. These were: companies known to employ women; childcare agencies, where women whose children needed day care while their mothers were doing paid work might be contacted; and trade unions with a relatively high proportion of female members. A direct approach was made to trade unions only when it was clear that unionized women would otherwise be poorly represented among the respondents. Because random sampling could not be used, there is, of course, a risk of bias in the sample. I show in the tables below the distribution of the women interviewed by industrial sector (*Table 1*), and by whether they were employed in the private or public sector (*Table 2*). Comparison of these tables and the statistics given in Appendix 1 about women's position in the local labour market reveals that there was some under-representation of women working in manufacturing, and a corresponding over-representation of women working in service sector employment. Whilst this should be borne in mind in interpreting the data, statistical generalizations are not made from these, and it should be noted that the women's varied employment careers (described in Chapter 4) indicate that confinement to one broad occupational category was the experience of only a small minority of the respondents.

I want now to describe the three main sources of my respondents in some detail.

Table 1   *Employment at time of interview, by sector — all respondents*

industrial sector	public sector no.	private sector no.	all no.
manufacturing	0	8	8
service	30	24	54
primary	0	0	0
construction	0	0	0
all	30	32	62*

* Three respondents were not currently in employment. Reasons for their inclusion are given in the text. One woman had two jobs, one in the manufacturing and one in the service sector (both jobs were in private companies).

Table 2   *Employment at time of interview, by local area — all respondents*

place of employment	manufacturing no.	service public no.	private no.	all no.
Maidstone	4	21	7	32
Canterbury	0	9	17	26
Herne Bay / Whitstable	4	0	0	4
all	8	30	24	62*

* See footnote to *Table 1.*

Companies   There were two of these, and I made direct approaches in the first instance to managerial staff. Fifteen of the respondents were employees of the first, a large and successful chain of retail stores which has outlets all over Britain. I shall refer to it throughout as 'the retail store'. Most of my interviewees worked in the sales departments and a few in the catering department. Seven of the fifteen women were full-timers, whilst the remainder worked a variety of part-time hours. All of them had agreed to be interviewed following publicity about the research in the form of posters and a circular letter from me which was given to all relevant staff by management. All the women who came forward in response to this publicity were interviewed, at their place of employment, where an office was made available to me for this purpose. The average age of the women interviewed in this first company was 37 years.

Four of the respondents worked for the second company, 'the engineering company', which employs approximately 600 people.

An approach was made in the hope of obtaining respondents from amongst both clerical staff and factory workers. In fact, all four women were clerical employees: none of the factory workers agreed to be interviewed. This poor response was initially puzzling, but was to some extent explained later when it was disclosed to me that the shop-floor workers had been the subject of another research project on a different topic within the previous year. It was also suggested to me by several of the clerical workers interviewed that relations between the shop-floor workers and the sections of management with which I had to deal were not good. This would have helped explain any unwillingness to co-operate, but I was unable to substantiate it further as I was not allowed to approach the factory workers directly. Three of the clerical workers interviewed worked full-time (37 hours per week), whilst the fourth worked 27 hours per week. Their mean average age was 39 years and 10 months, and they thus formed the oldest group in the entire sample. All four women were interviewed at their place of work.

Childcare agencies   The decision to approach childcare agencies was made in order to make contact with mothers of pre-school-age children. Very few of the women contacted via the employing establishments had young children, and I considered it important to fill this gap. A small day nursery was approached, and circulars explaining the purpose of the research were delivered by nursery staff to the children's mothers. Three respondents, all of whom were or had been lone parents, came forward following this publicity; their average age was 30 years old. One was in full-time employment as assistant manager of the local branch of a building society, one did part-time secretarial work for a charitable organization, and the third was a full-time student teacher. She was included, despite not being in paid employment, because of the full-time vocational nature of her studies. All three women were interviewed in their homes.

As only a small response was obtained from this source, a further approach was made, to the secretary of a local Childminders' Association, and she was able to put me in touch with a number of childminders and mothers of minded children. Through this approach a further thirteen respondents, employed in a variety of occupations, were found. They included factory operatives, clerical workers, shop assistants, and various other workers, as well as two non-employed women. One of these women currently worked for money only on a casual basis as a supply teacher, and the other worked part-time in her husband's business. Both of the women had previously been full-time working mothers when each had only had one child, and they were included because of this. The mean average age of the women contacted in this way was 31 years and 2 months. Six of the thirteen women worked on a full-time basis for their employers. Again, all thirteen women were interviewed in their homes.

Trade unions As very few of the women who were contacted via either the employing establishments or the childcare agencies were members of trade unions, I decided to seek further respondents with the assistance of trade unions. The unions were approached on the basis of their relatively high female membership, and their importance locally. In two cases, the unions (National Union of Public Employees (NUPE) and the Confederation of Health Service Employees (COHSE)) were contacted by means of letters and telephone calls to their regional offices. In each case I was given the names of local officials who would be willing to assist with the project. In the third case (the Civil and Public Servants' Association (CPSA)) an official of a local trades council gave me the name of an elected officer, who subsequently agreed to help me and put me in touch with members of both her own and other unions who were employed by a major public sector company.

Following communications with the South East Regional Branch of NUPE, I was put in touch with the union's branch secretary at a higher education establishment in Kent (subsequently referred to as 'the college'). After discussion with him, I attended a shop stewards' meeting of the union, and was able to ask stewards for support. Circulars were distributed to union members by some of the stewards, and as a result of this five women came forward and agreed to be interviewed. Of these, one subsequently dropped out for personal health reasons, and thus four women, all kitchen staff, were interviewed. (Only three of these were included in the final sample, as one woman proved to be over 45 years old.) The three had an average age of 38 years 4 months, and all were interviewed in their homes. The low response to my circulars (far lower than originally predicted by the branch secretary) can be attributed to various factors, including inability to offer women interviews in working hours, failure of stewards to distribute circulars, and an over-estimate of the numbers of women in the required age group and circumstances. This particular phase of the research was an object lesson in the frustrations of conducting empirical research: the optimistic and apparently enthusiastic response of the branch secretary misled me into believing this phase of the research would be much more productive than it eventually proved.

The COHSE was also originally approached via its regional office. Again, I was put into contact with a local official, with whom I had a long interview. This official was willing to lend support to my research within the National Health Service (NHS) hospital where he worked, but preferred me to enlist the support of management rather than to put me in contact with union members himself. I agreed to adopt this approach, and as a result three of the eighteen respondents obtained in this hospital were not union members. All responded to a circular distributed on my behalf by management, who also made available a room for interview purposes, and arranged the interview timetable. All the interviews took place during the respondents' working hours. All eighteen women were non-nursing hospital ancillary workers. Fourteen were domestic workers ('housekeeping aides'), and four were domestic super-visors. Two-thirds of them were employed for 40 hours per week, whilst the remainder had hours ranging from 15 to 30 per week (basic). The average age of these eighteen women (two further women were eventually excluded on grounds of age) was 35 years and 5 months.

The CPSA officer who assisted me in finding the remaining eight respondents was able to put me in touch with a number of employed women who were mothers and who fulfilled the age requirements. Four of these were clerical workers who were members of her own union. There were also two members of the Society of Post Office Executives (SPOE), both in medium-grade technical occupations, a member of the Union of Communications Workers (UCW), and a further clerical worker who did not disclose any information about trade union membership. These women were all employees of the same public sector company, but worked in a number of different establishments throughout mid and east Kent. Some were interviewed at work, and the remainder in their homes. Their average age was 36 years and 8 months.

The interviews

Because I anticipated each woman having a slightly different employment career to describe to me, I decided not to use highly structured interviews or (except in a few specific cases) fixed-response questions. Whilst I had clear ideas concerning the nature of the information I wished to obtain, it was evident from the outset that this would not lend itself to highly specific questioning. I thus conducted the interviews with a list of questions and topics for discussion which was intended principally as an *aide-memoire*, rather than as a formal interview schedule. I tape-recorded the interviews, as this was obviously the best way of recording the detailed information I expected to obtain (see Appendix 2).

Each interview began with the collection of basic personal details (age, marital status, composition of household, etc.), for which a standard form was used (see Appendix 2). The tape-recording of the interview began with the next part, in which I questioned respondents about their current jobs. This phase of the interviews was used both to collect basic factual data (what is your job? how many hours a week do you work? how long have you been in this job? etc.) as well as data of a more general nature (what do you like/ dislike about your job? would you like to be promoted? how long do you think you will stay in the job? etc.). Also in this phase, a few fixed response questions were asked, concerning attitudes to pay and working conditions. This first main phase of the interviews was considered important not only because of the data collected, but also because it was used as an 'ice-breaker', enabling women to relax and talk about themselves. All the questions asked invited respondents to disclose information which was very well known to them, thus putting them at their ease, and convincing them that the interview had relevance to them as individuals.

The second phase dealt with the women's current family lives. Details of household composition were checked, and questions asked about relatives outside the family household (how often were they seen? did they need/supply any kind of help? etc.), as well as about previous marriages where appropriate. Women were also asked to comment on the views of their parents and husbands on their current employment.

The third phase consisted, in effect, in inviting women to tell their life stories. I began by asking them about leaving school, and proceeded with prompts and probes to ascertain as many details as possible about their working lives. It was felt important here to encourage women to tell their stories in their own way (rather than to restrict them with close and rigid questioning which might have been inhibiting or confusing). This phase of the interviews thus (ideally) took on the form of a rather one-sided conversation, with the respondent doing most of the talking. Women were always prompted to disclose certain details about their employment histories which were considered important, but were also encouraged to 'digress' into details of their personal histories and to recount anecdotes about their working lives. Much important information was gathered in this way: the opportunity was given for women to discuss the progress and decisions of their employment careers in all their complexity, and this helped to eliminate the danger that the framework of my questions might impose external meanings and interpretations on the events which constituted a respondent's individual history.

In a few cases, the recounting of her employment career in this way finally brought the respondent to the point where we had begun, with her present job. More usually, however, respondents had employment careers which had been broken at least once (usually to raise children), and in these cases the interview went on to a further phase in which the women were asked to disclose their feelings about the break in their employment career, as well as to give full details about any moves in and out of the labour market and about any developments in their personal and family lives.

When the employment history was complete (in the respondents' eyes), I asked any supplementary questions, and checked any points which were unclear. The next stage of the interviews involved my raising a number of topics relating to female employment for discussion, and also included a number of probes relating to specific details of respondents' lives and work. All women were asked to describe a typical day, paying attention to both wage and domestic labour, and to give information about financial arrangements in their households. I asked them to consider what kind of a job they would seek if they found themselves out of work in the near future, and questioned them about their membership of trade unions and any participation in union affairs. The final (planned) topic which was discussed concerned the law as it affects women in employment: women were reminded of the recent legislative changes (Equal Pay Act; Sex Discrimination Act; Employment Protection Act) and what these meant, and were then asked for their views about these changes, as well as their assessment of how, if at all, they had been personally affected. All interviews were concluded with an opportunity for respondents to question me as an interviewer, and many did so. Most of their queries concerned the research I was conducting and its purpose, but sometimes I was asked my opinion about, for example, whether there was a causal link between juvenile delinquency and working mothers, or perhaps for information about married women's access to state benefits.

Most of the women were interviewed twice, followed by a short, postal questionnaire about a year later. In some cases, especially where women were interviewed at home or employers preferred it, the two interviews were condensed into one longer one. One of the important checks on the reliability of the data collected took the form of a chronology of key events in the respondents' employment history. This involved linking details of family events (dates of marriages, children's birthdays, etc.) with the details of the employment careers, and making sure that they fitted together. Once this chronology had been compiled by me I could go through it with the woman concerned at the second interview or send it by post for her to check and return. This technique proved most effective in clearing up any confusion resulting from my interpretation of the informant's original oral account of her employment and family history.

Where possible, details given to me in the interviews were checked with other sources (taking care never to break my respondents' confidentiality). Some impersonal details could be checked with managerial staff in their place of employment, other information could be checked using company reports, entries in telephone directories, and local newspapers.

All the taped interviews were later transcribed, and these written documents were used extensively in the analysis. The tapes were not destroyed however: it was felt important to keep them for future reference, and to remind me of the respondents' emphases, tones, and manners of speaking, all of which were crucial to a detailed understanding of the data which had been collected. I found it useful to refer to the tapes at various stages, including the final stage when the material was being written up.

3 Patterns of women's labour

Each of the women interviewed as part of the study gave an account of her 'employment career', in which she described her moves in and out of the wage labour force and the nature of her experiences as an employee. In giving this account, the women also supplied information about the organization and division of domestic labour within their family households, and about other networks of support upon which they had relied at various times. This chapter, in which the women interviewed are first introduced, describes the patterns of labour which they had adopted, and indicates some of the social factors by which these patterns were shaped. It also includes some material from the women's accounts of their motives, feelings, and attitudes with regard to changing jobs and to decisions to leave or re-enter the paid labour force. Where possible, I use the women's own words to illustrate my account, and in doing this, I hope to convey some sense of them as individuals. (The name used is fictitious in every case, with each woman being given a different pseudonym.) The chapter is concluded with the first of the three portraits, in the form of a 'coda'. In subsequent chapters I consider strategies for employment, looking both at characteristics of women's labour and aspects of the labour market, and at the social relations of household work.

The majority of the women (75 per cent) had followed in their employment careers a pattern which has been well documented by sociologists and recognized by policy makers as the conventional one for married women. Broadly, it consists of entry into the labour force as a full-time employee on leaving school or college, and continuing this formal participation in economic life through the period of courtship and marriage, leaving the labour force only when the birth of the first child is expected. There then follows a shorter or longer spell devoted exclusively to household responsibilities, and above all to child rearing, which is followed by a return to participation in the formal labour market, sometimes as a full-time, but very frequently as a part-time employee. A significant minority of the women in the study (25 per cent) broke with this more conventional pattern: their employment careers are discussed in detail later in this chapter. The fact that most followed the 'dominant' pattern described above should not mislead us into thinking there is nothing to be said about them, however, and in the section which follows I present sociologically significant information about their employment careers.

THE DOMINANT PATTERN OF WOMEN'S EMPLOYMENT CAREERS

The first phase: employment patterns before birth of first child

Most of the forty-eight women in this group left school at an early opportunity with no formal qualifications and immediately entered employment, although a few passed some examinations or went on to some form of higher education (*Tables 3, 4, 5, and 6*). A quarter of those who entered the labour force on leaving school stayed in their first job until they left employment several years later when expecting their first child. Only two of these had any educational qualifications, and all but one gave up her job when expecting her first child. (In most cases this first pregnancy was unplanned.)

How did they feel about their first jobs? Most claimed to have enjoyed them, although with the benefit of hindsight, some respondents were able to recognize the limitations of their jobs:

HEATHER *(on clerical work):* 'I enjoyed it while I was there . . . looking back on it . . . it was completely unproductive with no room for initiative or anything like that.'

The majority had received some form of training in these initial

Table 3 *Age of school leaving — dominant pattern*

school leaving	no.
left at 15	28
left at 16	14
stayed beyond 16	6
all	48

Table 4   *Destination on leaving school — dominant pattern*

destination	no.
employment	40
secretarial college	6
teacher training college	1
university	1
all	48

Table 5   *Formal qualifications before entering employment — dominant pattern*

level of qualifications*	no.
no qualifications	31
secretarial qualifications only	3
CSE grades only	1
one or more GCE 'O' level pass	10
one or more GCE 'A' level pass	3
all	48

* highest qualification obtained.

Table 6   *First occupations of direct entrants to the labour force — dominant pattern*

occupation	no.
clerical workers	14
sales workers	10
factory operatives	6
hairdressing apprentices	3
miscellaneous*	7
all occupations	40

* miscellaneous = telephonist, waitress, children's nurse, dressmaker, window-dresser.

jobs, with the exception of two factory workers (who had less positive memories of their jobs) and one of the clerical workers.

Three-quarters of the direct entrants to employment, however, changed their jobs at least once before leaving the labour market to raise children. *Table 7* indicates the reasons given by these thirty women for their job changes. I have categorized the reasons given for changing or leaving jobs as follows: *instrumental* (for better pay and/or benefits), *family* (in order to fulfil obligations to parents or husbands, or to care for dependent children), *dissatisfaction* (because dissatisfied with working conditions, treatment at work or

Table 7   *Reasons for job changes* — all direct entrants to the labour force*

reason for change	no. of changes	no. of respondents
instrumental	21	13
family	18	14
dissatisfaction	8	7
travel	7	7
dismissal	6	2
social	5	4
sexual harassment	3	3
redundancy	3	3
don't know / miscellaneous	5	5
total	76	30

* taking the 'main' reason given; obviously changing jobs may be the result of a variety of complex causal factors.

nature of duties), *travel* (to obtain more conveniently situated work), *social* (because dissatisfied with social contacts at work), *sexual harassment* (to escape unwanted sexual attentions at work), *redundancy, education* (to obtain further education or training), and *health* (of the woman concerned).

For many (seventeen of the thirty), changing their job had also involved changing their occupation. The case of Caroline, who began a hairdressing apprenticeship on leaving school, but was unhappy in her job and left, before completing her training, to become a sales assistant, illustrates this kind of job change. Those who changed jobs were mostly motivated by instrumental and family reasons, but other reasons were also important, as can be seen in *Tables 8* and *9* overleaf.

As already suggested, eight of the forty-eight women did not enter the labour force directly on leaving school, but engaged in some form of further education. Did their experience differ in any other important ways from the rest? The most striking difference is that none of these eight women moved from one type of work to another during their first phase of participation in the labour force. All but one, however, changed her job at least once over this period, during which time the eight women had between them a total of twenty-three jobs. The six who went to secretarial college all found employment in clerical and secretarial jobs, and Jenny, who went to teacher training college, worked as a teacher. Frances, who went to university, dropped out at the end of her first year, partly because she failed her examinations, and partly because she had married. Her two spells of employment following this, and prior to the birth of her first child, were both in sales jobs. Another important

Table 8 *Reasons for job changes — direct entrants to the labour force who had more than one occupation*

reason for change	no. of changes	no. of respondents
family	12	10
instrumental	11	8
dismissal	6	2
dissatisfaction	5	4
travel	4	4
redundancy	2	2
social	1	1
sexual harassment	1	1
education	1	1
health	1	1
don't know	1	1
total	45	17

Table 9 *Reasons for job changes, by type of work — direct entrants to the labour force who had only one occupation*

| | no. of changes | | | | |
| | clerical | sales | factory | | no. of |
reason for change	workers	workers	workers	all	respondents
instrumental	7	3	0	10	5
family	2	3	1	6	4
social	3	1	0	4	3
dissatisfaction	2	1	0	3	3
travel	3	0	0	3	3
sexual harassment	0	1	1	2	2
redundancy	1	0	0	1	1
don't know/ miscellaneous	1	0	1	2	2
total	19	9	3	31	13

difference between this group and the other women who had changed their employment during the first employment phase, is that *family* reasons were overwhelmingly the ones given for their job changes (see *Table 10*). These related primarily to marriage and husbands' job changes, but parents' job changes and health also played a part. Instrumental reasons, the most important explanation of job changes for the other thirty women, played a very significant part in shaping the early employment patterns of those who had gone on to further or higher education.

Table 10 *Reasons for job changes — women who engaged in further or higher education*

reason for change	no. of changes	no. of respondents
family	9	7
dissatisfaction	2	2
social	2	2
redundancy	1	1
instrumental	1	1
total	15	7

The detailed information given above (*Tables 7, 8, 9, and 10*) is summarized below in *Table 11*, which indicates the relative importance of the various reasons for changing jobs given by all those in the 'dominant' group who had two or more jobs during this first phase of their employment careers.

Table 11 *Reasons for job changes — all those who had more than one job*

reason for change	no. of changes	no. of respondents
family	30	21
instrumental	22	14
dissatisfaction	10	9
travel	7	7
social	7	6
dismissal	6	2
redundancy	4	4
sexual harassment	3	3
don't know / miscellaneous	5	5
total	94	37

Leaving the labour market to raise children

If the process by which women leave the labour market in order to raise children is to be understood, it is important to know to what extent, if at all, their departure from paid employment has been a consciously planned event. Women in the study were therefore asked to disclose whether the birth of their first child had been 'planned' or not. Twenty-three of the women in this group said their pregnancies had been planned, while twenty said they had been 'unplanned'. (The five women who did not give this information, or who claimed to have left the matter to 'chance' are not discussed in this section.)

All but four of those who had planned their pregnancies had conceived their first child at roughly the time they desired (the remainder all had some years to wait). On average, they had been in the labour force for about seven and a half years when they left to have their first baby. The plans which these women had made (often jointly with their husbands) frequently took into account such factors as a desire to have children whilst they were still relatively young, and a recognition that they were 'settled' as a couple.

> CHRISTINE: 'We had decided about then — we had our own house as soon as we got married, and we gradually sort of spent the four years . . . getting it all together . . . and we had decided that the time had come to start a family.'

Some of the women had mixed feelings about giving up their jobs to start a family, recognizing the passing of a relatively carefree phase of their lives, whilst others had looked forward to motherhood without reservations.

> TESSA: 'I was really pleased — I couldn't wait to leave work. I think it was — at that particular time — it was really what I wanted. I wanted the home and the family and I wasn't interested in going out to work or earning a living or anything.'

> ELIZABETH: 'I was a little bit reluctant to leave [my employers], but, you know, it was just one of those things. I mean I wanted a family just as well, so I had to make the choice.'

Only Carol disclosed that at the time having a baby was more her husband's wish than her own.

> CAROL: 'We got to the stage that I was doing supervision and my husband could see the point that if I didn't soon leave, I wouldn't want to leave at all. There were people [at work] that

were saying "You could go a long way . . . there's a lot you could do . . . . 'And he could see the point that I wouldn't want to leave — I would turn into a career person. He said, "I think we ought to start a family." '

Whilst their pregnancies and withdrawal from the labour force were thus in some sense 'planned', the idea of also planning for a return to employment had clearly not occurred to most of them.

TERESA: 'I didn't [think about it] at that time, no . . . I suppose I thought when my children were off my hands I would go out to work . . . . But I didn't even think of it then.'

Several had thought of returning to employment when their children started school or were old enough to look after themselves, and one or two even said that they had definitely intended to seek a job at this stage. However, none had made any plans about how she would organize this. Nevertheless, the average length of time spent out of the labour force before the first return to paid work was just under three years, and almost a third had less than eighteen months out of employment.

There were four women whose first child was 'planned' but who had to wait a number of years before conceiving. By the time these women left the labour force to raise children, they had been members of it for, on average, almost eleven years. All had been very happy when, after what was often a rather distressing period in their lives, they finally became pregnant. Although one began doing seasonal farm work when her child was only a few months old, the other three all had a much longer break of between four and a half and six and a half years out of the labour force.

Twenty of the women in this group had a first child as the result of an unplanned pregnancy. The average age of these respondents on the birth of their first child was just under 20 years, and the average length of time spent as members of the labour force before the child was born was just over four years. Five of the women in this group disclosed that they had become pregnant before marrying, and of these, two did not marry until after the child was born.

Despite the fact that their pregnancies had been unplanned, the women in this group expressed views about having a first child and giving up their jobs which were very similar to those expressed by the women whose first pregnancies had been planned. Many accepted their situation quite happily, and most either expected to be out of the labour force for some years, or had no thoughts about any future return to work.

BARBARA: 'Well, I'd always wanted children . . . . I thought perhaps that eventually I might get another job, but I didn't intend to work when the children were small. It was a struggle, but I didn't intend to anyway . . . it was . . . just a matter of drifting along.'

PRU: 'No, I didn't . . . it was purely accidental — I was quite shocked — it always happened to somebody else . . . quite honestly, I was on cloud nine — I thought I would never have to go to work again in my life.'

The main difference between the women with unplanned pregnancies, and the women who had planned their first child was that a minority (four of the twenty) had experienced very negative feelings about their situation. In some cases the feelings stemmed from a sense of being unprepared to start on family life, in others from a reluctance to give up a job.

MARGARET: 'I felt terrible. I felt I was too young to have a child really. I liked my job so much and I wasn't really very happy about having a baby at all.'

JENNY: 'Not very happy — we were living in a rented flat . . . and it wasn't big enough to bring up a baby in . . . we wanted to own our own house . . . it came a bit soon . . . . We didn't know what we were going to do . . . eventually, it got round that we could afford to buy a house . . . and it just arose, really, that I was going to go back to work.' (Jenny did not leave the labour force until the birth of her second child.)

Return to the labour force

By definition, the women whose employment careers had followed the 'dominant' pattern all moved from the first employment phase (described above) into a period outside the paid labour force. During the latter period, they were almost exclusively engaged in domestic labour, principally the bearing and rearing of young children. In considering their subsequent return to the labour force, as mothers seeking employment, it becomes necessary to distinguish between three groups, each of which has a different set of experiences.

The first consists of women who have only one child. Their return to paid employment is a relatively straightforward affair, often a once-and-for-all event. The return to paid work came sooner than many had originally anticipated, in most cases within three years. The initial return was usually prompted by either financial pressures or a perceived need for social contacts, or a combination of both.

For many of these women, some unanticipated aspect of their lives as young mothers prompted an early return. Gail was separated from her husband when her child was about a year old, and decided then to return to full-time employment.

> GAIL: 'I decided that if I ever wanted to be as independent . . . I would have to go back to work and get some money together.'

Another young mother found to her surprise that she was not perfectly content with being at home all day with a small baby.

> SHIRLEY: 'I don't like a lot of female company, so coffee mornings, tupperware parties — all of that — I just couldn't take, and basically that's the only thing you can do when you're at home with a baby . . . and nothing annoyed me more than somebody coming round and talking about how they washed their nappies, or something — it's just not me . . . I couldn't stand it . . . plus, I didn't like not being able to earn my own money.'

For others, the decision to take a paid job was prompted by both financial difficulties and a desire to escape the isolation of housework.

> ALISON: 'Mainly it was the money — we needed the extra money — and I was bored to tears at home . . . although I had my daughter, it seemed I'd never, ever seen anybody, I was indoors with my daughter all day.'

One of the women, however, was prompted to return to paid work after only six months out of the labour force because of financial circumstances alone.

> MARION: 'The only reason I've come back out again is because [my husband's] overtime was cut . . . I didn't have any choice . . . we were on a tight budget anyway, so there was really no question — either he had to get another job, or I did. And it seemed better that I should, because he already works six days, and for tax reasons as well . . . it was better that I did.'

About a third of these women took temporary or seasonal jobs at first, but once the return to permanent jobs had been made, job changes tended to be prompted by a variety of factors: instrumental, family, redundancy, personal health, and dissatisfaction. Wendy's account provides several illustrations of why women may change their jobs. She explained her move in 1971 from a part-time job as a shop assistant, to a full-time one in the school meals service.

WENDY: 'Well, we'd had a lot done to the house, and we'd used up any money we'd had, and really more than £2 a week was needed then — so someone said, "Try school meals", and at that time they were very short of staff and they were glad of anybody.'

Wendy stayed in the school meals service for eight years, accepting promotion to assistant cook during this time. Why did she eventually leave to become a full-time sales assistant?

WENDY: 'Well, school meals is really going down... and down... and down. When I first went in, the meals were — they had the best of everything and they didn't skimp.... I know school meals have always had a bad name, but it's not a case of how the meals were cooked. I mean, a lot of care and a lot of pride was taken in the meals themselves, especially where we were . . . and I enjoyed it like that... it was excellent, and the money was good... but then the money didn't alter, and I mean the conditions got worse . . . staff left . . . they were not replaced, and so your conditions were worse... equipment wasn't replaced... and the pride — I mean to them it didn't matter any more — you made do and mend . . . and now instant things are coming in . . . and what really made me decide to get [another] job was I was in charge, and I think we were really short of staff, and six came from ... top level and walked into the kitchen, purely looking at how we were working, and not one single one spoke. They looked round the kitchen, noses in the air, and they were just standing there, and I thought "this is it, out!" — no way do you have to work under those conditions.'

Wendy's vivid description of her progressive disillusionment with this job demonstrates her active membership of the labour force. Pride in her work, the need for her skills to be recognized, unwillingness to put up with being treated as if she were a machine rather than a person, all suggest a commitment to her job which breaks with the more conventional image of female employees as very passive members of the labour force. This attitude was by no means uncharacteristic of the majority of my respondents.

Clare's account of her employment career illustrates the commitment felt by many of my respondents to both their families and their job responsibilities. She explained why she resigned her job as a sales assistant when she was finding it necessary to have frequent time off because of her daughter's health.

CLARE: 'I worked from May until... December, then again [my daughter] started having trouble, and I gave my notice in and said it wasn't fair — although [the Staff Manageress] did say to me that they would be prepared for me to have time off whenever she was ill, but I didn't think it was fair to the other girls. I mean . . . it wasn't a long-term illness, but it used to spring up overnight and she'd be really ill for three or four days, and then be OK again. . . . I just didn't think it was fair to the company or to the girls I worked with to have to cover me.'

For almost all of those with one child, the kind of employment obtained after the break for childcare was of lower status and less well paid than that held beforehand. The post-childrearing phase typically included agricultural, domestic and catering, and sales employment, while the pre-childrearing phase had typically included clerical and secretarial, and sales employment.

The experience of women with larger families was different in several important respects, and these women form the second and third categories in the discussion here. The second group consists of those who took paid jobs in between the births of at least two of their children (about two-thirds of those with two or more children). For them, the 'return' to employment was not a single event, but involved a series of moves in and out of the labour market.

The majority of them had two children, while others had three or four. For most of those with two children, there had been only a short gap (of between eighteen months and three years) between the two births. However, in a few cases the gap was longer, either because the second child was unplanned, or because there was a child from each of two marriages. For the women with three or four children, the longest gap between births was normally that preceding the last child — which in several cases represented an unexpected, and initially unwanted, addition to the family. Nearly all the women took paid employment between the births of each of their children. Most commonly this work was agricultural labour ('field-work'), often of a seasonal and casual nature, or domestic and catering work. Factory jobs, and sales and clerical employment were also quite common. Most jobs were taken on a part-time or seasonal basis, and usually the first return to employment occurred within a year.

Overwhelmingly, the motivation for taking a job at this stage was the need to supplement the family's income. At this point in their lives, most of the women were married to men in relatively poorly paid or insecure occupations — construction workers, semi-skilled manual workers, tradesmen, drivers, etc. The few husbands who were in occupations with relatively good potential earning power (police officers, technicians, and a surveyor) were all at the outset of their careers, or in the process of moving into those jobs from less secure ones, and thus not earning high wages when their children were small. Most of the women were quite frank about their reasons for taking a paid job at this time.

> MARIA: '[My son] must have been about three or four months...
> and then I went out to work again... it was a situation where we
> bought our own home, and financially he needed support, so I
> went out to work . . . a part-time job, to help towards the
> home.'

> CHERYL: 'I had an early morning job when I used to take my
> eldest one with me. That was cleaning in a pub.... She was about
> fourteen months . . . we needed the money . . . my husband's
> wage was about £18 a week then (1968).'

Several women had been unsupported by a husband at this time, either because they were as yet unmarried, or because their marriages had broken down.

> JUNE: 'I did a little cleaning job, which was three days a week...
> for about two hours, I suppose, every morning... and then from
> there I used to go on the strawberry fields. [My daughter was]
> about three, I would say... she used to come with me.... At this
> time I was on my own.'

Some acknowledged that for them there were other motivations besides purely instrumental ones:

> ELIZABETH: 'She was ten months [when I went back to work] ...
> money got tight... there wasn't that much to keep me occupied
> really, and she was a devil when she was a baby, so I was quite
> glad to leave her in some ways.'

For those women who had more than two children, the arrival of a third or final child sometimes disrupted what had been the mother's gradual return to full participation in the employed labour force. Dawn, for example, had only just returned to her career in hairdressing after a seven-year break, when she had to leave because of a third, unplanned, pregnancy. She has not since returned to this occupation, feeling that her skills have subsequently become 'rusty' and old-fashioned. Pat's fourth pregnancy and temporary withdrawal from paid work came just as she had established herself in a permanent part-time job as a hospital bed-maker, following a number of years when she had only been able to undertake evening or seasonal work because of her family's needs.

Thus for two-thirds of those with two or more children, raising a family had by no means meant a complete withdrawal from the employed labour force. Much of the employment discussed above will not, of course, have been included in any official statistics on employment, but it is no less real or important for that. It should, however, serve as a reminder of the need to exercise great caution in interpreting official data about women's paid employment. For these women, finding a way of supplementing the family's income, by selling some of their labour power for wages, was an important part of what they saw as their family responsibilities. Most were only too well aware that if they were not earning, their families' standards of living would drop significantly and they might well sink into poverty.

The third category contains women who remained out of paid employment until they had completed their families, just over a third of those with two or more children. The majority of those in this category had been in employment for over four years when they left the labour force to raise children, and on average had spent about eight-and-a-half years out of the labour force looking after their families. As one would expect, the women with larger families tended to stay out of the labour force for longer than those with only two children.

When interviewed, all but two of the women were married and living with their first husband. In contrast to those in the second category, most of these women were married to men in white-collar occupations with relatively high earnings — technicians, managers, and administrators, for example. The fact that their husbands had been bringing home relatively good wages had obviously been important in enabling the women to stay out of the employed labour force whilst raising their young families, and in enabling them to adopt a particular ideology of family life.

> YVONNE: 'I believe that if you have children, then you should look after them, and I stopped at home until they went to school.'

I do not wish to suggest that economic considerations played no part in prompting these women's eventual return to employment. Indeed, for some, the need to earn an income was the decisive factor, placing them in a situation where they felt they had no choice but to get a job.

> TESSA: 'I didn't work at all until my second daughter was born .... My first marriage had broken up actually when I was still only six months pregnant ... and it was necessity rather than anything else. Social Security wasn't very much and my husband's

whereabouts were unknown. I took a part-time job in a local estate agent's . . . purely and simply because I needed the money.'

SANDRA: 'I [still] had two [pre-school children] . . . the youngest one and the one I foster . . . I got a bit fed up with being at home . . . actually it was a case of having to [get a job], because my husband was out of work at the time.'

Sandra's remark, made apparently only in passing, almost conceals the importance which male unemployment may have for prompting wives to seek work. She was not alone among my respondents in having this motivation.

Christine, on the other hand, took paid employment outside the home for slightly different reasons.

CHRISTINE: 'We were going through a very dodgy time, you know, marriage-wise, and I was trying to consider what to do . . . and I thought perhaps if I could get some sort of job, it would make me more financially independent, and help me decide what I would do.'

Others saw employment as a means of achieving a limited, but specific, material objective.

YVONNE: 'I started in September because I wanted to get two bikes for Christmas for them . . . and I thought I'll just go out to work and earn the money to get that . . . and I got a job in a hotel, and I stopped there for five years.'

Several women first began earning money again without needing to leave their homes, and in a few cases, husbands were active in providing their wives with income-generating work at home.

CHRISTINE: 'I used to work sometimes for my husband('s firm) on a casual basis, doing their typing at home — he used to bring it home — and that all started when [the youngest one] was born . . . instead of getting a temp. in they'd send it home to me.'

It would be misleading, however, to concentrate on financial motives for returning to employment to the exclusion of the other important factors. For a number of women, obtaining a job was a constructive means of escaping their social isolation at home and of defeating their sense of lost identity once their children began to grow older.

TERESA: 'I felt I needed something at that time. I was really getting into a rut at home and I felt I needed to be out. The children were both at school, and I needed . . . I felt I needed something different, it was really getting me down, so I thought, well, I'd have to do something . . . and that's when we decided that we'd go for the Christmas period, it would be a break — which several friends had done . . . . I stayed on there two years.'

How did their first employment on returning to the labour force compare with the jobs they had held prior to having children? Of the seven who had been clerical or secretarial workers before having their children, only one obtained such work when she first took a job afterwards. The rest went into sales jobs, factory work, and other manual jobs. Two other women had had jobs with specific skills in their first employment phase: Anne had been a telephonist, and Yvonne a dressmaker. Both re-entered the labour force as domestic workers. The two other women who became domestic workers at this stage had previously been employed in sales and in factory work. Thus for most, the break from employment resulted in a deterioration of their occupational status. Two women, however, were to find higher status occupations on their return to work. Tina, who had originally been a factory worker, found an opening in nursery nursing, while Frances decided to train to be a teacher. She explains how she finally reached this decision:

FRANCES: 'I [had always] said that I wanted at some date, when we were in a suitable place, and knew far enough ahead etc., that I would hopefully go back and do some form of further education, but . . . it's a very easy thing to put off unless you've got that extra bit of determination — and obviously [my husband's] leaving was the push I needed.'

The employment patterns of the women with two or more children are also of interest following their return to the labour force *and* the completion of their families. These patterns are best described in relation to the age of the youngest child, whether of pre-school, primary school, or secondary school age.

All but two of the nine women who still had a pre-school child when interviewed had returned to formal, regular employment, most working part-time: only two were in full-time jobs (one as a secretary, the other as a hospital domestic) and both of these women had previously done a spell of part-time work. Five of the seven women had been employed in domestic and catering work, and other employment undertaken included clerical and secretarial jobs, sales jobs, agricultural jobs, and childminding. Three of those in regular employment had been in clerical or secretarial jobs prior to having their families — however, when interviewed, only one had returned to using these skills, while the other two were engaged in domestic work.

Seven of the eight women with a youngest child at primary school were in regular, paid employment, while the eighth was a full-time student at a teacher training college. Four were working full-time, and three part-time, and all but one of the full-timers had previously been a part-time employee. Again, manual jobs had predominated in the post childbearing phase. Four of the seven were or had been engaged in domestic work, four in other manual work (in factories and warehouses), and two in agricultural work. However, when interviewed, the seven also included two sales workers, a clerical worker, and a telephonist. Like those with pre-school children, many of these women had also been unable to return to their former skills, especially in office work.

About half of those with two or more children (eighteen of the thirty-five) had a youngest child at senior school. Some had children in their late teens, or older ones who had left home. When interviewed, half were employed part-time, and half full-time, and all but one of the full-timers had worked part-time at some previous stage. Their occupations were as shown in *Table 12*, although at an earlier stage (after completing their families) seven had done paid work of a seasonal or casual nature, and four had done some kind of home work. Of the eight who had some kind of job-specific skills prior to having their children (clerical, hairdressing, dressmaking, telephonist), four had not obtained work using these skills after completing their families, and a fifth had only done so after taking a TOPS course (Training Opportunities course, funded by the Manpower Services Commission).

Table 12 *Occupations of selected respondents* at time of interview*

occupation	no. part-time	no. full-time	all
sales	3	3	6
domestic and catering	5	4	9
clerical	1	2	3
all	9	9	18

* respondents with a youngest child at senior school.

Although a few of the women with two or more children were unsure of their future plans, the vast majority of them fell into one or other of two categories: those who expected to stay in the job they were doing when interviewed until retirement, and who did

not intend to seek or accept any promotion or greater responsibility; and those who intended to remain in paid work until
retirement, but who also planned to seek promotion, further
training, or simply a better job.

How did the women who planned no changes in their
employment careers understand their future? Just over half were
employed part-time, the rest full-time. A third were in jobs where
they had some responsibility, a supervisory role, or recognized
seniority over more junior colleagues, while the remainder were in
the basic grade in their various occupations — primarily hospital
domestics and sales assistants. Many felt that they were happy in
their current job, and desired no further changes. Helen for
example, a full-time domestic supervisor in an NHS hospital, was
quite clear that she did not want any further promotion. She
enjoyed the close contact with staff which her job entailed and
knew that any higher grade job would not have this characteristic.
She expected to stay in her job 'until I retire' — a further seventeen
years if she retired at 60. Nancy, also a domestic supervisor, had
similar plans, but emphasized her lack of ambition in relation to her
job.

> NANCY: '[Promotion] just sort of fell into my lap . . . I've never
> been ambitious, to be quite honest with you, I mean, all I've lived
> for is my home and my children, but when you are here full-time,
> it's a long day, so you think . . . your opportunities are there, and
> I'm gonna take them . . . . I'm not one to keep changing my job —
> in my last job I was there eight years, I was made redundant,
> otherwise I expect I'd still be there . . . . I can't see me not working,
> quite frankly . . . I can't see that I'll ever be financially well enough
> [off] . . . to pack up work altogether.'

Teresa, a part-time deputy supervisor in a large retail store, also
emphasized that her employment career had to fit into her family
life.

> TERESA: 'I suppose really you can't be (promoted any further) . . .
> because I am only a part-timer . . . . I think as I am now it suits my
> family commitments very well . . . . I wouldn't want full-time
> work . . . . I'd be quite happy to continue as I am until, I suppose,
> retirement age . . . . I think if you have good working conditions,
> you adapt to them . . . that would be my only thing, if problems
> like that arose.'

Those who had basic grade jobs, and who were happy to stay in
them, made similar comments.

DAWN: 'I'm happy as I am . . . but, if they come and ask [if I'd like promotion] . . . I expect I'd say yes, I'd have a go at it . . . . I'd stay here, I should think [till retirement] — as I feel now, anyway.' (Dawn was a part-time sales assistant when interviewed.)

Mary would have been glad to have her experience as a part-time clerical assistant recognized by her employers, but was not ambitious in any other respects.

MARY: 'Because I'm part-time, my grades don't go up — I mean, I'm doing a more responsible job within the department, than when I came — but my grades don't go up . . . . I know it's perhaps silly, but it would be nice for them to say "You've done well, you're now a clerk grade whatever" . . . . I can't really see myself changing . . . basically, I feel that while the children are at home, you need extra money . . . but then, the way the situation is now, I think perhaps you'll continue to need extra money . . . I'll be fully happy to stay where I am.'

Another respondent, a part-time domestic, put it quite simply.

OLIVE: 'I suppose [I'll stay] until I retire . . . yes, I shall be working until then, yes. I don't think I'd like promotion or anything . . . I'm quite happy as I am.'

All but two of the women who had no plans to alter their jobs were married women, living with their husbands. The exceptions were Maria, divorced and living with her parents and one of her two small children, and Pru, who lived with her two late-teenage sons and her 'boyfriend'. Maria was not too certain about her future:

MARIA: 'I should think [I'll stay] until he goes to school — I can't see myself getting another job and changing it before then . . . and of course if anything comes of this supervisor [training] thing, then I would stay here and do it.'

Pru also anticipated possible changes in her personal life which might affect her employment career.

PRU: 'The possibilities [for promotion] could be there, but I don't particularly want it . . . . I don't want any hassles . . . . I just want . . . [to stay] as I am, because it suits home life . . . . If I could afford to, I'd leave because I prefer to be at home . . . possibly if I got married again, and finances were different, then I would probably try and leave.'

Nevertheless, many of the women wanted promotion, further training, or a better job. In other words, they were seeking further integration into the labour force. They fall into two categories: those who were already working for employers who made training opportunities readily available, and in jobs where there was an established career structure; and those, mostly in domestic and catering jobs, who recognized that their current jobs held little prospect of improved working conditions or employment opportunities, and who sought a future change of occupation as a result. Tessa, a full-time telephonist, was amongst those to whom job advancement was already available.

TESSA: 'I'm waiting for a vacancy to arise . . . because I sat an exam and a Board for promotion to Clerical Officer. I mean I could stay here *ad infinitum* and just do the same job, which I'm not really prepared to do . . . but I could go there as a clerical officer, and then do another exam perhaps and become an Executive Officer or a Higher Clerical Officer . . . really, I would like to . . . it's more of a challenge, and you're using a bit more of your brainpower . . . . I like this job very much, but it doesn't require a lot of initiative, as long as you're polite and tactful and know your procedures, it doesn't require an awful lot more from you.'

Heather, a supervisor in a retail store, had set her sights relatively high. She had returned to full-time paid employment once her two children were both at school.

HEATHER: 'I shall stay here till I retire . . . that's twenty-five years . . . . [After I'd been here a while] I thought I'd like to make a career of it, I'd like to go into supervision, when I then did . . . . I was promoted quite quickly — I intend to go on further, too.'

Maureen, a full-time personal secretary employed by a large paper-making firm, also wanted more than 'just a job', as her discussion of future plans illustrates. She felt fairly confident of obtaining more rewarding work with her current employer.

MAUREEN: 'I wouldn't mind staying with them (until I retire) . . . . If I can alter my job slightly — [to one that's] a bit more interesting, a bit more involvement, then I wouldn't mind staying.'

Anne, like several other women, was currently in a 'dead-end' job at the bottom of the occupational status ladder, and hoped for better employment opportunities in the future.

ANNE: 'I only do what I do simply for the money, really, I don't really like the work, you know . . . . [I'll stay] really until I can find an alternative job that I liked . . . it's just a matter of if a job was available . . . . I should think two years would be the limit I'd stay here. It would be a different type of work altogether that I would look for. I'm going to night school in September.... I'm going to take biology — I'm very interested in nursing... that's probably what I will do.'

Pat worked full-time as a hospital domestic, and like Anne, hoped to gain access to employment in nursing at some future date.

PAT: 'I love working here... but I can't say I like doing what I'm doing. Because it's all mechanical, and, well, you just don't need a brain.... So later on I would like to change... I thought about going as a nursing assistant.'

Although plans for the future might not be achieved, many of these women nevertheless bore little resemblance to the passive members of the labour force which women are so often taken to be. Those who lacked ambition for promotion mostly anticipated participation in the labour force until their retirement, and those who had become well integrated into their employment environment frequently demonstrated considerable determination to 'make something' of their jobs. Carol's and Cheryl's comments about their attitudes to future employment were illuminating. Both lacked the kind of aggressive career ambition which characterizes the 'male' stereotype, but neither was willing to accept a definition of their work as passive and non-assertive.

CAROL: 'I have been asked to do supervision, but up until now I've never had the confidence to do it.... But now I'm thinking about it, because my children are getting older and they're [shy] like me, and I want to show them that if you tell yourself you can do it, you can.... [I'll stay] probably until I retire.... I'd quite like to, because they are a good firm as regards pensions. It would pay me to stay here... I'd be silly to leave really.'

CHERYL: 'I always take it stage by stage... I was an assistant and knew I could do better, and I'm aiming at supervision. When I'm doing supervision I will then contemplate whether I am capable of doing better. But I never sort of say "Oh, I want to be a Departmental Manager" — I would love to, but I've got to take it in stages to see whether I am capable — just increase it gradually .... I've come back with the intention of working till I retire.'

The impact of marital breakdown

Fifteen of the forty-eight women whose employment careers had followed the 'dominant pattern' had experienced marital breakdown. Of these, nine had re-married following their divorce. All but two of the fifteen had at least one child when their first marriage ended, including in eight cases a child aged 5 years or younger. What effect, if any, did the break-up of their marriages have upon their employment patterns?

For Angela and Elizabeth, neither of whom had children, the break-up of their first marriage had little effect upon their employment careers. Angela continued working full-time as a secretary, and did not change her job. Elizabeth gave up her job as an audio-typist partly because she could not cope with facing her colleagues at work, and partly because she decided to move back to her parents' home in a different town. However, she only had a short break from employment before going back to work full-time as an office temp., and subsequently taking permanent secretarial employment.

For the eight women who had at least one child aged 5 years or under when their marriage broke down, the event either increased or prompted their participation in the paid labour force. Four had not been in paid employment: of these, two took part-time jobs, and one a full-time job when their marriages ended. The fourth began full-time training to become a teacher. Of those already doing paid jobs, two changed from part-time to full-time hours (but stayed with the same employer), one continued in her full-time job, and the remaining one took on additional casual and part-time work.

The remaining five women (whose youngest children were of school age when their marriages ended) had all been in paid employment, three working part-time and two full-time. All remained with their employers, and one of the part-timers went on to full-time work, as she explained.

> PRU: 'I got promoted to a supervisor . . . . I did that for about two and a half years . . . still 5 till 8 . . . . Then, because of finances — I got divorced — I needed more money. I had to take demotion, to go on to the forty hours.'

Paula, a clerical worker and one of the full-timers, stayed full-time, and after her divorce went through (shortly before our interview) applied for promotion to a more senior position.

The evidence of these women suggests that the impact of marital breakdown upon employment careers is fairly straightforward. Existing participation in paid employment tends to be maintained, and is frequently increased from part-time to full-time. Where women have not been engaged in paid work, the break-up of their marriage may prompt them to seek employment. Whilst instrumental motives are especially compelling at such a time, and the need to earn an income may appear to be paramount, women also recognize the social importance of their jobs at this stage, when self-esteem and confidence may be at a low ebb. The 'poverty trap' into which women who have access only to low-paid employment or supplementary benefit may fall[1] is one of which such women are well aware. But they may still choose to be at work. One woman who worked part-time explained what had happened to her.

> BRENDA: 'It wasn't enough to keep me and two children on . . . . I was on Social Security, and I had a few bills that I had a job to pay, and I ended up borrowing off my parents and getting deeper into debt. In fact I went up to Social Security one day, and they turned round and said, "Well, you'd be better off not working." '

> S.Y.:   *'How did you feel about that?'*

> BRENDA: 'Oh, I couldn't have given the job up, I had to have something to keep me going . . . I thought it was terrible . . . if I hadn't worked, the actual cash in hand would have been £4 less than what I was getting by working — and bus fares and other expenses were costing more than £4 . . . . If I did extra hours at work, Social Security stopped the extra that I'd earned, so I was no better off by doing any, and I did feel a bit trapped, but there was nothing I could do to get out of it. Even if I was working full-time, I couldn't have — well, at the time, I wouldn't have left the children alone, not for too long anyway, because they were upset as well, and I think they needed me as much as I needed them at the time.'

Brenda's account, which refers to 1976, expresses many of the tensions and ambiguities affecting an unsupported lone parent. She recognizes the need for time with her children, but also knows that her job is an important source of social contacts for her, and helps her to structure what at first appears as a shattered lifestyle. She wants to support herself, by earning what she can, but is caught by a bureaucratic social security system which lacks the flexibility to accommodate her particular needs.

A note on redundancy and unfair dismissal

In discussing patterns of women's labour, it is important to note that whilst many job changes made by women are (in the broadest sense) voluntary — women resign their jobs for personal, family, or instrumental reasons — this is not invariably the case. For the women in my sample, redundancy and dismissal (including various types of what may constitute constructive — and therefore unfair — dismissal) were also features of their employment careers.

Almost a third of the forty-eight women in this group had experienced redundancy. Shops or restaurants where they had been working closed down, industrial firms cut back on staff or re-located, small companies went into liquidation. Most accepted their experience of redundancy as simply a fact of an employee's life. Rarely did women mention any kind of resistance to redundancies, and where they did, actions had been unsuccessful. I do not wish to suggest that women in general do not, and have not, put up determined and effective resistance to attempts to deprive them of employment. There are, of course, numerous examples of such action, and the case of women workers at Lee Jeans in Greenock, Scotland, who occupied their factory when threatened with redundancy, provides a recent example (Ryan 1981). However, my respondents had not been involved in such struggles. Chapter 4 includes discussion of the women's trade union involvement, and their generally low level of union participation, indicating an individualistic approach to employment which is consistent with a failure to engage in collective action against proposed redundancies.

In the interviews, women were not questioned closely or routinely about sexual harassment at work — unwanted or intimidating sexual attentions in the workplace — and it is entirely possible that some women had experienced problems of this type, but did not disclose them to me. Nevertheless, three women described incidents leading to their resignation from a job which constituted clear sexual harassment. All had been in their teens at the time of the incident, two still unmarried, and one recently married. Sheila's interview illustrates the tendency for incidents of this type to go unobserved.

S.Y.: *'What happened to you when you left school — did you go straight into a job?'*
SHEILA: 'Yes, I worked at [the paper] Mill — my mother got me a job. The first job I had ... for four months — but it didn't work out.'
S.Y.: *'What were you actually doing there?'*
SHEILA: 'Making, well, no — sorting, paper.'
S.Y.: *'Why did you leave?'*
SHEILA: 'I left there because — you know, they kept saying, "Oh, your Mum works here", and all this ... I didn't like it ... you know.'
S.Y.: *'So you think it was because of that that you left, rather than because of the actual work?'*
SHEILA: 'I liked the work.... It was the foreman I didn't like ... where I worked ... he was dirty.'

S.Y.:   *'So it was the people that you didn't really get on with?'*
SHEILA: 'Well, this particular bloke. He used to touch all the young [girls] ... when the young ones used to start, they used to start in the cutter house, you know — they was all like fifteen-year-old girls, and he used to — you know — be rude to them. So ... I told me mother, and she more or less smacked him in the mouth, and that was one of the reasons I left, you know.'

Barbara's experience was not dissimilar.

S.Y.:   *'What happened to you when you first left school?'*
BARBARA: 'I went to work in the dispensary at [a large chemist's store] ... it wasn't what I wanted to do, so I was there a matter of three or four months I suppose .... I didn't settle in the job .... I felt that everything I did was wrong because I just didn't like what I was doing .... I was shut away in a little cubicle ... plus, I didn't like the manager that was there, he was a creep .... I wouldn't have found (the work) difficult if I hadn't had this creepy manager behind me, so I think he was mainly [why I left] ... you didn't have a proper office, you were just standing in this cubicle thing where they did the prescriptions, and I mean he was one of these people who'd come and smack your bottom, sort of, and in those days, you didn't turn round and tell him like they would today ... he was I think the main reason why I left.'

Brenda was more direct than the other two.

BRENDA: 'I worked as a stock control clerk in a garage ... up until I was married ... I quite enjoyed it.'
S.Y.:   *'You said you did that until you got married?'*
BRENDA: 'Until after I got married.'
S.Y.:   *'Why did you leave the job?'*
BRENDA: 'The stores manager started getting a bit fresh ....'
(laughs)

Thus in factory, shop, and office, these women had been subjected to intolerable pressure of an overtly sexual nature, from men in more senior positions than themselves, and this resulted in their resignation. The kinds of evidence now becoming available concerning sexual harassment[2] would seem to suggest that these three women may represent the tip of the iceberg. The optimism of Barbara's view, that 'nowadays' girls would not put up with the kind of treatment she left her job to escape in the early 1960s would appear to be unjustified by the emerging facts.

Several women disclosed that their employers had offered them an impossible choice about their working hours and conditions, which in effect constituted 'unfair' dismissal. One had been taken on to work evenings as a catering assistant, but later found her employer insisting that she work weekends also. As she had a young family at the time this left her with no choice but to resign her job. Another was forced to leave her job when her firm re-located about fifteen miles away. She was told she could travel daily to the new venue if she liked, and was prepared to work longer hours, but for a woman with both a pre-school and a school-age child, an extra burden of this kind was out of the question. A third woman, working part-time as a merchandiser, was faced with the choice of doubling her hours (to 40 hours per week) or giving up her job. Since full-time hours were impossible for her because of her family commitments, she too had no option but to lose the job.

It may be that one or more of these women would have had a case for unfair dismissal under subsequent legislation. However, it seems likely that they would not have brought a case, even if legally entitled and aware of their right to do so. One of the things employed mothers seek to avoid is 'hassle'. If they are to accommodate the demands of their families and go out to paid jobs, they must organize themselves in order to avoid spending time and effort in unnecessary ways (see subsequent chapters). Most of the women I interviewed lacked the extra energy and determination which would be required to bring legal action for unfair dismissal, regardless of their chances of success.

ALTERNATIVES: WOMEN WHO HAD NOT LEFT THE LABOUR MARKET

Six of the women interviewed had not left the labour market since joining it on completing their school or college education. When interviewed, most were in their late thirties, and all were living with their (first) husbands. Since their continuous commitment to employment breaks with the more common pattern of at least a short period at home with very young children, it is worth examining their experiences in some detail.

Three had left school at 15 with no academic qualifications, two had left at 17 with four or five 'O' levels, but had not gone on to further education, whilst one had left school at 16 with several 'O' levels and 'CSEs', and had subsequently attended secretarial college for a year.

When interviewed, most had been with their current employer for a number of years: three for over twenty years, one for thirteen years, one for five years, and one for just two and a half years. All were in white-collar jobs with established employers, five in clerical occupations (ranging from clerical assistant to accounts supervisor) and the sixth in an administrative grade which was considered to be an executive position. Three had jobs which involved supervising other staff, whilst a fourth had responsibilities which included interviewing members of the public in connection with their requirements for personal financial loans.

Interestingly, none of the six women was following an employment pattern set by her own mother. None of their mothers had been in permanent jobs whilst my respondents were children, and only two of these mothers had had permanent occupations outside the home after her family had grown up.

For most, there had been a delay of some years between marriage and the birth of their first child. Two had a first child within three and a half years of marriage, but for two others there was a five-year gap, and in the remaining cases the periods were seven and twelve years. These longer than usual delays between marriage and the first child's birth were significant in explaining their employment patterns.

In three cases, the respondents had planned their families so that they could continue in employment without leaving their jobs.[3] This involved not merely ensuring that the baby was born at a convenient point, but also making arrangements for the child to be cared for once it was born, and in one case, changing her job to one with less responsibility. I shall describe each of these cases in turn.

Sara was born abroad but came to England in 1966 on marriage. Her husband has been in the nursing profession throughout their marriage, and at the time of the interview held a senior position. On arrival in England, Sara did manual work for a couple of years, before obtaining a job as a clerical assistant in a public sector company in 1968. She was subsequently promoted to clerical officer. Her first child was born three and a half years after she joined the company, and she took two months maternity leave.

SARA: 'Well, we discussed it before we had children, and I've never liked the thought of staying at home, you know, I've always wanted children and wanted to work as well. So we discussed it then, you know, whether I would be able to do both. So we said, 'Well, we'll try — if we can't, then I'll pack up', you know. But as it is, we've managed . . . . He does his share of work, and I do my share . . . . We decided at first that my husband would go on night duty — we did that for a while . . . . He went to work at night when I got home, you know . . . . I found it ever so hard to leave a baby after four weeks, to come back — but it's one of those things — I had to come back.'

She goes on to describe how these arrangements were subsequently modified.

> SARA: 'We did that for a while, night duties, and we found out we were just saying 'Good morning', and, you know, going out the house. So, one of my sisters came, to go to college, so he went back on normal working, the shifts — you know, they do one week a morning, one week afternoons — and so my sister was studying at home and looked after the baby for a while, and then he went to do his normal work . . . . The second one, we did the same — and then my other sister came and we did the same thing — she went to college and helped us out during the day. When I had the third one, she decided she was going to get married, so I had to find a baby minder . . . . I used to take one to school, one to nursery . . . and then the other one to the minder, in the morning. But it was very hard, you know — I suppose if you want to do it, you do it.'

Geraldine left school at 15 with no qualifications and took a job as a punch operator. She worked her way up through various grades to a supervisory position, before marrying nine years later. After five years of marriage, she and her husband wanted to start a family.

> GERALDINE: 'Now a supervisor has a lot of week-end work, a lot of overtime, so I decided to switch to be a clerk, an ordinary clerk . . . . I found my childminder before I was pregnant . . . . I used to pop over before the baby arrived, she was the first one to know when I was actually pregnant.'

When the baby arrived, in 1976, she took seventeen weeks' maternity leave. She described her feelings about going back to work.

> GERALDINE: 'I didn't want to leave him – you don't. It's a terrible wrench. I would never advise anybody to do it – and it's hard, jolly hard, on you, because you're losing your sleep at night . . . of course you can't breast-feed if you're going back to work after six weeks; it's not fair on the baby, so I had to bottle-feed him.'

Both Geraldine and her husband come from large families, and have chosen to have no more than their one child.

Andrea also left school at 15 with no qualifications. Her father had recently died and she considered herself fortunate to have obtained a job as a telephonist. After about three and a half years she married, and at roughly the same time was promoted to a supervisory post which involved working shifts. Her first baby was born about five and a half years later, according to plan.

> ANDREA: 'I'd arranged that she would go to a nursery when I came here – I was on shift work then, as a supervisor – we used to do different duties, like eight till four, and either my husband or myself used to take her to the nursery in the morning, and one of us used to collect her at night.'
> S.Y.: *'And you never considered giving up work at that period?'*
> ANDREA: 'No. I'd always enjoyed work too much.'

The birth of her child was difficult, and because of this she decided not to have any more children — as she put it: 'It's best to have one that's perfectly all right.'

The remaining three women had not planned their pregnancies in quite the same way. Valerie was married for twelve years before the first of her three children was born. After a short spell as a shop assistant on leaving school aged 15, Valerie joined most of her male relatives, who already worked for the same public sector company, as a clerical assistant.

> VALERIE: 'I think it was just pressure from Mum and Dad. You know, "You ought to get that good little job", and all the rest of it. So I applied . . . . It's sort of family-orientated really.'

She married a few years later and was subsequently promoted several times. Why had she sought promotions?

> VALERIE: 'I just felt – I mean, you sort of work here, you just get caught up in it . . . and, I think, well, if I'm out earning, working, I want job interest . . . so, it was the natural . . . course of events to some extent . . . rather than . . . an inbuilt desire as always wanting to achieve this.'

She described how she came to decide to remain at work when she eventually had her family.

> VALERIE: 'It was just something at the time. We'd been married twelve years then, and you sort of acquire a lifestyle, and there was no way that we could continue doing the things we'd become accustomed to doing, if you like . . . and selfishly enough we weren't prepared to give that up. Although we'd wanted a family – had it been forthcoming, you know, in our early years of marriage, when we'd planned it, I would have left work like most mums do, you know, and had the children, and then come back to work. But having worked all that time, I was too old to get up and start scratching around really, because – you know, it *is* hard when you suddenly come down to one wage, and suchlike . . .

and so we just decided that, you know . . . as it happened, my
mum would look after them, and so it worked out like that.'

Valerie had three children, and took four months' maternity leave
from her job at each birth.

Neither Sally nor Louise had planned to start their families when
they did. Before her marriage, Sally was employed for six years in a
variety of jobs. A routine clerical job which she left after about a
year, mainly through boredom, six months abroad as an au-pair,
and several more office jobs, including assistant to a buyer in a large
mail order firm, and supervisor of fieldwork in the market research
department of a large company, her last job before marriage. This,
she felt, was 'probably the best job I've ever had – I was in charge of
the interviewers around the country.' On marriage she moved to
Kent and left her job. Although she tried to find the same kind of
work there, she could find nothing like it, so after a couple of
months out of employment she took a job as a shop assistant in a
department store.

> SALLY: 'I stuck it for two weeks – it was utterly boring – in many
> ways an absolute insult to anybody's intelligence, supervised by
> a woman who had no sort of intelligence either. The whole thing
> was a complete waste of time – utterly boring – I really was
> bored.'

Following this, she succeeded in obtaining part-time employment
as a market research interviewer, and was doing this work when she
first became pregnant. However, neither this nor her subsequent
pregnancy (eighteen months later), nor having two small children,
prevented her from continuing this part-time work. The hours
(about 20 per week) were flexible — 'you just sort of did it in your
own time' — and it was possible to make arrangements for the
children.

> SALLY: 'I used to strap [the children] in the back of the car . . .
> and there were quite a few friends who would have them for the
> odd hour or two – and sometimes, I would take them with
> me.'

She continued in her market research work for about six years, at
the same time running her own farm shop. Once her two children
were at school, however, she took a full-time clerical job with a local
engineering company. She explained why she made this change.

> SALLY: 'Really because my [self-employed] husband took a
> [second] job in the evenings . . . we did need the money – and he
> didn't used to get home until about half past eleven, really tired,

and things got to the point where the children were both at school and I realized that he just couldn't go on doing it. And I came along here for the interview . . . . And I sort of took over the earnings, if you like. My husband had to take [the children] to school, and he had to pick them up and he had to make sure they were all right till I got home. That was the arrangement – if I go out to work, he'd have to accept that responsibility.'

She was still working in this clerical job when interviewed, but has subsequently, after about four years there, changed her employer, going first to work full-time as administrative co-ordinator in an advertising agency, and later, after three weeks out of employment following redundancy, taking a part-time clerical/cashier job with a building society (for 20 hours per week).

Louise went to secretarial college after leaving school and worked as a typist with a building society for six years before changing her job on marriage. She explained:

LOUISE: 'I met [my husband] there . . . and you can't work for the same company[4] so I had to leave . . . [also] we moved . . . to London, because he got promoted.'

She described how she came to take her next job.

LOUISE: 'It was easy because it was London . . . I could have had almost any job but the reason – it's stupid really – but the only reason I chose [the company] was that we'd got a flat nearby and it was the most accessible place to get to. And I could get home in the lunch hours and start – you know, newly married, I thought get home and get the vegetables ready, and all this rubbish [laughs] – that lasted for about three days, but that was the idea. I thought . . . I wouldn't be able to cope with running a house and going up to town . . . I wanted a nice local job . . . it was very close to the flat, so I could nip home at lunchtime and do the shopping, that was why I chose the job.'

Louise's first child was born three and a half years after her marriage. At first she found her pregnancy hard to accept.

LOUISE: 'I asked, you know, if it was possible to terminate and [the doctor] wasn't very agreeable – but looking back, I probably wouldn't have done it, it was just that – I went to him because I hadn't come on, and he told me that I was pregnant. It was a bit of a shock. I did ask, but he – he lied in fact – he told me that I was sixteen weeks gone, and I wasn't, I was nowhere near that, I was about ten[5] . . . looking back [my husband] would never have agreed to it anyway . . . to me, having a baby meant staying at home and washing nappies and things like that.'

S.Y.: *'So you thought it was going to mean giving up work?'*

LOUISE: 'End of my life, in fact – yes.'

Through discussing what she saw as her predicament with other people, Louise came to realize that having a child need not mean leaving her job.

LOUISE: 'I thought about it before he was born. And weighed up lots of possibilities. . . . I got talking to a girl who happened to take my place on maternity leave . . . and she told me her child was at a childminder's . . . . She said, do you want me to put you in touch with this girl? And I went round to see her, and it was very clean, she was registered, obviously . . . I was happy with her and she was happy with me . . . he went there before, in fact, he was six months. They were short-staffed at the office, because it was holiday time.'

Louise felt confident that her decision to stay at work and take maternity leave had been the right one for her. She found the period at home with her young baby difficult.

LOUISE: 'I was not really very happy – my husband used to come home at night, we didn't seem to have anything to talk about . . . my mum still can't understand it, because she scraped and saved to, you know, bring us . . . up, and she feels that if she could do it – and they had no money at all – she doesn't see why I shouldn't.'

Since returning to work from her maternity leave, Louise has moved from London to Kent (because her husband has been promoted in his job). When this happened she was able to obtain a transfer within her firm, and had three weeks' leave of absence at the time of removal. During this time, she was able to make arrangements with another registered childminder for her son. Louise would like to work part-time, but her employers have a full-time only policy, and as she has been unable to find suitable alternative employment, she has chosen to reduce her workload by employing domestic help at home for four hours per week.

These six women, whose attachment to the labour force has been virtually unbroken since they joined it on leaving full-time education, all showed evidence of an active commitment to paid employment. They had had relatively few employers and most were currently well-satisfied with their pay, working conditions and with the nature of their jobs. Most had been able to take advantage of opportunities for promotion, and all planned to remain in employment until retirement. All referred to some difficulties in combining full-time paid jobs with raising children, but with the support of either husbands and other relatives, paid help, or the cooperation of friends and employers, these had not proved insuperable, and none suggested that she regretted the decision to remain in employment. The choices they made might not always be ones which other women would select, but many might benefit from a genuine opportunity to consider remaining in paid work as an option.

ALTERNATIVES: SOME EFFECTS OF INDIVIDUAL BIOGRAPHY

Whilst most of the women interviewed had employment careers which followed the 'dominant' pattern described at the start of this chapter, and a minority chose to remain in paid work despite changes in their family lives, a further minority had employment careers which were quite clearly affected by the special circumstances of their personal lives. None of these ten women had conformed to the norms currently governing family formation behaviour and the conduct of personal relationships. Thus for them the social processes of marriage and childbearing had differed in important ways from those experienced by the majority of my respondents.[6] Whilst marital breakdown has become a commonplace of contemporary relationships between the sexes, and had been experienced by well over a third of the women interviewed, frequent breakdown of personal relationships (whether marital or extra-marital), the bearing of children outside of stable unions, and the failure of women to marry, continue to constitute behaviour which breaks with normative expectations. These are the characteristics of the women in this group. Disrupted private lives can have important effects upon women's employment careers. Some women seek stable, full-time employment as a 'constant' in their otherwise changeable lives. This enables them to escape dependence on either the state or men for their economic well-being, and gives them a sense of maintaining control over their own lives. Others find that the personal insecurities of unstable and unsatisfying relationships, often complicated by ill-health (mental or physical) and unplanned pregnancies, keep them from permanent or full-time employment.

In four of the ten cases, attachment to the labour force had been strengthened. These women were all living alone with a child or children, and were, in effect, employed full-time.

Mavis was in her late twenties, had never married, and had an 18-month-old son. She was living in a small council flat, and gave every appearance of coping well with organizing her life and managing her responsibilities.

> MAVIS: '[It's] not really [a strain] . . . because I've always sort of sailed through things, and sort of not worried. Well, I do worry a little bit, but it doesn't bother me what other people think. . . I do what I want to do, and I don't care what anybody says.'

She had two paid jobs, working 40 hours per week for a food processing company, packing food, and 7 hours on Saturdays as a butcher's assistant. She had been doing this for nine months when I first met her, and was still doing so when contacted again a year later. In the week, her child went to a registered childminder, whom she paid £12.50 a week, and on Saturdays her neighbour looked after him. Her Saturday job was quite important to her, and she had worked for this employer on and off for eight years, going back there when the baby was 6 months old and she was living on supplementary benefit.

> MAVIS: 'That was a great help . . . because, also, he said "You know you can help yourself off the counter, like." So, I mean, that was an even bigger help, that was . . . things like butter and cheese, and your meat, and it did save me a lot . . . and after . . . doing it about three or four weeks, I didn't honestly know how I could have gone back to just being on Social Security alone – I couldn't – well, to think about it now, I don't know how I really did manage.'

Three months later she took the full-time factory job, and although she was toying with the idea of working shorter hours, she was aware of all the factors she needs to weigh up.

> MAVIS: 'Well, you see, you can gain and you can lose – at the moment, I can't claim for FIS,[7] because I am earning too much – but in November, they all go up again, so I can claim for them again.' (FIS = Family Income Supplement)

Kate and Cathy were both in their mid-thirties. Kate had four children, aged between 6 and 14 years, all living with her. She had been married three times, divorced twice, and said she was 'estranged' from her third husband. Cathy had been married and divorced twice, to the same man, and had three children. At the time of the interview she lived alone with the youngest child, a 7-year-old, while the elder two lived with their father. Neither woman was financially supported by a former husband, and both worked as hospital domestics. Kate worked a 40-hour week and did regular overtime of about 15 hours. Cathy worked part-time as a supervisor, but usually worked a 42-hour week including overtime.

Kate's first marriage had lasted two years, her second for twelve. She had one child from her first marriage and three from the second. Her third marriage was breaking down after only a couple of years, when we met. She described her estranged husband's attitude to her job.

> KATE: 'He doesn't like the idea – because of the independence side of it I suppose . . . . I was earning my own wage . . . so it gave me almost equal rights to him . . . and he didn't like the idea from the beginning.'

She was bitter about her past.

> KATE: 'I've always done everything myself, anything to do with the home, cooking, looking after the children, everything. I've always been the one . . . . I've even taken on the responsibilities of bills, always have done . . . . I don't feel at all happy about it, mainly because it should be a shared thing between husband and wife. I don't know if it's me, or if it's just the type of people I've married – it just doesn't work out that way.'

Her early experience of employment was in clerical work, which she found boring, and as a supermarket cashier. While her children were young, she worked for about seven years as an agricultural worker (working about nine months in every twelve), before having to give this up because of an injury, and taking a job as a hospital domestic. She planned to stay in this job 'quite a few years, I hope. All the time I'm able to, I will.'

Cathy's early employment career was inauspicious. In the first two years after leaving school at 15, she worked as a supermarket shelf-filler and counter assistant, in two jobs as a waitress, and as a factory operative. She was made redundant from one of these jobs, sacked – 'for being mouthy' – from a second, and left the others of her own accord. Before taking a fifth job as a trainee laundry worker, she also spent some time caring for her sick grandmother. Cathy's employment career was broken again before she completed her training, when she became pregnant and had her first child. She married for the first time nine months later, and did not return to paid work (this time as a 'casual' agricultural worker) until three and a half years after this, by which time she had a second child. She continued in this work for about six years, although in the meantime she divorced, and three years later re-married, her husband. She then had to stop work to have a third child, but returned to agricultural work again soon afterwards.

> CATHY: 'I done one season of potato picking-up, after I'd had her . . . . I've always suffered with my back, and that last spell of picking up potatoes just about finished me. I'd just about had enough. And then I decided that I would see if I could get a job inside . . . . I knew that there was one going (at the hospital) and I applied for it, and got it.'

Cathy's husband had no objection to her taking a more secure job.

> CATHY: 'He thought it was good that I was working . . . because then he could cut me housekeeping down, you see . . . no, it's the truth! . . . . He always told me to get to work anyway – I did as I was told.'

As this second marriage came to an end, things deteriorated further:

> CATHY: '[my wages] all went in the housekeeping . . . I mean, I kept them all, from last May – because he never gave me anything at all – I was having to keep him, 'n all.'

How long did Cathy plan to stay in her present job? 'Until they get rid of me, I should think.'

Susan was in her mid-forties, and had been living alone with her three children for over twelve years. Prior to that, she had been twice married and divorced. Susan's employment career began when she was 15, with a period of clerical work which lasted six years. During this time she married for the first time, giving up the job when she was expecting her first child. In the next three or four years, before her marriage broke down, she had another child and engaged in periodic seasonal work on farms, taking her children with her. After her marriage ended, she took on various casual jobs, including part-time clerical work and washing cars, before forming a relationship with the man she was later to marry. At first she lived with him, unmarried, but when she was expecting his child, she succumbed to pressure from her family, and, against her better judgment, married him. A few years later she obtained a part-time clerical job in the firm where her husband worked. This lasted for two years, until the marriage began to break down and she felt compelled to leave. After her second divorce, Susan gradually became more fully integrated into the labour force. She worked for a while in the school meals service, and then moved to a full-time office job. Finally, she took the advice of her sister, who worked for a public sector employer.

SUSAN: 'I applied for a job here — my sister is an Executive Officer here, and ... she'd brought up her family on her own. She said you needed to get into a secure job, because you want a pension — you'd got to think about, you know, bringing up your children on your own — and this obviously made sense.'

Susan had been in this job for ten years when we met. She had accepted modest promotions, and had become very involved in trade union work. At the time of her interview she was branch secretary of her union, and was also actively involved in Labour party politics, thus making the kind of link between her working life and her private life which is characteristic of male trade unionists. As she put it: 'What I do for the trade union here fits in with what I do in my leisure time — it's hardly separated.'

She expected to stay with her employers.

SUSAN: 'I hope until I retire ... all the time I'm fit ... I mean, I shall need a pension .... We have excellent conditions of service, and because the [employers] have always worked closely with the unions, we don't have the unfairness that you get where you don't have union representation ... [we have] flexi-time ... we have a good superannuation scheme, we've got a welfare officer, benevolent society — this sort of thing ... it's very secure.'

In many respects, the four women described here conformed more closely to the stereotype of a 'male' than of a 'female' employee. Working regular overtime, taking a second job, relying upon earnings as a sole means of support, and active involvement in trade union activities are all characteristics more commonly found among male than female employees. Of course these characteristics have nothing to do with biological sex. What these women's employment careers demonstrate is that where women find it necessary to think of themselves as breadwinners, and shoulder all responsibility for themselves and their families, they are likely also to follow what has often been thought of as a 'male' pattern of employment.

Three other women in this group were in paid employment when interviewed, but were only marginally integrated into the labour force. All were living alone with their children, but were not economically self-supporting in the way the four women already described were. Jackie was receiving supplementary benefit, as well as support from two men, her former husband and the father of her second child, while both Hilary and Jane were in receipt of Family Income Supplement as well as a small amount of maintenance from their former husbands. Jackie and Hilary were both employed part-time, while Jane worked a 40-hour week, and sometimes did 5 hours overtime as well. In what ways had their personal histories resulted in their marginal integration in the labour force?

Jackie's employment career had been severely disrupted by ill-health: several mental breakdowns, anorexia nervosa, and alcoholism. During the first three years of her employment career, she had three different jobs in residential homes for the elderly and handicapped, working as a care or nursing assistant. She left two of these jobs on account of her health, and the third following her marriage (when she was 21). After her marriage she took a full-time college course and qualified as a medical secretary, subsequently finding employment as secretary to a hospital consultant. She left this job after a year when expecting her much wanted first child.

She had not anticipated returning to employment for some years, but an opportunity to work 6 hours per week in the evenings as secretary to a general practitioner came up, and she took the job. After just two months she had to be re-admitted to hospital. Subsequently her marriage broke down, and after a short spell living alone with the baby she lost custody of the child to her husband, 'because of my drinking'.

JACKIE: 'When I got her back [four months later] I still wasn't working... and I just lived here on my own with her for a while, and I didn't work until the following year, until I got sober .... I started that about nine months after I stopped drinking.'

Her next job was secretarial work for a charity on one day a week, and she was doing this when we met.

JACKIE: 'I don't claim my money from there — which is £6 per week — until my telephone bill comes in — so it's purely for the telephone.'

She explained that a telephone was vital to her because of her alcoholism. Shortly before we met, Jackie had had a second child. She intends to stay on her own, and says that the baby's father now 'maintains him'.

Hilary, in her early thirties, with three children aged between 8 and 14, was married for just two years, although she has subsequently lived with another man for about four years. After leaving school at 15, Hilary had a number of short-lived jobs, as a factory worker and as a cinema usherette, before joining her parents, both agricultural workers. As she put it: 'I went on to the farm with Mum and Dad . . . I did quite a lot of farm work.'

She stayed in this work until her first, unplanned, child was expected.

HILARY: 'Well, it didn't upset my plans — because I never had
any plans — I never plan things anyway, it's no good . . . it's just
that I knew — this fella that I was going with — before I married
him . . . it wouldn't work. And I thought, you know, getting
married, it might alter him . . . well, it didn't. And then, when I
found that I was pregnant, I thought "Oh God, how are we going
to manage?" . . . and this is what it was.'

Her husband was unemployed throughout the two years of their
marriage. 'I was going to work to keep him.' After her marriage
ended, and following a spell when she lived on supplementary
benefit, she began living with the man who is the father of her
second and third children, a self-employed builder and decorator.
During the four years this relationship lasted, she was not in
employment, and her involvement in a car accident meant that 'The
very last year that he was with me, I couldn't walk.' Hilary felt that
neither of the men with whom she had been involved had helped
her to shoulder the responsibilities of raising a family: 'I've brought
my three up on my own, really . . . . Really, I mean, because the two
boys' father, we never used to hardly see him, anyway.'

When she had recovered from her accident, she took a part-time
job as a hospital bed-maker.

HILARY: 'I wanted to get out . . . I was just shut in, day after day,
and I just couldn't take any more of it. It was either come to work
or crack up in the end, I think.'[8]

With help from her family with childcare, she kept this part-time job
for over eighteen months. However, 'The reason I didn't stay was . . .
because of the children, you know the seven-week school holiday.'
Her next return to employment was as a part-time hospital
domestic, a job which she had held for over three years when
interviewed, despite a long period of sick leave, and a period of
working reduced hours so that she could visit her youngest child in
hospital following his injury in a road accident. She was not at the
time of the interview entirely satisfied with her situation at
work.

HILARY: 'I have been moved about, quite a bit, just lately . . . they
shove me off somewhere else. I fell out quite a few times with
[management] . . . . If I could find another job tomorrow, I'd go
to it.'

Hilary was not finding it easy to cope: her children were difficult to
manage, and she has had to call upon social services for
assistance.

HILARY: 'My children get me down . . . you know, sometimes . . .
they really do make me cry . . . to think that I'm trying as hard as I
can, to keep that house going and keep it nice, and they just don't
care.'

In the light of her past history, Hilary's expectations about her
employment future seemed rather unrealistic: she thought she
would stay 'until I find something else — or I get married — then I
won't have to go to work.'

Jane was a divorcee in her mid-thirties, with three children aged
between 11 and 15. She had been married only once, for about
seven years, and did not do so until after her three children were
born. She was divorced five years before we met. After leaving
school at 15, Jane was employed for five years in a variety of
different jobs before having her first child. She worked as a shop
assistant, in two factories, and as a bus conductress. She left the
shop for better pay, was made redundant from one of the factory
jobs, and left the other following an argument with the foreman.
She left the bus company because of her pregnancy. There then
followed a period of five years during which she did no paid work
and had three children. How did she feel about being a single
mother?

JANE: 'Dunno . . . I just had to shoulder the responsibility, as
with all three of them . . . it just happened . . . so that was
that . . . '

At first she lived with her parents, but towards the end of the five
years married and went to live with her husband. Her return to
employment was prompted by the loss of her fourth child soon
afterwards.

JANE: 'I was getting a bit depressed, you know, with losing the
baby and that, and I was sterilized — I had a Caesarean and
sterilization at the same time — so I took a job — that's
about it.'

She took full-time work as a hospital domestic, but left after a
year.

JANE: 'I started having problems with the old man . . . whilst I
was in hospital, he was carrying on with this woman . . . .'

After two years without employment she started working again, as
a barmaid in a pub.

JANE: 'I started there a couple of dinner times, and then did
three or four a week . . . and then several evenings a week. And

then we split up completely . . . the marriage had really broken down, and then, obviously, you know, I needed extra money, because of being on my own with three kids, so I took a job here.'

This time her job was again as a hospital domestic, working full-time. She had been in this job for four years when I interviewed her. Although previously her personal life had tended to limit her attachment to employment, she now recognized that she needed to continue earning a living. I asked how long she expected to stay in her job.

JANE: 'Well, as long as possible.'

S.Y.:   *[Until] you come to retire?'*

JANE: 'What can I say? . . . There's not a lot you can say about it, is there? It's a job . . . . The chance is, I might have to be.'

For these women, then, participation in the labour force had been reduced by the nature of their personal relations and health. Unlike the four women described earlier, Jackie, Hilary, and Jane had not used employment as a means of structuring uneven and disrupted personal lives, but found that their employment careers were limited and fragmented by them.

The remaining three women had personal histories which temporarily interrupted their employment careers.

Annette was gentle and softly spoken, a woman who looked younger than her 27 years. Although she was caring for two children aged 12 and 14, she had no natural children of her own and had never married. At the time of the interview she had been living for four years with Jim and his two children by his ex-wife. Jim's wife had 'walked out and left' the family some six months before Annette moved in. Annette worked full-time as a clerical assistant and had also taken on the role of mother to Jim's children, and wife to Jim. Her early employment career had been rather chequered. She left school at 15 and worked briefly in a factory, and then in a hairdresser's, finding both unsatisfactory. After this she took another factory job, this time wiring electrical goods. She stayed in this job for two and a half years, before being made redundant. After some weeks out of work, she obtained a job as an office junior.

ANNETTE: 'I learnt how to operate the switchboard, and went from being a junior to doing all the credit control and the wages.'

Meanwhile, she had applied for another clerical job.

ANNETTE: 'My sister worked there . . . I suppose that was really the reason I went there — plus it was more money.'

She was taken on, and stayed two years before starting to feel restless. She then gave in her notice, and took work for the summer at a holiday camp — 'getting away from home for a couple of months'. Afterwards, she worked briefly as a barmaid, before obtaining clerical work again, in a small company. By the end of the year, however, she had been offered her old clerical job back, and this time she stayed for almost three years, only leaving after moving in with Jim. She was quite keen to stop working, and Jim was anxious for her to do so: 'He's a bit possessive and a bit selfish, and he just wanted me at home.' After three years out of employment, however, Annette was anxious to return to her old job:

ANNETTE: 'The frustrations of being at home all the time had set in by then . . . [he] didn't want me to come to work at all — it was purely at my insistence — at which he is pleased now — but it did take quite a few months.'

She had been back a year when we met. What were her plans for the future? She explained that she had decided not to have children of her own, but that was not all.

ANNETTE: '[I have] distant thoughts of having a little business of my own . . . perhaps a little shop . . . . I think I like working better knowing that it's not something that I'm going to have to do for another forty years or whatever . . . if I wanted to give up, I can give up.'

Alice was a 40-year old divorcee. She had left her husband and three children five years previously to live with another man, but the relationship did not last. She then spent some time living with her father, and, since his death, with another man and, more recently, her elder son. Like many of the women interviewed, Alice had several jobs between leaving school and having her first child, and married during this period. She left employment to have her first baby, and during the next six years her second and third children were born. At this stage she engaged in seasonal agricultural work and took on evening jobs — as a factory operative and as a cleaner. After the birth of her third child, she gradually began working more hours per week, at first as a cleaner but later as a laboratory assistant (at the same place of employment). She worked in this last job for about four years, and eventually left her family to set up home with her employer. She explained that she had been unhappy about her marriage and her husband's attitudes to her employment.

> ALICE: 'It seemed to me that he would want me to work all day and all night... my money always went straight in the house — it was expected to go in there — it was never mine.... That's where I went wrong... I felt like a slave. He liked to have his drink, and I was working for him to have his beer. I would come home after working from ten till six... and he admitted he'd been up since half past four, but he'd been asleep all afternoon, and he hadn't bothered — he hadn't made the bed, he hadn't washed up, he hadn't done anything... and before that anyway — he was never capable of looking after me.'

When her new relationship failed, Alice had a breakdown. Afterwards, in her own words, 'I pulled myself together, and went to work.' The work was in a paper mill, 'cutting holes in paper' and she found it hard: 'It was bonus work... you had to do so much... you had to keep going.' After two years, during which time she was also caring for her dying father, she gave the job up and took work as a full-time hospital domestic instead. Two years later, at the time of the interview, she was still working full-time, often doing 11 hours overtime each week. She had no plans to leave: 'I think I shall be working here — well, I just think I shall always be here.' Alice's affair, divorce, and nervous breakdown had not severely disrupted her employment career, but had created a hiatus in its development.

Penny's employment career had been interrupted in a way similar to Alice's, although the change in her personal life which caused the interruption was different. Like Alice's, Penny's employment career followed a typical pattern for about twenty years. She took employment, married, and left to have her first child. She then did seasonal farmwork before moving into full-time permanent employment in sales after her child started school. She continued working full-time, although changing from sales to domestic work when her son was in his early teens. When he was 18, however, she found she was expecting another, unplanned, child. I asked her how she had felt.

> PENNY: 'I don't really know. I wasn't overjoyed, I wasn't bitter .... I always wanted another child.'

Having the child meant giving up her job, but also coincided with the breakdown of her marriage.

> PENNY: 'It finished .... And then, the hard times hit .... I had two choices — either live on social security, and poverty, or

come back to work, and get above — just a little bit above poverty.

She returned to her former job, again full-time, and was able to place her child in the workplace nursery. What of the future?

> PENNY: 'I don't think I shall change [my job] . . . I don't think I'd like promotion . . . I think I've come to a standstill in my life — I think I just like being as I am. I don't think I could take on any more responsibilities because I already have enough . . . I'll keep continuing as long as I can. I've got quite a lot of years left to continue work, and I still hope I can fulfil the years.'

As with Alice and Annette, Penny's employment career was temporarily interrupted by developments in her personal life. Having a child unexpectedly late in her life had a similar effect on her employment career as moving in to be 'mother' to an existing family had for Annette, or leaving a family to establish a new relationship had for Alice.

I have tried to show here that 'distinctive' personal histories such as those described do not have any simple effect upon women's employment patterns, but may influence them in a variety of ways. Some women use employment to structure their lives, while others may find changes and disruption in their personal lives spreading to their employment careers.

In this chapter, I have presented detailed discussion of the patterns of labour adopted by the women interviewed. Although most followed variants on a pattern usually regarded as typical (employment — childrearing — employment), two minority groups whose experience differed in important ways also emerged. In the first, women did not leave the labour force at all, but used maternity leave, or made other arrangements, to enable them to continue in their jobs. The second group consisted of a number of women whose personal histories deviated significantly from current norms governing personal relationships and family formation; in some cases this deviation had the effect of reinforcing integration into the labour force, in others of restricting it. It is important not to ignore the significance of the two minority groups. The former suggests a commitment to participation in the labour force with which women who are also mothers are not usually 'credited', while the latter tells us that there is no simple effect on employment careers which can be attributed to deviation from social norms concerning interpersonal behaviour.

The women in the main group (the 'dominant' pattern) had all left the labour market at least once to raise a child or children, and had returned to it at some subsequent point; none the less there were significant variations within this pattern.

Between leaving school and leaving the labour force to have a first child, most of the women in the group held more than one job; in many cases, changing jobs, even at this initial stage in the employment career, meant changing from one type of work to another, although this changing of occupation was uncommon amongst those (few) women who engaged in further education after school.

In establishing how women came to leave the labour force when expecting a first child, it was noteworthy that about half of first pregnancies were unplanned. These women thus had little opportunity to plan seriously for a future combination of domestic labour and wage-earning. These 'unplanned' first pregnancies reflect the fact that most young working-class women view marriage and a (first) baby as inevitable steps in the transition to adulthood. These steps are not usually subjected to rational economic planning, and often a 'the sooner, the better' approach is adopted. Once they are taken the individual can then get on with organizing her life around what are seen as its essential components — husband and children. Such economically irrational behaviour (which contrasts clearly with the career-oriented approach characteristic of the middle class) can best be understood in terms of the constraints and restricted opportunities of working-class life. Even amongst those whose first child was planned, little thought had apparently been given to returning to employment in the future, although many women said that they had had vague expectations about this at the time.

Most women were to return to paid work much more quickly than they had expected. The return to employment represented a new experience of work, and the next few years were mostly characterized by a succession of part-time, temporary, or seasonal jobs. Most were in low paid and insecure occupations, and many would have gone unrecorded in official statistics. For the minority of married women who had more than one child and who remained outside the labour force throughout the entire childbearing phase, the average length of time between leaving and returning to paid employment was about eight years. It was notable that these women tended to have stable marriages and relatively well-paid husbands. Most placed a high value on their mothering role, and many sought employment partly because of a sense of lost identity when their youngest child started school.

After returning to employment there was a tendency to engage in several part-time jobs over a period of some years before taking on full-time employment. Some women chose to remain part-timers, whilst for others full-time work was an aim which could only be achieved when the youngest child reached a particular age. Almost without exception, the women intended to remain in employment until retirement. For many this intention reflected the fact that they had finally found themselves an acceptable occupation, where they were treated with some respect, derived some enjoyment from their work or working environment, and were earning wages on which they had come to rely. An important minority of the women were more ambitious however, and they intended to seek promotion, further training, or a higher grade occupation. Many of these were women who worked for employers offering training and a career structure to all able members of staff. They had been made aware of the contribution they could make at work, derived a sense of self-worth from this, and had gained the confidence to pursue a career. Others were not positively motivated in this way, but rather felt undervalued and discontented in their present jobs. They knew they could do more demanding work, and recognized that they would need to change their occupation if their skills and abilities were to be used.

The evidence from the analysis of employment careers suggests that women may not be such passive members of the labour force as has sometimes been claimed. They have an experience of paid work which is fragmented and variable, but they also return frequently to employment, and intend to stay. Indeed, many have relatively ambitious plans for the future, and desire to be further integrated into the labour force.

CODA: BARBARA'S STORY

Barbara is 35, has been married to Frank since she was 18, and has two sons, Mark aged 17 and Philip aged 14. Mark left school recently and is doing an apprenticeship. Slightly plump, Barbara has a kindly, almost matronly appearance, and punctuates her conversation with the phrase 'I've been very lucky.' Looking back, she says that if a girl 'had a life like mine she wouldn't have a lot to complain about', although she readily admits that 'we have our ups and downs — but (that's) all part of life.'

Barbara's employment career has conformed to the traditional stereotype for married women: several years in full-time jobs between school and having children, then a complete break while her family were young, followed by a return to employment in part-time work. This pattern of employment reflects the traditional role which Barbara plays within her family. As she says herself, 'I'm not a great women's libber.' Of central importance in Barbara's life have been her responsibilities with regard to 'running her home', a phrase to which she returned frequently. She says proudly that she 'didn't start work (*sic*) until the children were both at school', and finds some contemporary attitudes towards raising children rather puzzling:

> 'I supposed I'm old-fashioned . . . if you're having a baby, then obviously my thought would be to stay at home and look after it — I wouldn't want to go and leave it . . . but if that is sort of what career women really want, then I don't understand it completely, but I would think . . . [the law is right to permit it].'

Although she has no wish to be at home all day now that her children are older, Barbara has always considered it important to plan her life around the demands of her husband and sons. She explained what having a job meant to her, and how she fitted it into her life.

> '[Having a job] makes me better-tempered in some ways . . . . You're so small-minded when you're at home, you just live in your own little world. . . . If it suits people, I mean, it's entirely up to them of course . . . obviously we all come out for the money, but I mean it is the company and the outside attachments . . . the friendships that you make as well . . . . Even if I was well off — obviously if you were filthy rich you'd probably have other things to entertain you — but . . . I would have to have an awful lot of money not to, I think . . . otherwise I think you get a little bit stale . . . . I've always been lucky . . . I've been able to find work where I can fit it in with family life . . . I've more organized my jobs round the family than the family round the jobs.'

It may be useful to indicate just how Barbara has been able to do this. After the birth of her first child in 1963 (she gave up her job as a shop assistant at the beginning of that year) she was at home full-time until September 1970 when Philip started school. Only once in these eight years did she consider taking a job: when Mark was just a few months old she started work as an assistant in a children's nursery, leaving the baby with her mother who lived nearby. She found the separation from her child too hard to bear, however, and after two days abandoned the job. The years at home with the children were not entirely dedicated to caring for the needs of her own household however:

'I used to look after an uncle ... we lived close by .... I looked after him for seven years ... he had his own place ... and I used to just go along and do his cleaning. When he got beyond looking after at home ... they put him into hospital ... and then he died.'

Barbara took this additional responsibility quite for granted. As she saw it, caring for an elderly relative was simply another aspect of a married woman's duties towards her family.

When both her sons had started school Barbara started to look for a part-time job. She faced some opposition from her husband, and her mother was not enthusiastic. However, she persuaded her husband to 'let' her take a job by offering it as a means of achieving a specific objective:

'I told [him], if he wanted a car .... It was really to get extras ... I mean, if we went out anywhere, it was either buses or we had to walk, and we thought it would be nice.'

This tactic was apparently successful; in any case, Barbara obtained Frank's consent, and made enquiries at a local college, where she started work as a part-time catering assistant: 'helping in the kitchens, clearing tables, serving meals, that sort of thing'. Barbara's mother had reservations about the idea of her daughter taking a job. She had never had a paid job herself, although as Barbara explained, 'she used to do little bits of needlework and that ... she was able to make herself the little bit extra.' Nevertheless, she was soon persuaded that the arrangement could do no serious harm, since she recognized the financial pressures on Barbara and her young family. (Frank has worked for the past fifteen years as a warehouseman in a retail store. Prior to this, he worked as a bread roundsman and as a milkman. None of these jobs is particularly well paid.) Indeed, Barbara acknowledged that her mother 'was prepared to help if she could', but added that 'I wouldn't have done it if I'd had to get her to look after the children a lot.' Rather she had 'helped out on odd occasions.'

The job at the college involved striking an individual bargain with management:[9] officially, working at the weekends 'was supposed to be compulsory'.

'When I went for the job, I said, "No, I can't take the job because you want weekends" — and he got me to work a couple of evenings [instead] ... and I ... used to have a young girl — she looked after the children for half an hour before my husband got home. She lived next door but one, and she just came in and looked after them.'

Later, this arrangement about weekend work was not allowed to stand, and, faced with what was for her an impossible choice, Barbara left the job in the following summer. Her comments about the incident are illuminating:

> 'They were insisting then that we work weekends — that was purely because some of them were being funny about it — and so they said, "You'll have to do weekends", and I said, "I can't do weekends because my husband's working every other Saturday." And I didn't feel it was fair to ask the family, so I gave that job up, and had the summer holidays off.'

This explanation reveals that there were other factors in the background influencing the choice which Barbara was forced to make. She had the summer holidays in prospect, and although she was not officially required to work during this time she knew she would be asked to do so (in connection with conferences at the college), and that she would have either to refuse, or to seek support from her mother. Her reluctance to call on her family for support was influenced by both her feeling that the children were essentially her own responsibility, and by her knowledge that her mother was already involved in helping her sister with childcare. Thus a variety of factors combined to produce her decision to resign the job.

As the summer holidays ended, Barbara started to look around for work again. She was experienced in shop work, but did not look in that area:

> 'I didn't think it was worth trying, because I knew I wouldn't get the school holidays . . . I had to sort of compromise . . . and I mean most shop work is Saturdays anyway.'

As the school term began again, she decided to try a different kind of work.

> 'I did two days as a crossing patrol person along by the school — but my nerves wouldn't let me do that. Oh dear, I couldn't put up with that. I did it for two days and I went home and cried my eyes out. I just said to my husband, "I just can't go up there and do it" . . . . A policeman is supposed to stand with you the first week apparently, and he was with me for one day — plus the other lady had left to have a baby, and the thing said "Stop Children" — and the comments I used to get . . . . Anyway, my husband went up and saw the headmaster, and said, "It's no good, she can't do it". And I began to wonder what I was going to do then, I used to look at the papers on Friday morning . . . and then I saw this little job.'

This account reveals something of Barbara's relationship with her husband, as well as of the difficulties which undertaking a new and unfamiliar task can entail. The failure to provide Barbara with proper training, and the vulnerability involved in performing a task in public, where there is no protection from the comments of passers-by, both contributed to her lack of confidence in a job which involves a serious responsibility for the safety of children. The involvement of her husband in communicating her decision to abandon the job illustrates the dependent nature of her relationship with him. As we shall see, it is not a relationship in which she has no power, but it is one in which she defers to his authority and wishes, especially in matters which concern the world beyond their family household.

Her next job (whose significance for her is neatly summarized in her use of the adjective 'little') was a part-time office-cleaning job. She worked at this for three hours each morning, making a 15 hour week. This job did not conflict with any of her domestic responsibilities, but as she suggests below, in discussing why she left it after two years, it had other disadvantages.

'We wanted to do improvements on the home which would mean taking up more on the mortgage . . . . It was only just three hours a morning, and it wasn't very well paid, and I looked for a part-time assistant job in the paper . . . and there was one [in] a wallpaper shop . . . I came for an interview . . . and they didn't want Saturday work. . . I used to work from 9am till 1pm — I was there about six years — and then I changed the hours to suit myself, as gradually the family were growing up.'

Barbara was to stay in this latter job until she knew the shop was about to be closed down. It offered a good arrangement for her because she was able to have the children in the shop with her (when necessary) during their school holidays, and had some flexibility in the hours she worked. It also gave her the opportunity to work on her own initiative and to take on responsibilities of which she had no previous experience. Although she had worked in shops before having her family, she had worked then as a counter assistant, mainly in two small shops, a grocer's and a baker's. Barbara enjoyed the challenge which this job represented for her, but found eventually that it began to impose rather too much upon her home life. She contrasted it with the duties of her current job, as a sales assistant in the retail store where her husband works:

'I had a lot of responsibility in there — management relief when management was off, responsibility as far as ordering goes, plus I mean, the nature of the work is completely different... you really are serving customers there . . . here, it's just a matter of they come and take what they want and come through the tills.'

Had she preferred the more responsible job?

'Yes, in a vain way... but no, not really, because it was beginning to ... interfere with home life ... we didn't get the staff, and the only... action... was that I gave more hours, which I did... then the manager... was off five weeks sick... and I had to take over for five weeks full-time, and you just hadn't got any home life... I enjoyed it, as I say, from a vain way... if I was single and hadn't got any other responsibilities, then fine... but this job does work much better.'

Despite this assessment, Barbara finds some aspects of her current job unrewarding, and misses the control over her job which she had previously:

'Sometimes you feel if you were just left alone you could get on with the job as you would like to — it's like everything else, there are so many rules and regulations, because of the conditions that they expect — it sometimes gets a bit much — but you understand why it is.'

As I have suggested above, Barbara prefers to fit her job around the duties of 'running her home', and chooses part-time work as her strategy for employment rather than the alternative of enlisting the support of her family or of the immediate household. I asked her about her husband's role in the work at home:

'He's always willing to help... when I've been doing it full-time, or something like that — washing-up, he's always been one to give a hand ... if he knows I'm really pushed he will help me do the cleaning — but I'm a bit independent that way ... I get the extra time off, and it's nice to get work done then, so we can share the time together.'

Barbara's 'independence' with regard to the home is a measure of the extent to which she sees this as 'her' domain. She is confident of her abilities to keep it running smoothly, and, unlike her dealings with the outside world, she sees this as a place where she manages and organizes matters as of right. In addition, she enjoys her husband's company, as their decision to have the same weekends off work suggests. In general, Barbara does all the cleaning, washing, ironing, and cooking herself, and she has a clear routine, involving doing particular jobs on set days, and ensuring that tasks like ironing, for example, do not 'pile up'. She prepares her sons' lunch-boxes daily, and is willing to cook twice in an evening if it suits them to have meals at different times. In addition to these tasks, she also does sewing: 'I'm making men's pyjamas at the moment. That I usually fit in at weekends or on my days off.'

Barbara has given some thought to the changed social arrangements whereby increasing numbers of married women have taken on paid jobs. She is not entirely happy about this development:

'The thing is, these days, I think they've *got* to — this is the sad part about it.... If they want... a home of their own... mortgages are so high . . . plus, they do take the wife's wages into consideration now, don't they? When we first started ours, they didn't — in some ways it seemed cruel to us, but I mean it was a lot kinder because you can manage on one wage... I feel so sorry for them... they can't start a family when they want to, perhaps . . . we encourage our boys to save as much as they can, mainly with that thought.'

The child of older parents herself, Barbara is sure that having a family while young is the best arrangement:

'Had my mother been younger, we could have done different things... I was always told I'd led a sheltered life and... I feel it more *now* .... I look at different people and they've got a wider experience of things than I have... my parents were very sort of protective.'

In fact, Barbara's adolescence involved a very straightforward transition from dependence on her parents, and an acceptance of their authority — 'I was the type who did what I was told. I mean, that's what I'd always been brought up to do, and I didn't rebel or anything' — to dependence on her husband and deference to him — 'I was only 15 when I met my husband, I just (wanted to) leave school and . . . get married and have a baby . . . . I had no real ambitions to do anything.'

Her early experiences of employment tended only to reinforce her sense of herself as powerless and as needing the protection of her parents or a husband. Not only was she driven from her first job by the unwanted familiarities of her boss (see earlier in this chapter), but her second employer, a shopkeeper, also treated her with no respect: 'He made you look very small plenty of times.' Significantly, her departure from this job was at the prompting of her parents:

'They were putting on me rather a lot... I used to have to take a lot of writing work home, and the family thought it was getting a bit much . . . . He didn't really want me to leave — he made it very awkward, and had me in tears, but . . . I wasn't staying.'

As Barbara's husband had worked for a large retail store which employs many married women on a part-time basis throughout the past fifteen years, I was curious as to why she had not sought work there until so recently (she had been employed there for less than a year when we met). She explained:

'I'd always said I wouldn't before. I think when I was younger, I was more possessive. I think we were both probably a bit possessive. I didn't think it would work. . . . But then . . . one of the foremen suggsted to me, "Why don't you apply in our place?" — and we'd always said we wouldn't, so I thought it over for a while, and eventually I said to my husband, "What do you think?"'

In the end she decided to apply for the job, 'for the security really', her confidence that it would have this characteristic stemming from her husband's experience.

Barbara has had no hesitations about staying at home if either of her sons has been unwell or has needed her for any other reason. I asked her how she felt about doing this:

'It was just the natural thing to do. Luckily again, wherever I've worked, they've realized that the family came first.'

In Barbara's experience, the standard arrangements with her employers in such an event have been either that she loses pay for the hours not worked, or that she makes up the lost time. 'I've been lucky . . . . If I couldn't work certain hours, I could do it at some other time.'

Barbara's earnings represent a significant contribution to the family budget. When we met in early 1980, she was earning approximately £30 per week (basic), while her husband's basic wage was approximately £69 per week. Their weekly household income was thus about £100, subject to deductions for tax and national insurance, and supplemented by a small contribution from their elder son. Their wages 'all go into the same bank account'. I asked Barbara if they could manage without her earnings:

'At the moment we run two cars — my son is having one of them soon — so obviously the first thing to go would be *my* car. It would mainly be the family holidays and the car — we might perhaps go for a smaller car . . . and just sort of a normal cutback — sort of fizzy drinks and biscuits, all the little extras in that line . . . entertainment, probably — since I've been here we've been going out a little bit more.'

Barbara and Frank are buying their own home, so have a mortgage ('we don't have hardly anything to pay now') as well as the usual household bills to pay. Barbara says they have 'most of what we need — we've been doing the home up now for a couple of years', but the house is less well-equipped with domestic appliances than many homes. It contains a washing-machine (twin-tub) and a fridge-freezer, but lacks items — tumble drier, automatic washing machine, a large food freezer — which other women find valuable. In general, their standard of living is modest, but it is difficult to see how they could maintain this level without Barbara's contribution.

Barbara plans to remain in employment until she reaches retirement age. She thinks it likely she will stay with her present employer and she says she may seek a modest promotion (to Deputy Supervisor), when she has been in the job a little longer. She has no intention of working full-time in the job, however, a decision which in itself effectively bars her way to any further promotion. It seems probable that Barbara and Frank will now complete their employment careers in the service of their current employer. The firm has a reputation for its benevolence (see Chapter 4) and has a paternalistic style which accords well with the ideological framework which supports the couple's domestic arrangements. It seems entirely plausible that they are both regarded by their employers as model employees, just as, conversely, they (if Barbara's views can be taken as representative of them both) look upon theirs as an exemplary employer.

Strategies for employment: 4 employment and the labour market

One of the objectives of the study was to identify how women with children organize their lives so that they can undertake both paid work and family responsibilities. What kinds of strategies for employment are available to them? And what are the structural features, of the labour market, and of the social organization of child and family care, which place limits upon those strategies? In this chapter I look at the nature of women's employment experience and at conditions in the labour market, and consider how these factors shape, and indeed are also a product of, the strategies for employment which women have developed.[1]

In the first section I document ways in which the women's experience of employment was varied, by type of work, hours and conditions of work, and opportunities for collective action. This is followed by a second section in which I present evidence from the interviews which demonstrates the women's flexible approach to employment, and in which I consider ways in which this characteristic may be useful from the point of view of capital. (I am not suggesting that this flexibility results from functional requirements of capital: amongst other problems, such an argument would ignore the various situations in which capital seeks rather to repress flexibility.) Finally I consider some of the implications for the future of the variation and flexibility of female labour — especially with regard to labour market opportunities — and suggest ways in which these characteristics both impose limitations on women's participation in the labour force, and indeed are themselves subject to important limits.

There are two main ways in which a person's experience of employment may be said to be varied: it may (a) include periods spent in a variety of different types of work and (a related factor) working for a variety of different employers; and (b) it may include periods spent working under a variety of working conditions. Although these two aspects may sometimes be related, they can be regarded as logically separate and are therefore discussed separately below.

Type of work experienced

I want to make clear from the outset that I am not claiming that women's experience of employment tends to be varied across the whole range of occupations undertaken by both sexes in Britain. As in other advanced industrial societies, occupations in Britain are sharply sex-segregated and most occupations are classed as either 'women's work' or 'men's work' in the popular imagination. My respondents had not experienced employment outside the sphere of traditionally 'female' jobs, and this was entirely as expected. What I am claiming, and will attempt to demonstrate below, is that *within* the sphere of 'female' employment, women tend to have experience of a wide variety of different occupations.

In order to analyse my data on this point, I classified the various occupations of my respondents under a number of headings.[2] I then calculated how many different types of work each had been engaged in. (This of course did not necessarily correspond to the number of jobs each had held.) Only a small minority (six out of sixty-four women) had experience of only one type of work for money. Over three-quarters of the women had experienced employment in three or more different types of work, and over half in four or more different types. Of those with the most varied experience, Wanda, aged 28 and with no formal qualifications, had had seven different occupations — agricultural work, clerical work, domestic work, driving, factory work, sales work, and homework (knitting and making toys for sale). Lucy, another woman with varied employment experience, had worked as a sales assistant, a packer in a factory, a cleaner, an agricultural worker, and a tourist guide. *Tables 13* and *14* give detailed information about the variety of types of work experienced.

The minority who had experience of only one type of work included a school teacher, two women whose only work experience was as shop assistants, two who had always done clerical work but whose experience in this field was in a variety of jobs (as secretary, clerk, typist, etc.), and one woman who had done a range of different clerical jobs in a computer department.

Table 13   *Number of respondents with experience of employment in each type of work*

clerical and secretarial	35
sales	39
domestic and catering	36
hairdressing	4
communications	5
factory (manual)	30
childcare and au-pair	6
nursing	5
agricultural	23
waitressing and bar-work	6
delivery and driving	2
demonstrating	2
teaching	2
junior managerial	4
technical	3
market research	1
miscellaneous	15
all types of paid employment	64

Thus most of the women had an experience of paid employment which, although limited by the traditional sex-labels which define those jobs which are 'suitable' for women, was extremely varied, rather than concentrated in one particular sphere of 'women's work'.

Table 14   *Variety of respondents' employment experience*

no. of types of work experienced	*no. of respondents*
one	6
two or more	58
three or more	49
four or more	33
five or more	9
six or more	3
seven	1
all	64

For only the exceptional few was it a case of 'once an office worker, always an office worker', and even where women clearly preferred to take employment within the area of work they already knew, they were prepared either to take other work if none was available in their preferred field, or to take on jobs at a lower level from those they had previously held. Thus Elizabeth, having progressed from an office junior through typing and clerical jobs to a position as a personal secretary, later took a job as an audio-typist. Likewise Christine, who had held several responsible secretarial positions both before and after having her family, was employed, when interviewed, as a clerical assistant, pricing and ordering goods in a warehouse. (It should also be noted that, on average, each woman had had between five and six different employers.)

Hours and conditions of work experienced

This varied experience of paid employment had been compounded by the women's experience of working an assortment of different hours, under a variety of conditions of employment, throughout their adult lives. All of the women had spent some time working in what they described as full-time employment (usually at least 35 hours and frequently 40 or more hours per week).[3] They had all worked at some time between leaving school and bearing a first child, but in addition twenty-seven were employed for 40 or more hours per week, and thirty-five for over 36 hours per week when interviewed. The experience of having a part-time job was also a very common one, and over three-quarters of the women had at some time been employed on a part-time basis. The term part-time employment comprises a variety of different experiences. For some, part-time work had meant a 5-day week with short days while for others it meant a shorter week — perhaps one, 2 or 3 days per week, often working a full 7- or 8-hour day. Some types of part-time employment (particularly cleaning, bar-work, waitressing, etc) involve evening work, perhaps just a few hours each night, and twenty-seven of the women had experienced this, including some who had been factory operatives on shift-work. A smaller group (seven women) had also experienced early morning employment, typically as cleaners in offices or shops, often for just a couple of hours, perhaps from 6.00 to 8.00 a.m. Thus part-time employment had frequently involved working hours outside of the 'conventional' working days of 9.00 a.m. to 5.00 p.m. (for white-collar workers) and 7.30 a.m. to 4.30 p.m. (for manual workers). In addition to this, about two-thirds of the women had experienced employment at weekends — Saturdays in particular, especially for sales workers, but also Sundays, notably for domestic and catering workers. Weekend working was frequently a condition of both full- and part-time jobs. Many women reported that they worked alternate Saturdays, or had one weekend in four free. Some, hospital workers for example, received modest 'overtime' payments for weekend working, but this was frequently not the case, especially for sales workers.

Conditions of employment had also been variable for most of the women. All had held permanent jobs, but well over half (thirty-eight) had also held temporary, seasonal, or casual jobs, for instance seasonal agricultural work, sales jobs in the run-up to Christmas, and temporary secretarial or clerical work (often obtained through a specialist agency). About one in five of the women had at some time done work for money at home, including four women whose status at this time is perhaps best described as 'family workers', since they were working in family-owned or -managed shops, and in one case as a clerical assistant to a self-employed husband. Apart from these activities, paid work at home involved mainly typing and childminding. Other women had done dressmaking, toy-making, and had taken in lodgers or guests as a way of earning some money. There is now substantial evidence concerning the relatively low rates of pay and poor conditions of employment for part-time workers, and especially for casual and home-workers.[4] In general, the experience of my respondents who had worked on any or all of these bases confirmed those findings. Most women who had worked for money at home recognized that such work was poorly paid, but had found it convenient at a particular stage in their lives. They rapidly realized that home-working would not make their fortune.

> WANDA: 'I've had the sort of thing when you send away . . . to earn cash at home . . . making things. It was a lot of hard work for hardly anything . . . . Making the sort of foam dollies that stand on your dressing table . . . nightdress cases, that kind of thing . . . the way it was advertized, it was — oh, there was hardly anything to do . . . and you could sell them for quite a good price . . . which was true, it did turn out that way, you could make them in a matter of about ten minutes . . . I had to pay for the kits, and then I had to sell them to make a profit . . . . That [didn't last] long . . . because other than selling them to neighbours and friends, it would have meant me walking round the estate, going further afield to sell them, and that wasn't what I wanted in the first place.'

Numerous women confirmed the evidence concerning employment conditions for part-timers. Many explained that, as part-time workers, promotion of any kind was unavailable to them, and some that they were ineligible for certain fringe benefits, such as membership of pension schemes, leave entitlements, etc. Teresa was working part-time as a sales assistant and deputy supervisor when interviewed, and had been with her employers for ten years.

TERESA: 'We've been trained as a deputy [supervisor] . . . when the supervisor's off, we take over their duties for that day, or a week, whatever . . . I thought it was quite a nice honour, to be just a part-timer and to be asked . . . it's always been full-time staff [who] have . . . done it prior to that . . . . There's quite a few of us now.'

Her pay was higher than that of an ordinary sales assistant, but 'not the same rate as the supervisors'. I asked if she would like to be promoted further.

TERESA: 'I suppose really, you can't be, because I am only a part-timer — [not] unless you're a full-timer.'

Another part-timer experienced a different disadvantage:

RUTH: 'There is a pension scheme, but as a part-timer, I can't belong to it, which is fair comment.'

Other women gave indications of the divisions which may exist between part-time and full-time workers in a company. I had asked Dawn if there was anything she disliked about her work as a part-time sales assistant.

DAWN: 'Well, we all have our moans . . . the thing I don't like mostly is having to get down and clean right underneath the counters . . . it's got to be done, but I feel it always seems to be the part-timers and not the full-timers . . . *we* do it.'

For many of those who had experienced periods in casual work, the poor and erratic pay and insecurity of the job had been factors leading them eventually to seek alternative work. This was particularly true of casual agricultural labour. Whilst many women had worked the summer seasons on fruit and hop farms, others had been employed all year round, and it was these women who saw their experiences as agricultural workers in the starkest terms.

PAT: 'I went out in the fields . . . I'd never do that again . . . the last time we went picking up potatoes, we were picking them out the ground frozen . . . it nearly killed me . . . . I didn't know, but I'd got gastroenteritis starting up . . . they [all] thought I was putting it on . . . I wasn't . . . I was half dead . . . I thought "Oh, no more, no more . . . I'm going to get myself a regular little job." '

The following account of casual agricultural work includes an insight into the resourcefulness which working women must often display, and their pride in this.

PRU: 'Over the winter . . . we were in a big shed . . . slicing apples — Oh God, what a job — you know, tinned apples and God knows what ... into apple pies .... They had a big barn, and [the children] had the top part of it ... we used to take turns in looking after all the children, and we used to pay so much a day to whoever was doing it ... it was quite revolutionary at the time — it was even on television!'

Carol had also worked virtually all year round as an agricultural worker.

CAROL: 'It was convenient, that was why I did it ... farm work has never been very well paid. You could earn good money piece-work, I pride myself that I could work quickly piece-work, and you did earn good money .... A big disadvantage was ... if [the farmer] needed other work doing when there was fruit-picking piece-work, he would tend to keep you on a day rate, hoeing and doing other jobs, and he'd have lots of people come and stay in caravans to do the piece-work. This to me was very unfair, you were working there for eleven months of the year, and we thought we should have the benefits as well. We discussed it with him, and he reluctantly gave us some piece-work which we did — it didn't last very long, but the money was very good if you worked at it, we worked Sundays as well .... There was also jobs with no interest at all, sort of weeding and fiddly bits of pruning, and then when there was no work in the packing shed — you go a certain time in a year when it's not worth opening another store .... I couldn't afford to be out of work so he used to let me go and I'd prune currants in the snow, and this sort of thing — it was gutty, quite honestly, but you still got paid at the end of the week. And if you want money at the end of the week, you're prepared to do virtually anything ... I've froze ... I can remember freezing to death out there, sitting out in the middle of a field eating your lunch, but you do it, you don't realize how bad it was until you look back on it.'

The fact that many of the women had experienced the relatively poor pay and conditions of casual and part-time employment, and in some cases home-working, is important in explaining their relative satisfaction with the permanent (and mostly full-time) jobs in which they were working when interviewed. The tables below (*Tables 15* and *16*) show how the women responded to questions about their current pay and working conditions. With the main exception of the hospital workers (whose low rates of pay gained some notoriety a few months after the interviews took place during the 1982 health service dispute), most of the women were relatively satisfied with their pay. Over three-quarters described their pay as

Table 15   *Description of pay in current job*

job category	assessment of pay				
	excellent	good	fair	poor	very poor
retail store					
sales and catering assistants	2	8	1	—	—
supervisors	2	2	—	—	—
hospital					
domestics	—	—	6	6	2
supervisors	—	1	2	1	—
engineering company					
clerical workers	—	1	1	1	1
college					
kitchen assistants	—	1	—	2	—
public sector company					
junior grades	2	2	1	—	—
supervisory and junior					
managerial grades	—	3	—	—	—
others					
junior clerical workers	—	2	2	—	—
senior clerical workers	1	3	—	—	—
manual workers	—	1	1	1	—
sales workers	—	—	2	—	—
all*	7	24	16	11	3

* 61 respondents were in regular employment when interviewed.

'fair' or better, and half said it was 'good' or 'excellent'. The women who worked in the retail store, and for the public sector company, were predominant amongst this group. Whilst the sales workers in this store were receiving relatively good pay compared with other women doing similar work, they were not in fact very highly paid. In 1980,[5] sales assistants were earning a maximum of £1.53 an hour (gross) if they were over 18 years old. (They also received a Christmas bonus equal to four weeks' pay, which, calculated as an addition of one thirteenth of their pay, brought their hourly earnings to approximately £1.65.) This can be compared with an average hourly rate for women of £2.06, and for men, of £2.81, in the same year (Equal Opportunities Commission 1981a).[6] Many of the women themselves made the point that they thought their pay 'good', because it compared favourably with their previous earnings which had often been from casual work. Carol pointed out that as a sales assistant with this company 'I've virtually doubled my money'.

Satisfaction with working conditions was even more pronounced. Two-thirds of the women described their working conditions as

Table 16 *Description of working conditions in current job*

job category	assessment of working conditions				
	excellent	good	fair	poor	very poor
retail store					
sales and catering assistants	8	2	1	—	—
supervisors	4	—	—	—	—
hospital					
domestics	1	6	7	—	—
supervisors	—	3	1	—	—
engineering company					
clerical workers	—	2	2	—	—
college					
kitchen assistants	—	1	1	1	—
public sector company					
junior grades	1	3	1	—	—
supervisory and junior managerial grades	1	2	—	—	—
others					
junior clerical workers	1	1	1	1	—
senior clerical workers	1	3	—	—	—
manual workers	—	—	1	1	—
sales workers	—	—	—	2	—
all*	17	23	15	5	0

* One of the 61 respondents who were in paid employment at interview did not answer this question.

'good' or 'excellent', and almost all said they were 'fair' or better. Why were so few women dissatisfied? The retail store has a reputation for the high standard of its employment conditions and services to employees. Medical and other personal services (e.g. hairdresser) are provided for staff, there is a good quality subsidized catering service, and employees have a pension scheme (open to all permanent staff, whether full- or part-time) and a profit-sharing scheme (open to all staff with five years' *unbroken* service). Much was made (by some employees and by management) of the good relations between all levels of staff, and in particular the accessibility of the staff manageress, who could apparently be approached at a moment's notice. The women I spoke to mostly valued the cleanliness of the store (which was impeccable) and the attentiveness to details of health and safety procedures. For women who had in the past been employed as kitchen assistants, cleaners, agricultural workers, etc., these working conditions seemed almost too good to be true. They were not getting any benefits which are not currently commonplace for male white-collar workers, but they were mildly amazed that any employer should make such things available to them.

One initially puzzling point concerned the fact that ten of the hospital workers described their working conditions as 'good' or 'excellent' and the remaining eight as 'fair'. In material terms — fringe benefits and the condition of the buildings and of the equipment in which and with which they worked — their conditions could hardly be so described. However, in asking a deliberately general question I had hoped to elicit responses to a wide range of the women's employment circumstances. This technique proved effective, for it became abundantly clear that while frequently dissatisfied with reduced staffing levels, impoverished material surroundings, and a dearth of fringe benefits, there was something about working as a hospital domestic or supervisor which made the women prefer this to many of the jobs (in factories, as agricultural workers, as sales assistants, and as clerks) which they had done in the past. What they found in the hospital was a kind of 'occupational community': not in the sense of a mining village, but in the sense that all hospital workers — nurses, doctors, and ancillary staff — must work to some degree as a team, responding to crises and taking account of the constantly changing needs of patients. Further, they are able to gain a considerable degree of satisfaction from doing their jobs because they can see their labour as directed towards genuine human need. Unlike their previous jobs — in several cases as factory operatives making paper bags for instance — they did not feel alienated by their work, but, on the contrary, it was possible for their employment to give some meaning to their lives. I include below a sample of the many positive comments made by the hospital domestics about their work.

OLIVE: 'The present ward I'm on [has a] friendly atmosphere.... I suppose that's all it is really — nice people to work with — that's the basis of it I think... you get on with everybody you're working with ... it makes it an excellent place to come to each day... [the] satisfaction of having done something . . . doing something for others.'

NANCY: 'I like the job.... I mean that's why I stick it... if it was for the pay, I mean, I wouldn't be able to put up with it. It's a nice job because you're meeting people all the time . . . you know . . . I worked in a factory before, and there's no comparison. You're just like a zombie all day, but here it's something different all the time, and you're dealing with people and not objects.'

SHEILA: 'Well, I like the patients .... I never thought I would like the patients in a mental hospital, but I do. They're well, they're nice. You feel as if you want to help them, you know? . . . to a certain extent . . . I know you can't, because, well, I'm not a nurse, but you — well, there's little things you do for them.'

PENNY: 'I think it's caring for people. I mean, I know we do the domestic side, but — on our type of ward — we come into contact with patients all the time — little things, you know? You care . . . and I would say that's the main thing really — you're caring for something and someone.'

Thus, within the confines of 'women's work', the women's employment careers had mostly encompassed a broad and varied experience of wage labour. They knew what it was like to work for money full-time, part-time, and (sometimes) at home; and to be employed both on a regular basis and as casual, seasonal, or temporary workers. They were used to a variety of working conditions and rates of pay, ranging from the very poor (as when working as cleaners and farm labourers) to the relatively good (as for some who worked as secretarial staff and junior managers in financial institutions and public corporations, and as sales workers in a large and successful retail store). Inevitably, their experiences in the past tended to colour their assessment of the present (just as their experiences in the present coloured their views of the past). As Carol pointed out, 'you don't realize how bad it was until you look back on it'. In conversation with the women, I was sometimes told that (for example) 'you can't improve on' the conditions of service provided by employers in the establishments where conditions were felt to be 'excellent'. This was, of course, patently untrue: paradoxically, it is one of the lessons to be learned from living in a capitalist society that standards of material comfort can never reach a point where further improvement cannot be imagined, or a desire for it instilled. There was, of course, plenty of room for improvement in conditions of employment (better pay, shorter hours, a workplace nursery — 'No one's ever suggested it', the staff manageress said) and ample scope for it in the company's substantial profits. What the comment really meant was that the speaker did not feel she was entitled to any improvement. It is an indication of capitalism's highly resilient nature that it is able to persuade individuals of the need perpetually to 'improve' on private material standards of living, but to accept that public standards, and what individuals can be offered in return for their labour, are always subject to limitation. The creation and legitimization of needs (or their absence) is a complex process of ideological manipulation through which capitalism displays considerable versatility, and the ability to generate a distinction between private and public needs is an especially interesting (and for capital, fruitful) paradox.

So far, I have not examined collective bargaining in the workplace: I now turn to this subject and report on the women's experience of trade union membership and participation throughout their employment careers.

Trade union membership and activity

Although a majority of the women interviewed had at some time belonged to a trade union, slightly less than half were in trade union membership when interviewed. All but three of these were contacted through their trade unions (see *Table 17*).

Table 17   *Membership of trade unions, by trade union, whether past or present, and level of involvement*

trade union	membership		involvement in present union		
	present	past	attend meetings only	hold, or have held office	other
COHSE	15	1	7	3	—
NUPE	2	2	—	1	—
NALGO	1	4	—	—	—
CPSA	4	—	—	2	—
UCW (UPW)	1	2	—	1	—
SPOE	2	—	2	—	—
TGWU	1	2	—	—	1
SOGAT	—	4	—	—	—
TASS	—	1	—	—	—
NUAW	—	1	—	—	—
NUT	1	1	1	—	—
other*	—	2	—	—	—

* Two respondents were unable to specify the union to which they had once belonged.

Key: COHSE: Confederation of Health Service Employees; NUPE: National Union of Public Employees; NALGO: National Association of Local Government Officers; CPSA: Civil and Public Servants' Association; UCW: Union of Communication Workers (formerly Union of Postal Workers); SPOE: Society of Post Office Executives; TGWU: Transport and General Workers' Union; SOGAT: Society of Graphical and Allied Trades; TASS: Technical, Administrative and Supervisory Section (of the Amalgamated Union of Engineering Workers); NUAW: National Union of Agricultural Workers; NUT: National Union of Teachers.

A few of the women who were union members had a high level of participation in union affairs.

PRU: 'I started off as an ordinary member, and then I became assistant secretary, shop steward, health and safety rep..... I do the ancillary meetings with management — you name it, I do it . . . . I usually try to put in 3 or 4 hours a week, sometimes more . . . some weeks it might be 15. [Since two weeks ago] I'm just an ordinary member. Because I found that too much, at home . . . really a lot of pressure was being put on me . . . I mean, I had a week's holiday, and my phone didn't stop going at home, and you need to be so dedicated, you know, in a thing like that. You've *got* to be prepared to put a lot of your own social life into it.'

Pru made it quite clear that one of her reasons for giving up union work was the unsympathetic attitude she met at home — her son was not interested, and the man with whom she lived was 'very anti-unions'. Some of the women who were elected representatives appeared to lack full commitment to their unions. Tessa was an elected assistant representative.

TESSA: 'I've got very mixed feelings about (unions). I certainly wouldn't go on strike for pay — and I'm not too sure I would go on strike for conditions either. It would . . . depend.'

Nancy illustrates several aspects of the women's trade union experience in her comments. She highlights both the lack of encouragement she had received from men already established in the union, and the fact that when she did get involved it was as a response to her fellow workers, rather than through 'political' motivation.

NANCY: 'I don't hold with unions quite frankly . . . you're advised to [join] because . . . you're so vulnerable here — no way would I join otherwise. I think I've got a tongue in my head, and I know how to handle management anyway. If I didn't like the job, I'd pack it in. It wouldn't be the union that would make changes . . . . I was elected to shop steward . . . . I asked to go on a course because I didn't understand it — it wasn't a very good set-up here at the time and he [the branch secretary] — he didn't put nobody forward for a course, so I didn't — I wouldn't go to the next meetings . . . . But again, that's not political motivation, that is just all my colleagues going — "Oh, go on Nancy, you'll speak up for us" — and it was just really through a group thing . . . . I think it's too powerful at the moment, and it's gone away from what it was all meant to be.'

While Nancy's comments reflected a very common attitude to the trade union movement, it would be quite inaccurate to portray hers as the only view. Several women were strongly behind their union. Beth felt she was at an advantage as a union member.

> BETH: 'Even today, shops don't have a union — the little shops in the street — you've got no union, no one to fight for you . . . . I believe in unions, I think unions are a good thing . . . they can't tread all over you — you have got someone you could go to to fight for you . . . a union is a good thing — because otherwise they'd still have the kids up to sweep the chimneys and the kids down the mines. No, I believe in unions.'

As indicated above, most of the women were not currently members of trade unions. The retail store where fifteen of the women worked was not unionized, and many of the women working in clerical and secretarial jobs were in a similar position. Most of those who worked in the retail store felt there was no need for trade union representation in their place of work.

> TINA: '[In this company] . . . I just don't think it's necessary at all — it wouldn't serve any purpose. I think everybody's wages — as far as I know — are quite good — and the conditions are fantastic . . . . If I wasn't happy, I'd leave.'

There was considerable hostility to the whole trade union movement amongst the women interviewed in this store. Many held strongly individualistic views, and were against collective action under almost any circumstances.

> HEATHER: 'I think we've come a long way in this company without a trade union, and I think it . . . would cause havoc if people started to try and do something like that . . . the only things they could strive for, I know the thing that some of the girls don't like, is the discipline over appearance and attitude, that sort of thing . . . . We have very much a hierarchy . . . but to me, it's quite acceptable, it's part of — what's the word I'm looking for? — freedom of enterprise. We can all strive for those positions, but some people will prefer to just moan and groan about it . . . I think that's the sort of people that you would get in a trade union in this company, because the majority are just here to get on, do a day's work, be paid a good wage for that job, and that's it . . . . I've always tended to accept what I've got, and if I don't want what I've got, then I go out and change my life individually. I know a lot of people can't do that, they're working *en masse* in industries, but once having joined a trade union . . . you're no longer as an individual responsible for your own actions — you have to follow the dictations of, again, the

hierarchy that are dictating what you want and what you need, and it might not be what you want and what you need personally.'

Other women were quite frank in admitting their ignorance about trade union affairs.

TERESA: 'No, I've never been approached about that subject at all. I've never really gone into the trade unions and that . . . . My husband's never spoken about it at home . . . I don't know any details about it really.'

Ignorance about trade union matters was not confined to those who were not union members. Jane, a hospital domestic, was a COHSE member and had previously belonged to NUPE.

JANE: 'I'm still a bit green about it now . . . I don't really know [why I joined] . . . . I just automatically joined it . . . . I go to all the meetings, but half the time I don't know what they're on about anyway.'

The commitment to an individualistic approach was common and strong, and found amongst many of the women, again including some union members.

SHIRLEY: 'No, I fight my own battles.'

SALLY: 'I just feel that any advancement is my own personal responsibility . . . . If I can't personally achieve something, there's no satisfaction in somebody else doing it for you.'

While it is, of course, important to recognize the significance of these views, it should be noted that least hostility to trade unions was evident amongst the women who were most familiar with trade union representation at the workplace, and vice versa. Some of the women who had experienced working in both unionized and non-unionized occupations were able to compare the two situations.

LORNA: 'If anything happened, they would give us a fair deal and stick up for us . . . I think perhaps they go too far in some things, but I mean they're good to have around, I think they help you.'

Valerie's comments highlight some of the problems facing employed mothers who wish to participate in trade union affairs, as well as the pressures which management and employers may sometimes apply.

VALERIE: 'I used to be on the committee. And — chairman at one stage . . . I enjoyed it actually . . . but, once I got my promotion, there was a bit of blackmail from higher management, you know

— "You really can't camp this side of the house *and* that side of the house" — but also really from my own point of view, with the promotion, I'd then got a child as well, and I couldn't have made the committee meetings in the evenings, so it wasn't just his blackmail if you like, that I opted out — plus the fact too that for your first year of promotion it's rather difficult actually to wear two hats as it were — you need to sort of concentrate your efforts a bit till you're well established, and so on . . . now, I think I've sort of got out of it, the kids are growing up a bit now, but I doubt whether I'll ever become that much involved again.'

I asked if she had ever taken any kind of industrial action.

VALERIE: 'Oh yes . . . I've been on strike . . . my view is really, we're here, we've got a trade union to represent our pay, working conditions and so on, and I pay them such and such — I can't negotiate my own — they're going to do it for me. If I strongly oppose what they were asking me to do or whatever, I might well withdraw from the union, or put a proposition in the next conference — this sort of thing. But . . . I feel that we're quite a modest trade union anyway, and so far I've not had to feel that our demands aren't worth meeting, so I've been able to go along with them quite happily.'

Valerie was not alone in experiencing management discourage-ment of union involvement. Ruth, a non-unionized clerical worker, explained that there had recently been a recruitment campaign by the trade union in her place of work but 'we got a £5 a week pay rise not to [join] — so we didn't.'

A FLEXIBLE APPROACH TO EMPLOYMENT

The fact that the women's experience of employment was varied in the ways described above is in itself an indication of a flexible approach to paid work on the part of the individual women concerned. This flexibility was further illustrated in the interviews by the women's comments about their varied employment experience.

MARGARET *(who had been employed in a wide variety of jobs)*:   'I quite adapt myself to anything really, I don't find it too difficult.'

MARY *(on first taking a job as a waitress)*:   'Again, I liked it — I suppose I'm quite adaptable. I fit in to what I'm doing, and, you know, I did like it.'

WANDA *(on an early morning cleaning job)*:   'I didn't like it a lot . . .

but there again . . . I think as far as I'm concerned, it doesn't really matter what work you're doing, if you're getting on with the people all right, you know, and sort of have a laugh and a joke, it makes it all worthwhile.'

Evidence of a flexible approach

In an attempt to discover how flexible the women were prepared to be, I asked them to imagine they were currently looking for a job, and to select from a list the characteristics which that job would have to offer. Items on the list included 'work you have done before', 'something completely different', 'a job where you could learn new skills', and 'suitable hours for your needs'.

A minority of the women (less than one in five) did not really want to consider work of which they had no experience. In some of these cases there was an active desire to return to a former occupation. Maria, for instance, was a hospital domestic who had formerly worked as a secretary: 'I would like to go back to my old job — which was interesting, and it had prospects.' Predominant amongst this group were women who, like Maria, had some kind of occupational skills, or who, like Lynne, had gained unskilled experience in a field to which they wished to return for training. Lynne's experience as a nursing auxiliary had left her with the conviction that 'I know what I want to do'. Jackie wanted to stay in the occupational field for which she was qualified, but wanted to build on her experience.

> JACKIE: 'A job where I could acquire new skills — I mean, I don't think that I've explored everything that I could do as a medical secretary . . . . I'd like to work in some sort of medical research, and there are hospital specialities that I'd like to work in.'

While most of these women had positive reasons for wanting to continue working in a field which they knew, one or two had more negative motivations. Mavis simply felt that 'it's easier to get a job if you've done the job before' while Yvonne was reluctant to explore pastures new — 'I don't like change of any kind' — and she wanted 'something I know I can do'.

A further small group (seven women) said that they would prefer work they had done before, but would be willing to consider other work if necessary.

> MARY: 'Work I'd done before I'd most probably go for, because, it's a case of — you know it. And I'm not that interested in, as I say, promotion or branching out. Mind you, if I couldn't get it, I'd

have a go at something else — but yes, I think I'd be more likely to go for something that I know.'

By far the largest group, however, either expressed a preference for a different kind of work from anything they had done before, or claimed that the issue did not matter to them either way. More than two-thirds of the women came into this category. In some cases, their attitude sprang from a willingness to take any opportunity for paid work which was presented. As Lorna said, 'When I came into this job, I'd never done it before — I don't think it particularly matters.' Others felt that by taking up new opportunities, it might be possible to find work which could be unexpectedly satisfying.

JUNE: 'I think if there's a job advertised and you're looking for work and anything comes up, you think, "I don't know, I think I'll have a go at that", and sometimes you can go, and it's something that you've never done before, and you find it quite interesting.'

For other women, the willingness to consider alternative types of work reflected a sense that their current and past employment had demanded little of their abilities.

TRACEY: 'Something quite different — I don't know what I would do, but I'd like to do something different from what I'm doing at the moment — I'm sure I am capable of doing something different from cleaning and making salads.'

A number of women explained that they liked a challenge in their job, and that they sought work which held interest for them and kept them busy.

TESSA: 'I don't think it would matter to me what I did really.... [I'd like] "interesting and demanding" work, because otherwise I feel I'm wasted — I feel I could be doing better things at home if I'm not fully employed.'

Lucy's attitude was shaped by her awareness that she lacked occupational skills.

LUCY: 'I think (I'd like) a job where you could acquire new skills ... as someone that hasn't got any qualifications for anything... if there was anything going with training that I was capable of doing, I'd like to have a go.'

In one or two cases, however, the willingness to undertake new or alternative employment was undermined by the lack of self-confidence which has often been noted by writers on married women's employment. Olive was working as a hospital domestic when interviewed. Although she had held a number of secretarial posts before her children were born, she had not felt able to return to this work. Her self-doubts were quite apparent.

> OLIVE: 'It would be nice to do something quite different — that I've never done before . . . [but] I don't know . . . at my age, I'd probably be panic-stricken doing something perhaps I couldn't cope with.'

The women were less adaptable in their answers concerning the hours they were prepared to work. For many, the working hours of a potential job were important, since they had to fit in with their other (family) responsibilities. Often, as I have demonstrated, accommodating these other responsibilities meant that they had experienced working a variety of different hours in the past: at particular stages in her employment career a woman might find working part-time, or in the evenings, or full-time, or at home, especially convenient (and perhaps the only way in which she could combine employment and domestic 'duties'). It is thus an apparent paradox, but an important feature of their real lives, that women should have a varied experience in this respect, bearing witness to a *personal* flexibility, yet still be limited at particular points in their lives to accepting jobs only under certain special conditions because of the burden of family responsibilities.

Flexibility of approach, then, emerged as a theme throughout the interviews: I believe it is a crucial feature of female labour in contemporary Britain. It is important, however, not to confuse a willingness to turn one's hand to anything which is required with passivity. As shown in the next chapter, women (and their families) often make considerable adjustments in their domestic lives to enable them to take paid employment. Rather, women's flexible attitude to paid work reflects the way they must work at home, slipping easily between washing, shopping, tidying up, bathing children, ironing, preparing food, cleaning, disciplining and playing with children, repairing clothes, etc, as the need for such labour arises. Given prevailing conditions, their flexibility in employment is perhaps their greatest asset, both from their own point of view — many of my respondents would have been unable to find employment after raising children if they had stuck rigidly to their original occupation — and from the point of view of employers.

I want to emphasize that the flexibility of female labour, and the related factor of women's varied experience of paid work throughout their employment careers, are functions of the subordination of female labour under patriarchal capitalism. The women interviewed had not had the kinds of employment careers described because they had made unfettered choices about ways of selling their labour in a completely free labour market. During the period of these women's employment careers, capital has made quite specific use of women workers, often using them both as a reserve army of labour (see Chapter 2) and as employees whose labour is most profitable to capital when it is not required on a permanent, full-time basis throughout the individual's adult life. The coincidence that, for example, part-time work, or temporary work, may be perceived by women with children as an especially convenient way of selling their labour (in conjunction with the role currently assigned to them in the family household), should not be allowed to conceal the exploitative conditions under which female labour is exchanged with capital.

Attractiveness of female labour for employers

In specific contexts, then, female labour has a number of attractions for employers. Not only is it available relatively cheaply, it is also available on terms which individual employers can set, rather than, as male labour currently is, on terms which are set in a context of collective bargaining and which follow 'agreed' social norms (e.g. 'firms should employ male workers on a regular full-time basis').

This point can be illustrated by reference to the retail store where one group of my respondents worked. This store has an employment and training policy which has been at least partly responsible for its relatively successful weathering of the current recession. I want to draw attention to two aspects of its policy: the use of part-time labour, and the practice of training employees to do work other than that in which they are normally engaged.

On average, over the year 1979-80, the company employed approximately 45,000 people, of whom approximately 60 per cent were part-timers.[7] I knew from my interviews with employees of this company that part-time staff frequently had 'basic' hours which were less than the hours they normally worked. Management explained that part-timers are employed on low basic hours, and that this enables the company to respond to the needs of holidays, peak periods, etc., by asking part-timers to work additional hours as required without paying overtime rates or being overstaffed at other times. The system, management maintain, is dictated purely by the commercial needs of the store, although they believe it also happens to suit the needs of part-time employees.

The company quite commonly gives its sales assistants training in a 'second skill' — to work in the offices, in the catering unit, or in the stock rooms, for example. They can be trained in one or more of these skills, for which they receive extra pay. This policy enables the company (which is non-unionized) to make flexible use of its employees. In particular, 'second skill' training is given to employees who show 'ability', but refuse the extra responsibility of becoming supervisors, and those of my respondents who had direct experience of this practice appeared to be happy with it.

The company's success in using female labour to generate substantial and consistent profits has also allowed it to persuade its employees that it is remarkably benevolent, as I have shown above. It is worth noting, however, that the company is quite frank about its policy of 'enlightened self interest'. A recent edition of the company's annual report and accounts stated:

'Our good human relations policy is based on care for the individual. Personal commitment and involvement of our staff results in good morale and *hard work*: *staff stability* is high and *absence* is low. Our policy, together with the *effective use of staff* enables the Company to be a leading employer.' (My emphasis)

Over the years 1977-78 to 1979-80 staff pay and benefits represented approximately 10 per cent of the company's annual turnover. In the company some benefits are available to all permanent staff (full- and part-time), for example the non-contributory pension scheme, whilst others are confined to employees who fulfil certain service requirements, for example the profit-sharing scheme, open to staff who have completed five years' unbroken service. It is notable that shares are made available to staff under this latter scheme only when the company's pre-tax profits exceed £100 million. (In 1980 pre-tax profits were approximately £170 million and approximately £3 million was made available for the scheme.)

The company's employment policy is successful not only in that employees report favourably on their pay and conditions (as shown above) but also in creating a public image which it (apparently correctly) calculates is attractive to customers. Thus an internal company news report, picturing employees in receipt of dental care, hairdressing services, and the attention of a chiropodist, could comment that these company-provided benefits 'are all available for us to look, and feel, our best ... from top to toe'. On the opposite page a large photograph of a smiling and immaculately groomed sales assistant serving a customer is accompanied by the phrase: 'No wonder our girl here has a smile worth a billion and a half (that's our sales last year).' Just in case employees should doubt the justice of the company's substantial profits, the house newspaper also carries an article by a financial journalist, from which I quote:

'If you work for a profitable firm you can be pretty sure that you are doing a good job for the community. Profits are an acid test of whether people really need your services. Of course, there are exceptions: drug peddling and pornography are highly profitable, but it's easy to prove they are evil. Schools and hospitals don't normally make profits, yet it's easy to prove that they're good for the community. But in between those extremes anything that makes an honest profit can claim that it is serving the public.'

VARIATION AND FLEXIBILITY: IMPLICATIONS

Having described the variation and flexibility of female labour, I want now to consider some of their likely effects upon women themselves and upon their families.

Labour market opportunities

Women whose employment careers have spanned the period since the early 1960s have witnessed important changes in the kinds of employment opportunities which are available in the formal labour market. From their point of view, the most significant of these have been the expansion of the service sector of the national (and local) economy, and the extension of part-time jobs.

The nature of women's domestic role, which involves the servicing of the needs of men, children, and (from time to time) the sick and elderly, has made it especially convenient for employers to buy female labour to perform tasks involving some skill, but for which no training need be given (e.g. the work of a kitchen assistant involves tasks for which persons unused to the preparation of food would need to be trained, at a cost to the employer). The variety of skills which women employ with considerable flexibility in the domestic context has made them highly attractive workers for the expanding service sector. However, it is a measure of the subordination of women in patriarchal capitalist societies that women themselves frequently do not recognize the tasks of domestic labour as involving skill. Nevertheless, liberal feminists have recently drawn attention to the 'relevance' of homemaking skills and experience for management and executive careers:

> 'Management has all the hassles and frustrations of looking after small children . . . . But most male managers would be astonished if a woman tried to argue that childcare was relevant experience in applying for a managerial job . . . . Next time you are on duty at the local playgroup . . . try not to think of it as a maddening waste

of a promising career. Think of it as a sandwich course in management instead.'

(Cairncross 1982a)

Of course, as Richards points out, this kind of argument can be deeply reactionary, and patronizing to women. She argues: 'It is silly to console someone with being a cook (for all you know a bad one) if she hates cooking, but would have been rather good at ballet dancing or car mechanics' (Richards 1982:202–03).

Further, we should not be surprised to find that the link has rarely been made between the domestic skills of working class women, and the use which is made of their labour when it is exchanged with capital. It is interesting to note that current technological develop-ments render obsolete many of the highly specialized skills once greatly valued by capital. Arguably the trend now is towards a requirement for skills of a different kind — the ability to adapt and be flexible, to learn *new* skills, and to demonstrate general, rather than highly specialized, aptitudes. We may make a connection here with the 'flexibility' which women display, the origins of which lie in an ideology which values women as competent all-rounders and men as specializing experts. Shaw compares the 'disorganized, episodic and fragmented' nature of most women's lives (which she links to the need to combine childcare with paid and unpaid work) with the relatively 'predictable, cumulative' and continuous lives of men. She concludes her discussion of gender and models of learning in school by suggesting that 'discontinuity and interruptions are . . . an institutionalized and essential part of . . . (girls' education and women's lives)' (Shaw 1983:101).

It is clear that part-time, intermittent, and temporary employment all have specific uses for capital. Not only are they mechanisms whereby labour can be obtained cheaply (and thus highly profitably), but they are also, as I suggest above, especially effective ways of using labour. It has been established, for example, that hour by hour part-time workers can be more productive than full-time workers.[8] And the TUC Women's Conference Report (1979-80) has noted:

'Employers were attracted to the idea of part-time employees, because part-time workers could be used to cover peak periods of business, without the need to pay for a full week's work . . . Labour costs could be cut, making it cheaper for the employers, especially if part-time workers' hours could be kept below the National Insurance threshold.'
(Trades Union Congress Women's Advisory Committee 1980:38)

Freeman has observed that the needs of mothers who wish to participate in the formal labour market 'are ignored by public society'.

As a result, mothers are forced 'to seek an individual bargain with their employers', who, she argues, make available part-time work and other variations from standard conditions of employment mainly in response to labour shortages. Drawing on Hunt's data (1975) she concludes: 'The general picture is that by 1975 in the worsening employment situation there were few "understanding" employers among medium-sized and large firms at least.' Her next point has particular salience for the present discussion: 'From the employer's point of view, it makes sense to be understanding if, and only if, it seems likely to pay' (Freeman 1982:144).

Stromsheim, writing about part-time working in Norway, makes an important point when she debates the relative merits of policies which seek to standardize employment conditions across the labour market, and those which seek to promote 'greater flexibility and variation'.

'Standardization has the advantage that it to a large extent ensures equal treatment, equal rights and considerable political influence. At the same time, standardization entails that people and groups that cannot participate on the given terms are either excluded, or relegated to working conditions that entirely lack regulation. Flexible adaptations, on the other hand, promote labour force participation for a broader range of groups. In practice, this often takes place *at the expense of job security, pay, job opportunities, and promotion possibilities.*' (My emphasis)
(Stromsheim 1982:30)

The expansion of labour market opportunities 'for women' is a phenomenon which now appears to be of the past. Unemployment amongst women has been rising rapidly in the past few years, and there is some evidence that employers are making disproportionate redundancies amongst women.[9] Can women's varied experience and flexible approach help them to preserve their access to employment in this situation? Is variation and flexibility still an effective strategy for employment?

It certainly seems possible that it will be relatively easier for women, especially those who have the broadest experience of employment and who are most flexible in their approach, to obtain paid work, than it will be for many men. The changing needs of modern economies and developments in production technology are certain to mean more job changes for individuals (including changes from one type of work to another) than have been the experience of many workers in the past.[10] It follows that adaptability and willingness to learn new skills will be important characteristics in all members of the paid labour force.

Already it is apparent that what has sometimes been seen as women's failure to identify their paid occupations as central life interests (in which they are unlike many men) may have unforeseen effects. If a large minority within the British labour force must face either long or intermittent periods of unemployment in the coming decades, such an attitude to employment may well mean that women are better fitted than men to cope with the changing social conditions.

I do not wish to put forward an unduly optimistic picture of women's future labour market opportunities, however. The importance of taking account of factors, especially ideological ones, outside of the internal mechanisms of the labour market has already been noted. In the present context it is crucial to recognize the potential for a resurgence of patriarchal ideology which, superficially at least, was seen to recede in the 1970s. (Witness the achievement, from a feminist viewpoint, of the passing of the 1970 Equal Pay Act, the 1975 Sex Discrimination Act and the 1975 Employment Protection Act.) Whilst it is economically irrational for employers to select males as employees rather than the (currently) relatively cheaper females, and to 'waste' women's considerable skills and talents, it may be that patriarchy and capitalism will yet be able to forge a further 'unholy alliance' in the face of insufficient employment opportunities. This would involve capital's recognizing that the *de facto* sexual subordination of women makes their exclusion from employment less dangerous (in terms of social 'problems', domestic conflict, etc.) for the status quo than the alternative exclusion of men or of men and women equally. If this is the case, then those relatively isolated, but nevertheless powerful, voices which are currently calling for a return to 'family life' and questioning paid employment as an appropriate activity for women, especially for mothers of dependent children,[11] may not be relics of a bygone age, as feminists fervently hope, but may herald a return to a deeper subordination of women.

The limits and limitations of variation and flexibility

Of course the varied experience which characterizes women's employment careers is limited by structural constraints, and indeed may impose its own limitations. The limits to variation and flexibility are to be found principally in the sex-segregated structure of the labour market and in the socially constructed economic dependence of women on men. In addition, the variation and flexibility of female labour are characteristics which comprise their own limitations, both from the perspective of individual women and of women generally, because they lay women open to the interpretation of being transitory workers, and reduce their opportunities both of building up long-service employment records and of engaging in collective action.

The sex-segregated nature of the labour market is a crucial factor limiting the extent to which women's employment careers may be varied, or indeed their approach to paid work flexible. For many women, the socialization process has been so effective that they cannot conceive of taking on 'men's' jobs; and even where this is not the case, it is highly unrealistic for most women, especially those without the advantages of formal educational qualifications, to seek labour market opportunities outside their traditional sphere. Training opportunities are rarely available to them, and they can expect to encounter hostility from both potential employers (Benett and Carter 1982) and prospective male colleagues (Coote 1979). Thus while women's experience of employment *is* varied, this variation is firmly set within quite specific limits.

The social construction of women's economic dependence on men (which is sanctioned by the state) also acts as an important constraint on women's flexibility in the labour market and on the variety of their employment experience. First, it provides a powerful ideological justification for their confinement to low paid occupations. While men are the ones permitted access to relatively higher earnings (and state benefits in time of sickness or unemployment) and women lack economic independence, it will continue to be women who must shape their employment careers round the needs of men, and around the activities of domestic labour. Because they are defined as economically dependent upon men, it will be possible to deny women access (in a plethora of subtle and not-so-subtle ways) to labour market opportunities beyond the realm of 'women's work', and thus to place a quite definite limit on how varied women's employment careers can be. Second, women's economic dependence on men has considerable practical force. As Spender has noted:

> 'There can be no doubt that in education in general and schools in particular, women are encouraged to choose a vocation which — not coincidentally — helps to make them economically dependent. Such dependence helps to ensure that male authority is minimally challenged.'
>
> (Spender 1982:104–05)

Women who are economically dependent upon men need not be paid wages sufficient to maintain themselves and their children and so women's lower pay is in practice bolstered by its corollary, men's higher pay. For most women this means that variation in their employment experience will be possible only within the confines of low paid occupations.

It is quite evident from both unsystematic observation and carefully organized research (e.g. Hunt 1975) that employers tend to view women's varied employment careers and flexible approach to jobs in negative terms. In particular, these characteristics are taken as indicators of women's low level of commitment to their jobs, and to support judgements that it is not 'worth' providing occupational training for women who will 'only leave'. Whilst the data from my respondents in some cases constitutes a convincing challenge to such assumptions, there is no denying the fact that women's labour market opportunities are restricted by them. As has previously been noted, part-time work — an important component of many women's employment careers — is not treated as serious participation in the labour force by most employers. The experience gained in such work is not considered relevant in the context of management decision-making about promotions, and in almost every respect, part-time workers are judged by their employers to be second-rate employees, whose main concerns and loyalties lie elsewhere (at home). The injustice of such assumptions — many of my respondents made every effort to avoid having time off work in connection with the domestic responsibilities assigned to them — in no way reduces their power to limit the options open to women in the labour market.

Because most of the concessions and benefits obtained by workers from employers have historically been negotiated by men in the context of collective bargaining, it is unsurprising that those concessions and benefits are available to employees on terms which are more easily met by men than by women. In particular, length of service with an individual employer is the crucial criterion used in conjunction with pension rights and protection against redundancy. The typical male employment career has begun on leaving school or higher education, and continues unbroken (except in cases of sickness or unemployment) until the retirement age is reached. Because most women's employment careers have not been like this, and because few women have been in positions to influence negotiations about such matters, women normally find themselves with little in the way of pension rights at the end of their employment careers, and virtually uncushioned against the effects of redundancy. I am not suggesting that women's employment patterns are intrinsically problematic in this respect, or that it would not be possible to award pension rights and protection against redundancy on grounds other than length of service. It is indisputable, however,

that *under current employment conditions,* women's intermittent
employment careers operate to their disadvantage in these respects.

Recent writers on women and British trade unions have pointed to
a number of practical and institutional constraints which limit
women's participation in trade union affairs (Coote and Kellner 1980;
Stageman 1980). Some of these findings were borne out by the
experience of my respondents. Attention has also been drawn to the
tendency for women to work in occupations and workplaces which
are non-unionized, and which by their nature present considerable
obstacles to attempts at unionization. The retail trade, and clerical
work are two cases in point. Again, the women studied bore witness
to the salience of this point. When these factors are further
compounded by the varied nature of women's employment careers,
and especially by their tendency to engage in a variety of different
types of work, it can be seen that women's opportunities for collective
bargaining are severely limited. As a result, the channels open to
them for improving their pay and conditions of employment are few
indeed. Small wonder that the women I interviewed were more
familiar with an individualistic approach to employee-employer
relations than a collective one. Because women find it hard to
organize collectively, they are rarely able to secure good pay and
conditions of employment. Their very flexibility in the labour market
militates against their chances of obtaining these, and gives capital
ample scope to perpetuate their subordination.

Although I would claim that in most cases, my respondents'
employment behaviour bears witness to their commitment to
participation in the paid labour force, it also underlines clearly the
importance which women place upon their family lives. The variation
and flexibility of female labour are characteristics which have
developed through women's efforts to minimize inconvenience to
their families (particularly the young and male members) and
through their experience of taking responsibility for childcare and
household work. It cannot always be in women's best interests for
this to happen. The fact that most women (employed or not) continue
to shoulder the main responsibilities of childcare and homemaking
has a detrimental effect upon the development of their employment
careers, and this cannot be alleviated by even the most generous state
provision of maternity leave and benefits and childcare facilities
while these are seen as assistance to *women* workers. Until the policy
issue becomes 'working parents' rather than 'working mothers',
parents of both sexes and their children will continue to be more or
less confined to sex-roles which will not always suit them: women, to
achieve this, will have to cease relieving men of family responsibilities.
(Most evidence suggests that even when both husband and wife

work outside the home, it is the wife who continues to shoulder most of the responsibility for child rearing and domestic work. (See Derow (1982) for example.) Failure to do so will ultimately make a nonsense of feminist claims for genuine equal pay and the removal of sexist fiscal and social security policies.

CODA: MAUREEN'S STORY

Maureen is 31 years old, has two children, Clare aged 9 and James aged 3, and lives with her police officer husband Michael in a comfortable modern semi on a pleasant suburban housing estate. Her home is well-furnished and recently decorated, and contains a smart kitchen equipped with most of the modern appliances: automatic washing machine, tumble drier, food freezer. When I called there was a newish family saloon in the drive, and Michael was about to leave for work on his motorbike. It was mid-evening and the children were both in bed, all signs of their existence tidied away, partly, no doubt, in preparation for my visit.

In the fifteen or so years since she left school in 1965, Maureen has had thirteen paid jobs, eight of them after the birth of her daughter. The two-year break from employment which surrounded the latter event has been her only long period without a job.

Maureen's experience of formal education was in a Kent technical school in the early 1960s. She recalled the opportunities it had offered:

'The only choice we did have, after I think the first year, you either went on the technical side, which was for the teachers or the nurses, or the commercial side, which I chose to go in. But always in my mind was this idea that I wanted to be a hairdresser.'

At 16, her parents reluctantly allowed her to leave school and start a hairdressing apprenticeship. But like other women I had interviewed, her experience of hairdressing was a great disappointment. In her memory, the unpleasant aspects of her year in this occupation were all couched in the personal relationships which the work entailed:

'It was the manageress — I just couldn't get on with the manageress of this particular shop . . . she was a bit of a nasty character. It wasn't *just* me, she bought the shop just after I started there, and she was very unpleasant . . . . I was so upset about it, I just didn't want to go to work — you know, I wanted to get away from it.'

Leaving hairdressing (an act which entailed her parents' loss of the money they had paid for her apprenticeship) left Maureen in no position to argue further with her parents: '[My parents] said, "Right, now you'll do what we wanted you to do in the first place .... Get back to office work." ' Her first office job however, working for a retail trader as an accounts clerk, was short-lived:

'They went broke after a few months. The boss was very good ... he did all he could to find people vacancies, and he heard of this one — it was receptionist/typist for a firm of land agents, and I started there.'

Because she had left school early, Maureen had not obtained the short-hand and typing qualifications typically acquired by girls following commercial courses at technical schools. She was thus fortunate that in this next job she was able to develop her secretarial skills:

'I wasn't very long doing the receptionist/typist and then I started helping out on the commercial side, and doing some more typing, and I said "Can I try a bit of shorthand?", and the chap was very good and went slowly — it gradually built up and I became his secretary.'

She stayed with this firm about two years, consolidating her skills, but finally becoming dissatisfied with her relatively poor pay. She moved from this job to work as a shorthand typist with a public sector company. At the time, she had clearly seen this as a superior position, although it had meant working in a typing pool: 'They were quite difficult to get into — you had to do a test — it was the place to get into if you could, and the money was much better.' When she had been in this job for something over a year she married Michael, and they moved to a small town a few miles away where they were buying their first home. Although she kept her job on for a little while, the travelling was tiresome and as soon as she could she obtained another, local, job, this time as secretary to a bank manager. Although this job change was a result of her altered personal circumstances, she was able to interpret it as a move forward in what had become her secretarial career. 'I went into a bank then, so I sort of crept up the ladder — you know, I was working for the manager — that was quite good.'

Thus she understood the events of these early years in her employment career, in 'career' terms. Nevertheless, this interpretation was not powerful enough to compete with the normative expectation that on marriage her husband's employment career would assume primary importance and she would shape hers around the demands both of his job, and of domestic labour. It was in the early years of their marriage that Michael joined the police force: as Maureen explained, this move was essentially part of a search for job security.

> 'Michael had been made redundant a couple of times, and we ... felt a bit unsettled. . . . Then Michael joined the police ... he was posted to (a different town).'

The move (which entailed Maureen's resignation from her job in the bank) coincided with her first pregnancy. Although she claimed that they had planned to have their first baby after two years of marriage, her comments hinted at the semi-conscious decision which often characterizes a first pregnancy:

> 'As we were moving, I'd given up my job ... I just sort of — you know, you drift into these sort of things — but we did say that we would wait about two years. . . . It never occurred to me at that time — you know, the chance of being able to do a job and have a child.'

When Clare was just 18 months old, however, the combined pressure of Michael's low pay — 'the money was very bad at that time' — and the boredom and social isolation of being a 'police wife' prompted Maureen, together with another friend, to seek part-time evening work washing-up in a private school. Often, depending upon his shift, it was possible for Michael to look after Clare while Maureen went out to this job. One of his shifts coincided with Maureen's hours however, and on these evenings she made other arrangements for Clare.

> 'My neighbour had her ... she would lay on her settee or whatever . . . it wasn't a good arrangement because the child should have been in her bed . . . it was just a friendly thing.'[12]

Conscious of what she felt to be the inadequate nature of this arrangement, Maureen started to look around for other strategies which would enable her to have a paid job. Before long she became aware of the advantages of engaging a childminder, and once this had been organized she registered with a secretarial agency. She was sent as a 'temp.' to work for a large manufacturing company where, after a few weeks, she accepted a full-time post as a shorthand typist. The childminding arrangements were working out well:

> 'In fact I think it did her a lot of good. Because, being the only child at that time, it did her good to be in a set-up with other children, be one of a number — and she took to it, you know, fine.'

Maureen was especially appreciative of the minder's attitude towards her work:

'Even to a family funeral, she would never say, "I can't have the child" — she had a neighbour that would have Clare for a couple of hours — she always took the responsibility — it was something she'd agreed to do, and she made sure the service was there.'

However, Maureen's return to secretarial work was not an especially happy one, and she left after about a year:

'I was so *bored*. I'd just never read so many books in all my life. I would go along to my boss who was the Chief Accountant... and I'd be in there two hours and we would just *talk* — he didn't have anything to do. Occasionally I'd have a couple of letters ... I've even come out of there without a thing in my book — we'd just chat about a few things and I'd just come out and sit back at my desk. And the strain of trying to look as if you're doing something, and jumping every time somebody comes in — you know, to hide your book — it was ridiculous. So I started looking around, and I applied for a job ... and ... got it ... went from the sublime to the ridiculous, I was so busy in the other one.'

Maureen's dissatisfaction with the undemanding nature of this job, and the life of idleness which she was expected to lead there, need not surprise us. Her previous experiences of secretarial work were indicators of her liking for challenging work, and the sense that one's skills are not being used or that one is not being given a chance to do the job for which one is being paid are responses which are to be expected in a society whose values are still permeated by the work ethic. But further, we might expect Maureen's frustrations to be intolerable because, as a woman and a mother, she would be constantly aware of the tasks of domestic labour which awaited her when she left her day's employment. How frustrating to be unable to use the hours of idleness in a productive way! The preference for being 'kept busy' in a job, rather than 'having an easy life', is one which I have heard many women express. It offers an example of how those Marxist analyses of wage labour which fail to identify the specific nature of female labour in our society may miss the fuller understanding of this particular phenomenon. Women's resistance to being allowed to remain idle when 'at work' can only be understood in the context of their entire experience of labour, which embraces both wage labour and domestic labour.

Maureen's new job was much more to her liking, and in describing it to me she laid considerable stress on the sense of involvement which she valued:

'It was for a pharmaceutical company .... They were just setting up a new company — a subsidiary of a foreign company — so I was really in on Day One, and it was very hectic, but I enjoyed that.... The money was very good, and the boss was very good. I think he realized the work I was producing, and I had ... pay rises ... every few months.'

Having found herself a challenging and rewarding position, however, Maureen again came up against the obstacle which disrupts the career of many women: when she had been with the company for eighteen months, her husband was posted to another town. 'I tried travelling for a little while, but it was almost an hour's journey at each end of the day, and it just got too much for me.' Although the move had its attractions — 'we were moving to a much nicer house so I wanted to come here' — losing the job she had so much enjoyed was a considerable blow, whose impact was not softened by the new job she found as a secretary with a local newspaper:

'It was just a large, open-planned office, and I'd been so involved in this [other] job, and so happy ... it was just horrible at the newspaper — nobody wanted to know, everybody went about their own way — you just sat in your little corner — I just hated it .... I got very low; I think it was that job, and the move, and all the rest of it ... [I stayed] a couple of months, and [then] I had a few months off.'

Her spell away from employment ended when, through another 'police wife', she found part-time secretarial work with a national charitable organization. This job coincided with the birth of her son, which was unplanned — 'a complete surprise/shock' — and she worked at home during her pregnancy and up until her son was 1 year old. Redundancy followed, and six months out of employment, but Maureen was keen to return to paid work:

'I started him off at Denise's — just two mornings a week, and then three ... I hadn't started work, it was just ... he was getting very clingy ... [it] gradually built up, and then I got a part-time job as a merchandiser ... going round filling up racks for certain products, but I found I was doing practically full-time hours, *and* I was driving ... I was exhausted. Denise had said she only really wanted part-time children ... but I explained the position to her, and she said, "Well, I don't mind, he's so good". I just couldn't get a part-time job anywhere. The agencies just didn't want to know.'

For many women who feel part-time work for one reason or another is essential, this is the point at which moves into other types of work occur. Part-time work is often available in factories, shops, and in domestic and catering jobs, but, it seems, only more rarely in the secretarial field. Maureen's commitment to using her existing skills led her to make a choice which many other women reject. She chose to return to 'full-time' work. The job she found was with a printer's, working from 8.45 a.m. to 4.30 p.m., hours which suited her well. However, certain other characteristics of this job combined to make her feel she had been less than fairly treated:

'I started with them around October-time . . . and after Christmas they said they thought they'd be moving the office — the other part of the firm was [about twelve miles away] and the managing director said something like, "Anyone who's prepared to come won't lose out on it". Well, it got down to two days before we were due to go, and he still hadn't said — because we were supposed to be going to get petrol money, etc. — and it wasn't until the day that the vans were there that we actually got him to make a decision, and he said, yes, he would pay petrol money, but he wasn't having any odd hours, it was 8.30 till 5.30 or lump it . . . and it turned out, I'd been there I think twenty-six weeks — if it had been twenty-eight I'd have had him, he wouldn't have been able to alter my hours.[13] I think they took me on knowing that they were going to be going . . . . I couldn't get anything in writing from them, I didn't have any terms and conditions, and that was it. There was no way, with two children, that I could do it, and they knew that . . . so I just left that afternoon . . . . When I started going round the agencies, they all said, "Oh, not them, they owe us money", they had quite a reputation. I was out of work for about a month, and then I got this job that I'm in now.'

Her latest job, which she had held when interviewed for a little over a year, was as a personal secretary in a manufacturing company. Maureen had no intention of leaving this company, and was still there a year later. She was able to work convenient (full-time) hours and found the pay and conditions quite good.

I was interested to know how she presented herself at an interview for a secretarial job. Was she asked questions about her children, and how did she respond?

'In this last job, the one that I'm in now — and I have done it before — I've *lied*. I've admitted to Clare, and they've been very wary of that, a school child, but I've never admitted to the baby . . . I mean, James was only 2. I told my boss when I'd been there about six months, and he said, "Well, you've proved your point, you obviously can hold down a job" — but if I'd have put it on the application form, I don't think I'd have got it . . . . It annoys me. I know that I'm more reliable than a lot of the youngsters that I've seen, that have a day off for a headache practically every week . . . if it's not them it's their family . . . or the car . . . I think they've probably had some bad experiences with women and children, but I haven't done it.'

She stressed that she never took time off work if she could possibly avoid it:

'I would get my mother to look after them as first choice — in the position I'm in, I don't think it's fair to a boss, and I wouldn't expect him to keep me on, if I took a week off for this and a week off for that . . . you just can't . . . . I would feel I would have to say I'll take a week's holiday . . . because they're paying me good money to do a fairly senior job. I wouldn't like to have to do it.'

As her employment career demonstrates, Maureen does not challenge the assumption that Michael's job is more important than hers. She has changed jobs to accommodate his career in the past, and is prepared to do so again in the future, although she is quite happy in her current job. While she expressed no resentment about this, she is clearly grateful that his postings to different places are likely to be infrequent:

'It's always possible in Michael's job — he can be moved — but they don't really like to do it too much when you're in your own home, because they have to pay your expenses — it tends not to happen too often.'

With the support of reliable childminders and of her mother, Maureen has been able to hold down a full-time job for most of the years while she has had young children. From the details which she disclosed to me, it was apparent that she is primarily responsible for developing the strategies whereby the family household can operate with both adults in full-time employment. Maureen is mainly responsible for performing the household duties, although she acknowledges Michael's role — 'if he didn't do his part of the morning, I would never get out at 8 o'clock.' Nevertheless, while Michael deals with making the toast for the children, Maureen is making the beds, tidying up, preparing Clare's school things, and reminding her of the arrangements she has made for after school: ' "Do you know where you are going after school? — You're going to Nanna's, or Nanna will be here." ' Housework and shopping are also Maureen's domain. She has 'a blitz' every weekend, and shops regularly on a Thursday evening. She explained Michael's attitude to her job:

'Oh, I think he understands — he does very long hours, and I was always bored at home — obviously he likes the money — the extra money that it brings in.'

The money which Maureen earns — she brings home between £70 and £80 per week — goes straight into the couple's joint account — 'much to my mother's disgust'. This she says, enables the family to have a 'decent' car, means that she can 'spend a lot on the children, on treats', and affects her spending on food and clothes. Without it:

'I'd probably be more sensible with food — I wouldn't buy such convenience things . . . . I think I would cut down on clothes for myself — but I don't spend an awful lot anyway.'

In general, Maureen presented herself to me as a person basically satisfied with the arrangements concerning her job and family. She had been relatively successful in formulating effective strategies enabling her to work full-time, and these had not been unduly upset by unforeseen events such as redundancy, Michael's postings, and her second pregnancy. She possesses the skills necessary to cope with such events, and is competent to deal with employment agencies and childminders. Family planning was well under control by the time we met, as, following the birth of their son, Michael had had a vasectomy. Maureen thus manages her life in an organized and effective way. Nevertheless, she is aware that existing social arrangements do little to support women such as herself:

'I mean, it's getting easier now with these childminders, but it's been dreadfully difficult . . . . I think it's awful that you do have to struggle so much to make arrangements to go out, it's not easy. It was very difficult to find a childminder, there weren't vacancies . . . . I think [the] Childminders' Association is very good, and I hope there will be more and more of them . . . . I wish there was an arrangement for after school, because that's going to be a real snag.'

Strategies for employment:
5 the social relations of household work

I turn now to the arrangements which women negotiate with members of their families, and others, to free themselves from certain of the childcare and household duties normally assigned to women in contemporary British society, in order to take up paid employment. In addition, I present data on the personal adjustments which women must frequently make as individuals in order to combine unpaid domestic labour with wage labour. In the discussion below, I have grouped these 'strategies for employment' under three main headings — 'household', 'family', and 'personal'.

HOUSEHOLD STRATEGIES

Most of the women interviewed were, or had been, able to enlist some practical support from other members of their households (principally husbands and children), either on a regular basis, enabling them to combine childcare and household duties with paid employment, or as a means of coping with crises (e.g. sick children) or periodic difficulties (e.g. supervising younger children during school holidays).

Role played by husbands

All but two of the respondents were or had been, married; however, when interviewed only three-quarters of them were living with their husbands (and in nine of these forty-eight cases this was a second husband). The remaining women were mostly living alone with their children, although three were co-habiting and one was living with her parents. There was thus a substantial minority within the sample for whom the sharing of domestic tasks and childcare with husbands was currently impossible. When it is remembered that some of the women currently living with their husbands had also spent time living alone with their children in the past, it can be seen that the sharing of domestic tasks with husbands is not even a theoretical possibility for many women, at least periodically. In fact about a third of all the women reported that they had at some time been living with their children but without a husband. This was usually after marital breakdown, although in a few cases the women concerned were single mothers. For some this arrangement was temporary, perhaps lasting just a couple of years between the breakdown of one relationship and the formation of another; for others it was virtually permanent, lasting for a decade or more. I draw particular attention to this phenomenon in order to stress that the sharing of childcare and domestic responsibilities between spouses is a strategy for employment which is not available to all mothers at all times. I need hardly add that, as I demonstrate below, there will also be cases where the husband is (theoretically) available, but the strategy is not. In some families husbands (and occasionally wives) continue to put up much resistance to the idea of male participation in the tasks of domestic labour.

What did my respondents have to say about the role played by husbands in the work at home? I think it important here to distinguish between the tasks associated with the care of children, and the aspects of domestic labour popularly referred to as 'housework' — cleaning, cooking, washing. Where young children are concerned, their care is a 24-hour job, although of course this does not mean 24-hour labour for the person caring for the child. Some of the caring for children can be done while one is asleep, or watching television, or performing almost any household task. It consists of 'being at hand', and ready to respond to the infant's sometimes unpredictable needs. Other aspects of childcare, of course, involve labour of a kind which can be physically exhausting: attending to the bodily needs of infants, keeping them in clean clothes, and playing with them or watching over them while they play. These are all tasks which those who care for children will confirm are often hard work indeed.

About half of my respondents reported that their husbands took (or had taken) a part in caring for their children. Frequently, the husband's willingness to do this — sometimes under protest — was the key factor in enabling a respondent to take a paid job. Husbands might care for their children on Saturdays, while their wives worked as sales assistants for example; or in the evenings, so that women could work an evening shift in a factory or take a part-time job as a hospital domestic. They might be willing to 'keep an eye on' the children first thing in the morning so that their wives could go out to clean offices or pubs. Whilst some of these husbands were no doubt relieving their wives of some of the *labour* of childcare, in many cases they were merely undertaking to 'be at hand'. For example, wives might find their husbands prepared to stay in from 5.00 to 8.00 each evening while they went out to work, but still themselves have to perform the labour of childcare. Lynne's husband was of this kind:

> LYNNE: 'He likes more or less everything to be done as he gets home — apart from he washes up . . . but I have to do the baby, get him ready for bed and that.'

Ruth's experience had been similar. When her children were very young she worked in the evenings, as a barmaid, and as a tupperware demonstrator:

> RUTH: 'My husband would do a lot of things, but — I think he has changed one nappy, because, as he says, he doesn't think that's a man's job, which I suppose is fair enough. So even when I went out [to work] you see, the children had to be changed and virtually ready for bed, or in bed preferably, before I actually went out.'

Some husbands were willing to take on some of the labour of childcare — but they were most definitely in the minority. Sara, who had never left the labour market, despite having three children, had a husband who was prepared to share this work with her. His occupation (nurse) had made him more familiar with the tasks of caring than are many men. Sara feels they are both able to work full-time, only because they have a high level of co-operation at home.

> SARA: 'He does everything when he's there — like looking after the baby, changing nappies, everything . . . when he's on morning [shift], on the way in he will take the children to school, and he'll pick them up . . . . There's nothing that he will say — "Oh, that's not my job." '

Such husbands, according to my respondents, were few and far between. More common was the response given by Yvonne.

> YVONNE: 'Well, he hasn't sort of given much time to the children, or to the house. He doesn't do a lot really.'

Doreen made a telling point when she contrasted her husband's willingness to participate in household tasks with his attitude to childcare.

DOREEN: 'Caring for the children? . . . When they were very small he was frightened of them — when it came to changing nappies — and things like that — he just didn't, at all . . . . He did what I call the easy side of caring for the children — making sure they'd their pocket money and so on — I tended to look after the children more, where he helped with the house.'

The 'easy side' of childcare certainly seemed to be all most husbands had been prepared to undertake. Being 'at hand' when the children were small, and being willing to take on some of the organizational tasks associated with older children, was all most women seemed to expect of their husbands.

HEATHER: 'He does a lot with the children, which I'm thankful for. He will mend the bikes and run round buying things for them, sorting things out. You know, if Steven wants football boots or something, *he*'ll do it . . . this sort of thing, which relieves me . . . . At Christmas he has most of the school holiday off, of course he has to organize the children then . . . which I think has been very good for him, because when the children were babies I felt totally responsible, especially for Steven, because he was still working his way up. I did everything for Steven, and I think now, looking back, we both agree that I shouldn't have done, it took away some of the joy from him, just because I thought it was my duty to do it. So I think he's reaping the benefits now — we lived a little bit in isolated compartments before.'

Husbands, then, had frequently been crucial in enabling women to take on employment (especially part-time jobs), but had only rarely been prepared to perform the more laborious tasks of childcare. In all but a few cases, the husband's role in caring for children was specifically related to the fact of the wife's employment. A small minority of husbands were willing to supervise children during school holidays, and an even smaller group would take time off work to care for a sick child.

What had been the extent of the husbands' participation in the tasks of housework? About half of the women reported that their husbands played a significant role in the performance of domestic and household duties apart from childcare. This usually meant that their husbands would do washing up, and perhaps some preparation of meals, or household cleaning. A third of the women felt their husbands made (or had made) a really important contribution to the general tasks of housework. Such men were described as 'very

helpful', 'very good', or 'sharing'. The nature of their participation
varied between a willingness to do anything their wives requested,
to genuine sharing of duties, and more independent activity.

> ELIZABETH: 'He used to have Tuesdays off . . . so he used to do
> the house right through for me from top to bottom — you know,
> the hoovering and dusting and everything . . . when I was full-
> time.'

> ANGELA: 'We share everything . . . [he does] washing up,
> cooking, hoovering, polishing, bathing Jane, making beds.'

Some women explained that their husbands carried out certain
tasks on a regular basis. Of the women currently living with a
husband, two-thirds had husbands who regularly did washing up,
and about half husbands who would do some meal preparation
(occasionally preparing entire meals but more frequently just
preparing vegetables, or heating up meals previously prepared by
the wife). Just over a third had husbands who did some household
cleaning. A few husbands (six out of forty-eight) did the weekly
shopping (alone), while a mere three would regularly make beds.
Of all the women interviewed, only one said her husband would
sometimes wash clothes, and none reported that her husband was
willing to do ironing. Meryl's husband was more than usually active
in performing household duties.

> MERYL: '[He does] half easily . . . he often does the shopping — I
> don't think my first husband knew what a shop looked like from
> the inside — he takes care of the money, which is lovely because
> I've done that for years and it's wearing . . . he does cleaning in
> the house, and so on . . . he cooks meals — curries and spaghettis
> — but I do most of it . . . washing I suppose I mainly do — [today]
> I pegged one lot out and there was some more and I said, "I'll call
> in on the way back from the dentist and do it", and he said, "Oh,
> I'll do it" — which he would.'

Several explanations were given for the more limited participation
by husbands which was more common. Some husbands were (or
were perceived by their wives to be) incompetent at performing
such tasks. Feminists may suspect a male conspiracy of 'studied
incompetence', but it was clear that the process sometimes
developed with the collusion of wives.

> BETH: 'I prefer to do the washing, because they always seem to
> shrink it — I don't know why, but they always do. Shopping,
> again, I'm very fussy and I like to see what meat they're farming
> off . . . . He got me some steak once — I'll always remember, 2 lbs

of chuck steak — and when he brought it home, I wouldn't even give it to the dog . . . I took it back — oh, I was angry . . . and cooking — no, no-one can . . . I prefer to do my own cooking, thank you.'

Other men were reluctant to undertake tasks which they identified as 'a woman's job', and several women reported their husbands' refusal to do any domestic task which was publicly visible.

HELEN: 'The only thing he won't do is hang the washing on the line . . . "I don't want women looking at me hanging the washing out" . . . . If anybody comes to the door, if he's wiping up he'll put the towel down and go and sit down.' (*laughs*)

A minority of the women were, or had been, married to men who took no part at all in household duties. Carol's apparent approval of the arrangements in her home was thrown into question by her unguarded remark 'Ah, sore point actually'.

CAROL: 'Although I believe we should share — I am earning virtually as much as what he's earning — it is my duty as a wife to clean, polish, see the children are OK . . . and I wouldn't want him to go to work and say "I had to do the washing because my wife's doing full-time work". If I could not manage to do full-time work and run my home, I wouldn't do it . . . . [When] he knew I wanted to come back . . . he said "if the housework starts to go, you've had your chips".'

It is important in attempting to understand the sexual division of domestic labour to recognize it as part of a domestic bargain between spouses (see below). This means that a husband's attitude to his wife's employment (and earnings) is highly significant. I asked the women how they thought their husbands felt about having a wife with a paid job. Many husbands were apparently happy about their wives' employment because they appreciated the importance of their earnings in either enabling the family to make ends meet, or having a higher standard of living.

LUCY: 'Really, he's all for it, because otherwise we just couldn't manage . . . or there would be a lot of things which we would definitely be without if I wasn't working.'

GERALDINE: 'He likes it — it gives him a bit extra to play with, doesn't it?'

While sometimes the extra income was seen as beneficial for the whole family, in many cases it was made clear that the husband saw his wife's earnings as bringing a direct material benefit to him.

Cathy made this point more clearly than any of the other women:
'He thought it was good . . . because then he could cut my
housekeeping down, you see.'

A further quite common response was that husbands were
willing to tolerate their wives' employment, on condition that the
women did not allow standards of domestic labour and childcare to
'slip'.

> RUTH: 'He said all the time that I can keep the house clean and
> tidy, keep the children nice, as long as I've got time for the
> children, then I can keep the job. But, he says, once one or the
> other starts going — don't get me wrong, he doesn't expect me to
> do the painting and this, that and the other — but he does expect
> the house to look nice and tidy . . . once I start slipping on that,
> then I can start thinking about giving up.'

Similarly, some husbands disliked their wives having paid jobs
because it meant they had to participate in domestic work.

> SHIRLEY: 'He wasn't particularly keen about it being full-time . . .
> he had to do more of the things at home.'

Although some of those who reported such an attitude were quietly
critical of their husbands, many accepted that men had a right to
make such demands of their wives and to exercise their authority in
this way. Some made it quite explicit that they had sought their
husband's *permission* before taking employment.

> NANCY: 'He said, "Well, you can go to work, provided you do
> something with it" . . . . So what we've done with it, is we've
> literally ploughed it into our home.'

A small group of women reported considerable resentment on
their husbands' part. These men either disliked the idea of their
wives earning money, and felt that men ought to be the family
breadwinners, or were hostile to their wives having jobs because
they saw the arrangement as a challenge to their authority.

> LINDA: 'He doesn't like me working . . . he thinks he earns
> enough to support us . . . a bit of pride there, I think.'

> PRU: 'He didn't like it — he didn't like it because that way it
> would give me a certain independence, and I wouldn't be, you
> know, the woman stuck at home.'

It would be inaccurate to leave the impression that all husbands
either opposed their wives' employment, or liked it only for the
additional income. Some women claimed that their husbands were
content to see them go out to work, because they knew it made

them happier. No surprisingly, such husbands were mostly amongst those with the highest participation in household tasks.

MARGERY: 'He'd rather I be out at work, because he knows that I'll get really bored and fed up at home.'

WANDA: 'It relieves the tension in the house . . . I think he likes me going out — I don't get so miserable being indoors all day.'

Finally, it should be noted that a small number of women were married to men who took it quite for granted that they should be in employment.

RACHEL: 'He feels it's essential . . . . It makes me a person . . . in his eyes, people who don't work are sponging on society.'

VALERIE: 'He likes me working — he wouldn't have it any other way. His attitude is "I've got to work till I get my pension, why shouldn't you?" '

Interestingly, these two women could expect very little assistance from their husbands with domestic tasks.

Of course, some women reported a variety of responses from their husbands, and ones which changed over time. Many of the husbands who were initially hostile to the idea of their wives having a job came to favour the arrangement as time passed, usually when they became aware of the advantages of additional income, or on finding that they could gradually escape involvement in domestic tasks.

PAT: 'He wasn't keen . . . he wasn't keen on me coming back out full-time . . . . Now, we're managing to buy a house and all different things, he's quite agreeable.'

GERALDINE: 'He started off doing the housework and cooking meals — and having my meal ready when I got home — but of course now David has got older and things have got easier he tends to leave it to me. He used to do shopping as well at one time.'

In my view, none of the couples so far described resembled the 'symmetrical family' anticipated by Young and Willmott (1973).[1] There was, however, some scant evidence of marital egalitarianism. In a tiny minority of cases, women claimed that in their marriage, everything was shared, and that their employment was part of an agreed arrangement.

TINA: 'We always do things together — he's never said to me

"Don't go to work".... We've never looked upon it as yours and
my job. I think he's that sort of man — he doesn't look upon me
as being the head cook and bottle-washer. A lot of wives are
looked on like that, aren't they?'

Despite this however, the overwhelming impression of the marital
bargaining over the question of wives' employment, was that
husbands held the balance of power. This came as no surprise, but
the evidence was quite clear: in general, wives sought husbands'
permission, or at least approval, in taking a job. They got it,
especially if husbands were to be involved in domestic tasks (that is,
usually when full-time work was involved), only when the material
reward in the form of the wife's wages could be seen to be of benefit
to the family, and in some cases to the husband himself, or when the
husband recognized that a more contented wife would be a
pleasanter companion, and one better able to make his home, to
borrow Lasch's compelling phrase, 'a haven in a heartless
world'.

Children as a source of support

When interviewed, forty of my sixty-four respondents had at least
one child aged ten years or older living with them. Although there
was no prompting about the role of children in the interviews, just
over half of these women mentioned the part played by their
children in carrying out domestic duties. It was clear from their
comments, however, that in most of the families children performed
only very few duties. Most frequently mentioned were: making
their own beds, keeping their own rooms clean and tidy, washing
up, hoovering, and preparing vegetables, or sometimes meals. A
few women had children, mainly daughters, who would undertake
washing, ironing or shopping, while two had an elder daughter
who would take care of a younger child after school hours. (Of
course in most families there was not a large enough gap between
the births of children for this arrangement to be possible.)

A few explained that they paid their daughters to help at
home.

DOREEN: 'My daughter's been old enough — and now the
second one ... it's been a paid job with them to cook our evening
meal . . . . This is the benefit of the children getting older
now.'

This practice could also reveal an interesting sexual division of
child labour.

ANNETTE: 'Usually, Saturday mornings, Jill (aged twelve) and I
will do the housework between us — we've got a thing going....
Young Kevin (aged fourteen) goes out and does the car-washing,
by which he earns himself extra money. Jill isn't old enough, but
wants to earn extra money — she has her pocket money — she
takes the dog for walks, you know .... I think she does the brass
and silver for that as well ... things like washing up don't count. I
usually do the washing up, but occasionally I'll say "Oh, come
and do the washing up for me", and they'll do that. But apart
from that, like I say, she does housework — household chores,
polishing, floors, you know, dusting, hoovering, on a Saturday.
We quite often do it between us and I pay her 35p an hour, which
has got quite a bit of fun with her. She writes it down and she has
it in bulk when it's three or four pounds.'

Indeed, daughters were more often relied upon for support than
sons. Annette's comments, and the following extract, provide
illustrations of this.

DAWN: '[My daughter] does all her own ironing — she does do
some of my ironing — I mean, she doesn't have a lot of time,
she's at college. She goes out the house 8 o'clock and she doesn't
get in till 6. [Also], she's got a week-end job ... my youngest, if I
say to him go up the shops or something, he does. The boys
make their own beds — I do stress that.'

In only a very few cases, however, did women rely at all heavily
upon their children for support or assistance with domestic
responsibilities. Kate, who lived alone with her four children, was
one of the few women who had made a specific bargain with a
daughter in connection with the sharing of household duties. She
explained to me how she had talked matters over with her
daughter (aged 14) before taking a full-time job:

KATE: 'My eldest daughter ... she's ... always been — very
sensible, very adult. I said "Shall we try it?" Actually it was her
that pushed me into getting out of the house ... and she said that
she could manage — because she'd always learnt to cook, she
wanted to do it on her own. And I said "Well, we'll see how it
goes and if it doesn't work, then I'll take a part-time job" .... she
does the cooking and any light washing ... she cooks the meal,
and she'll make cakes — anything that's going .... She's been
doing it on her own since she was nine — she's done very
well.'

Kate's arrangement was exceptional, however. Many women
expected very little from their children, often suggesting that they

felt it unfair to ask them to participate in household chores.

> PAULA: 'I don't ask [my son] to do very much because I have
> one of these complex things... I go to work because I chose to go
> to work... I shouldn't put my chores on to them when they've got
> their school work.'

In a few cases, women expected assistance from their children, but
stressed that this was because it was 'good for' children to help,
rather than specifically because it would lighten their load as a
working mother. As Rachel explained: 'He does do those chores,
not because I need him to, but I feel he should do.'

In summary, then, it was evident that, in many households,
children were not expected to play any significant part in domestic
duties. However, a few women made statements which offered a
challenge to the prevailing ideology concerning the sexual division
of domestic labour.

> MARGARET: '[My son] does cooking, and tries to do a bit of
> cleaning... I think the mother should teach her son as much as
> she should her daughter.'

In most families, though, the status quo in this respect was under no
serious threat, and indeed was in many cases being systematically
reinforced and reproduced.

Other household members

Three of the women's households included a parent or parents.
Wanda had her father, and Andrea her mother, living in the family
home. Both of these women were married and living with their husbands. In neither case did the parent make any really significant contribution to the domestic duties: Andrea's mother usually prepared
vegetables for the evening meal, and Wanda explained that her father
kept his own room tidy, often did the washing up, and sometimes did
the hoovering. Neither parent required any special nursing or other
care.[2] In Wanda's case, the arrangement was temporary, while her
father waited for a council flat, and in Andrea's, her mother was a permanent member of the household, but lived a relatively independent
existence in a 'granny flat' linked to the family home.

Maria, a divorced woman, had lived with her parents and one of
her two children since the breakdown of her marriage. All three
adults in the household were in full-time employment, and Maria
made it clear that she found the arrangement both convenient and
beneficial. She and her mother shared the domestic chores between
them, which lightened the load for them both.

MARIA: 'I have very, very, smashing parents . . . . I don't pay them nothing. . . . I'm not that extravagant being at home . . . only a meal in the evening. My Mum cooks for Dad, and she gets an extra meal for me and the child. . . . She does the shopping as well . . . . I'm off [work] this afternoon — I'll go home, if there's any washing to do, I'll do it, general tidying up . . . then I pick up Mum from work . . . and start the cooking, so it makes it easier on [her] . . . when she has her days off, she looks after my boy — I don't bring him in the nursery then, she has him at home.'

Three women in the sample were living with men who were not their husbands. They included Annette and Alice (discussed in Chapter 3) and also Pru. Pru had lived alone with her sons for three years following the breakdown of her marriage, and the present arrangement had existed for less than two years. She said that in her household 'everybody mucks in now', and that both her sons and her 'boyfriend' gave her money. Nevertheless, she did all the main tasks — cooking, washing, cleaning — while the men simply helped out with washing up and odd jobs.

When women take on paid jobs, then, some sharing of domestic tasks with household members often develops. Certain duties may be off-loaded on to husbands, children, and occasionally other adults, but for the most part women themselves continue to take the responsibility for, and indeed to perform most of the labour of, childcare and household work. Amongst the women interviewed, there was considerable variation in the role played by husbands (from making no contribution to, in a very few cases, taking an almost equal share), but children and other household members rarely did more than assist in minor ways. Husbands were often crucial, however, in enabling wives to take part-time jobs when there were young children at home. As shown below, women often have to adopt strategies other than sharing work with household members in order to combine employment with the domestic responsibilities assigned to them. In almost every case, these strategies involve women and not men.

FAMILY STRATEGIES

I use the term 'family strategies' to describe those arrangements enabling women to combine paid employment and domestic labour which involve kin who are not members of the household. As expected, female kin were the most important extra-household source of support for most respondents, in addition to or as an alternative to support from household members. However, a minority of my respondents had no access to this strategy for employment. A few women lived at a considerable distance from their kin while others had no kin, or no contact with them, because of death, estrangement, or simple lack of kin (e.g. no brothers or sisters). In addition, women whose kin were themselves in full-time employment (especially mothers and mothers-in-law) usually found that they were denied access to this strategy.

Nevertheless approximately two-thirds of the women had been able to rely on family members outside the household for support. In many cases they lived in or near their place of birth, sometimes having parents or other relatives living in the same or the next street. This situation permitted frequent contact with kin. With a few exceptions, arrangements with kin were exclusively to do with childcare: caring for pre-school children while the respondent and her husband (when she had one) were at work, looking after children between the end of the school day and their parents' return from work, and taking care of children during school holidays, or when they were ill. Except in a very few cases, where respondents' fathers were involved, the support provided came from female kin: principally mothers and mothers-in-law, but also sisters, sisters-in-law, aunts, and grandmothers. Of those who reported family support, about half had, or had once had, regular arrangements whereby kin cared for their pre-school children throughout the time they were at work. This arrangement was especially popular as a means of enabling women to take part-time employment, although in a few cases women received such support when in a full-time job. A few women had arranged for kin to care for their school-age children after school hours. Family support was also important in enabling women to overcome the problems associated with school holidays and children's illnesses. Some women had relatives living at some distance who cared for children at holiday times, either by inviting them to stay, or by coming to look after them. Locally-based relatives were of course particularly important in helping out when children were sick.

Arrangements made with kin were often specific to a particular job, and usually had to be modified as children grew older. Sometimes they were temporary arrangements, used by mothers while they undertook seasonal work, or perhaps to cover the period between finding a job, and finding a suitable childminder. Inevitably, family strategies were also vulnerable to the vagaries of personal relationships.

MARIA: 'My mother-in-law used to look after them . . . . Of course, as soon as my marriage broke off, she didn't want to know any more, so then I had to find my own. That is when I asked them for a place in the nursery here.'

Only four women reported assistance from their kin with aspects of domestic labour other than childcare. Anne had had a younger unmarried sister who came to her home and prepared the evening meal on the days when Anne was employed. Valerie had paid her mother to come to her home and care for her children, from when they were small babies. After they reached school age, her mother continued to come to the house as before, but now did housework and washing, etc. as well as looking after the children when they came home from school. Because of her full-time job, Pru's mother had not in the past been able to assist her daughter with childcare but, now that she was retired, Pru explained, she 'comes down every week to do my ironing for me'. Heather's is perhaps one of the most interesting cases of kin being involved in a strategy enabling both the respondent and her husband to take full-time paid employment. When interviewed, Heather was working as a supervisor in a retail store, having joined the company some three and a half years previously when her husband Paul was temporarily out of work. She described her attitude to paid employment at that time (when her children were aged 10 and 8).

HEATHER: 'It was something I was looking for, but at that time I was still thinking of [a job with] school holidays, that was the thing that was holding me back . . . . I could take this job because it was over the Christmas period, and Paul would be there. And then having found that I could manage it, and my mother-in-law offering support, then I took the plunge and said, "Yes, I'll go into a job that hasn't got school holidays. I recognize the fact that there will be some days when the children are poorly and I've got to work, but with my mother-in-law's support, then I can do it." '

In fact, support from both her own parents and her parents-in-law was such that she fairly quickly took on additional responsibilities at work.

HEATHER: 'They look after the children when I'm not there . . . my mother and mother-in-law are in the house by the time the children come home. They cook the evening meal. Both fathers come over and eat the evening meal with us, and then they go home about 7.30 after we've eaten.'

Later she explained how she felt about these arrangements:

HEATHER: 'My job is important to me. The children I feel are quite adequately looked after and they're growing up in a loving community — well, group, family unit — with grandparents, myself and Paul. I like it. It's good for me and I think it's good for them.'

In general, the support of kin, especially other women, was clearly crucial in enabling many respondents to undertake paid employment. It is noteworthy that without exception, respondents saw it as their own responsibility (rather than a responsibillity which they shared with their husbands) to make suitable arrangements for the care of children. This point was further underlined in connection with the commercial childcare arrangements which are discussed below. In a few of the cases where mothers provided substantial support, women reported considerable hostility to these arrangements from other members of their families.

VALERIE: 'My brothers and their wives — two of them in particular — took tremendous exception, so much so that they stopped speaking to my mother for four years because they objected so strongly to her looking after my children. They thought that I should leave work, etc. . . . for four years my eldest brother didn't talk to his mother . . . they weren't directly involved . . . nobody was asking them to do anything, and they never have done.'

PERSONAL STRATEGIES

By 'personal strategies' I understand all those strategies for employment adopted by individual respondents which did not involve the assistance or active co-operation of members of their households or their kin. Women have recourse to a variety of such strategies, and included in the discussion here are commercial and *ad hoc* arrangements (principally in connection with the care of children); part-time employment and homeworking as 'solutions' for women who find standard full-time employment impractical; and the personally demanding strategy of engaging in long hours of labour, both paid and unpaid, which is a strategy adopted by, or sometimes forced upon, many employed mothers.

Commercial and *ad hoc* arrangements

Most of my respondents had at some time made use of non-family sources of support, either on a regular, commercial basis, or in the form of *ad hoc* arrangements with neighbours or friends in times of difficulty. As I have suggested above, obtaining such support was usually considered to be the responsibility of women themselves rather than their husbands. However, just as women tended to seek the permission or approval of their husbands in obtaining jobs, so they might find that they needed their husbands' consent to specific arrangements of this type. Maureen, for example, described how her husband checked out the 'suitability' of the childminder she intended to use. She first heard of the minder through another employee at her evening washing-up job.

MAUREEN: 'I got in touch with this lady who said . . . she had a vacancy . . . my husband went round first — I told him about it . . . he went round and saw [her], and spoke to her, and saw the set-up, and he said "Yes, you'll have to go round yourself, it looks OK".'

Two-thirds (forty-two) of the women had turned to persons or agencies outside their families at some time during their working lives. Sixteen had paid childminders to care for their children for some or all of the time they were out at work, usually when children were of pre-school age, but including a few children who went to childminders during the school holidays. Children of seventeen of my respondents attended, or had attended, nursery schools or day nurseries. Eight of these women had had access to nurseries provided by their employers while they were engaged in agricultural work or hospital work.[3] Registered childminders and employer-provided day nurseries are relatively cheap ways of obtaining care for small children. In 1981 the childminding rate for full-time care for one child was £12.50 per week and in early 1982 the hospital day nursery used by six of the respondents was charging £1.40 per day. Childminders were highly valued by most of the women who had used them. In particular, their flexible attitude to the care of children, and their provision of 'family' rather than 'institutional' care was considered important. Many childminders were prepared to care for sick children, or to take children early in the morning and keep them into the evening when required. This kind of flexibility can be crucial to women who are sometimes trying hard to keep their jobs in difficult circumstances. Many childminders were also prepared to give children extra meals, to wash babies' clothes and nappies, and to take older children to and from school, or care for them during the holidays. The experiences reported by respondents, and in some cases witnessed by me in visiting childminders, did not seem to bear out some of the more sweeping criticisms which are sometimes made of them. This experience may well have been atypical (and consisted only of registered childminders) but it may be useful in offering a limited corrective to some of the harsher generalizations which have been made. Many of the women found their childminders through personal recommendations.

> RUTH: 'A girl that used to live opposite me, her daughter used to go to Jane, and she had just mentioned . . . "If you do go back to work, I would get in touch with Jane, because in actual fact she is a terrific" — as I have found out since, obviously — but she said, "She is a terrific childminder, you know, if you don't just want to leave your child with anybody" . . . which I — well, once again, my husband wouldn't let me . . . . [It works] very, very well . . . she also has my little boy during the school holidays . . . . [My daughter] is starting school [soon] . . . and then they are quite welcome to go back there during their holidays, which is nice because it means then that I can carry on, you know, as per normal.'

Half of the women who used non-family sources of support (twenty) had neighbours or friends to whom they could turn, either on a regular basis or in an emergency such as children's illness, while fifteen women had at times been able to take employment only because they had a regular arrangement with a friend or neighbour who provided childcare for all or part of the time they were at work. In some cases neighbours cared for children after school, or perhaps looked after toddlers while their mothers were out at work. Sometimes neighbours or friends could be relied upon to take children to and from school or 'keep an eye on' older children who were thought to need a little supervision from a distance at holiday times or after school. Without exception, those giving such support were female — usually other married women, but occasionally the teenage daughters of respondents' friends or neighbours. Respondents usually paid for regular assistance of this kind, but not for occasional help.

All of these supportive strategies were put into effect outside the respondents' homes. However, a small minority of the women paid other women to come to work *in* their homes. Although such labour can usually be obtained relatively cheaply, women who are themselves low paid cannot normally afford to make such arrangements. For most of the women interviewed, paying for non-family domestic labour within the household had never been thought feasible or seriously considered as an option, and only three women had paid strangers to come to their homes to perform some kind of domestic labour. Doreen and her husband ran a shop whilst their children were still young, and during this time Doreen paid a woman to 'come in to clean the house and so on'. This relieved her of some chores, enabling her to work in the shop instead. Rachel started a full-time job shortly after moving to a new area, and needed someone to supervise her 9-year-old son after school.

> RACHEL: 'I paid a lady to look after my son, an old pensioner. . . .
> I put an advertisement in the local newsagents. . . . I didn't want
> her to do any housework, I just wanted her to be there.'

Louise had tried to cope with her full-time job and domestic responsibilities after her son was born, which worked well while she and her husband lived in a small flat. However, when they moved into a larger house, this became difficult. After weighing up various possibilities, she decided to employ domestic help.

> LOUISE: 'I looked around for a part-time job, you see — that was
> the idea . . . but there wasn't anything . . . [now] I have a lady in
> two days a week . . . it was either that or a dishwasher, and I
> haven't got room for a dishwasher, so I have a lady come in, and
> she does the ironing on Tuesdays and on a Friday she hoovers
> through and does the bathroom and the kitchen . . . . [my
> husband] was a bit against it, because he thought we could do it,
> between us, but we tried it for a couple of weeks and I think he
> realized just how much it does involve, and in the end he sort of
> knuckled down to my way of thinking, and I advertised in the
> shop window . . . she comes two mornings a week, for two hours
> . . . I pay her £5.60 a week.'

With a husband in a managerial job, and herself bringing home between £70 and £80 per week, incurring such expenditure (in addition to childminding fees) was no problem for Louise. This would not have been the case for most of the other women in the study, however, especially those single parents who were perhaps most in need of extra help. Paying other women to work in one's own home was a 'last resort' strategy, to be adopted if other strategies were unavailable or did not work, but one which was not especially popular, even with the minority who could afford it.

Part-time working and homeworking as a 'solution'

The majority of the women interviewed had found in part-time employment and/or homeworking[4] a way of combining paid employment with family responsibilities. I have already detailed the extent of such employment in the previous chapter, and discussed it as an important component in women's varied experience of employment. In the present context, I consider these two types of paid work as strategies for employment, and look at the ways in which women find it practical and convenient to work for money in these ways.

Regardless of why a woman with children wants a paid job, once she has made this decision, she will need to develop a strategy enabling her to bring her intention to reality. For women with young children (those not yet old enough to be left alone at home), the central issue is inevitably their care. Where those strategies already discussed are not available, or not felt to be appropriate or complete solutions to the difficulty, women often choose to take employment on a part-time basis. When such employment is combined with the care of school-age children, it frequently removes the need to involve others in their care, except perhaps in cases of illness or at holiday times. A high proportion of the women interviewed had found part-time employment the only arrangement which they could manage while they had young children at school. This was especially true of women who lacked female relatives who were willing and available to look after their children. In some cases, employers had introduced special conditions of work, as well as special working hours, in order to attract married women.

> DOREEN: 'I managed to get a "Mum's shift" in a factory, which was marvellous, because if the children were ill you just rang up and said "I'm not coming in", and it was accepted. I worked 9.15 till 3, so you could get the children to school, get to work, and you could leave in time to go and fetch them.'

Other women chose to combine part-time work with caring for pre-school children, some working at their jobs when their husbands could be at home to look after the children, others leaving their children with relatives or childminders.

> LUCY: 'I started back again when the baby was about two or three months old. My husband was then at home during the day because he works evenings . . . so I took a little job for a couple of hours in the morning while he was there . . . it was housework, cleaning.'

For some, the decision to adopt the strategy of part-time employment involved their recognition that the tasks of domestic labour fell overwhelmingly to them. Women who felt themselves solely responsible for the care of their children and the running of their homes, and who did not receive substantial assistance from other family members, sometimes stressed that a part-time job was all they could cope with.

BRENDA: 'The number of hours [is fine] . . . I have been doing more lately, because of holidays and everything else, and I do find that gets me down a bit . . . that it is a bit too much.'

An examination of the total workload of women who choose a part-time job as a strategy for employment, reveals that this is no easy option. The hours of domestic labour when added to the hours of paid work constitute a demanding full-time set of responsibilities. Linda's case was typical. When interviewed she was married and lived with her husband and three sons, aged 18, 16, and 14. She had a part-time job as a sales assistant, working 17 hours per week basic (mornings only), which in practice often rose to 24 hours per week (including some afternoons). She outlined a typical day's duties.

LINDA'S DAY

6.30 a.m. get up
   cook breakfast for the family
   prepare sandwiches for husband and three sons
   make the beds
   dust, put the sweeper through
   tidy bathroom
   check sons are ready to leave for school/college
8.15 a.m. leave house, driven into town by husband
8.30 a.m. arrive in town, do any shopping required, as have time
   to kill before work
9.30 a.m. begin work
1.30 p.m. lunch (at work)
2.30 p.m. arrive home

'I usually do some washing if I'm at home in the afternoon . . . and just clean a room or turn out a cupboard . . . (if I work any afternoons) . . . . I don't usually sit down until about half-past nine, because I like to keep things — you know, as far as possible — up to date. I like cooking, you see, and the boys like . . . cakes, so it's always cooking cakes . . . I prepare the meals at night and leave them if I'm working.'

Whilst it was common for women to move from part-time employment into a full-time job, some, under pressure of domestic work, found it necessary to make the opposite transition. Lorna had worked full-time in a factory while her son was at nursery school.

LORNA: 'I was really concerned about him going to school

because I felt that I had to be there when he got home. I mean, 5 is
no age to say "Here's a key, get in". I left that job, and went to a
firm that would let me have school hours and fit in the time that I
wanted . . . another horrible job.'

Elizabeth went back to full-time work when her first baby was
almost a year old, but after several months there were problems.

ELIZABETH: 'I had to go from full-time to part-time . . . there was
just too much pressure on me, you know . . . I went to the doctor's
and he said, "I really think you should do less work". I asked
them if I could do part-time work — luckily they said yes.'

In discussing 'who does homework', in the context of her study of
homeworkers in West Yorkshire, Allen has pointed to the
inadequacies of those '*ad hoc* explanations [which] are based on
characteristics of the homeworkers' family situations'. In particular,
she notes some 'homeworkers combined homeworking with
outside employment' (Allen 1982:80-1). Whilst I have used the
term here to cover a broader range of home-based activities than
did Allen (including childminders and self-employed shopworkers), my findings lend further support to her argument. My
sample, too, included women who combined homeworking with
part-time employment. June, for example, worked as a part-time
caretaker in a community centre in addition to being a full-time
childminder. There is indeed no simple link between onerous
family responsibilities (several small children, sick or elderly
relatives, etc.) and homeworking. Nevertheless, such conditions in
the home frequently do apply, and must be seen as *part* of the
explanation for the phenomenon. Several women had worked for
money at home at times when they were confined to their homes by
young children.

HEATHER: 'I did typing at home . . . I'd fit that in probably when
the baby was asleep . . . . I then had a student for a little while, I've
done that about three times now . . . and I did childminding —
[my daughter] was about 4 . . . I had a little boy from 8 o'clock till
6 at night.'

To illustrate the complexity of the homeworking phenomenon,
however, it is worth quoting the case of Maureen, whose employers
themselves changed her conditions of work.

MAUREEN: 'I got a job typing in a small office . . . 9.30 till 1.30 . . . .
After a couple of months there the lease was running out on the
premises and they approached three of us that were doing it and
asked if we'd be interested in doing it at home. Well, just before I

left that job, before the lease ran out, I found out I was having [a baby] — there were two of us pregnant, as it happened — so we didn't let on, we came home, to our respective homes, and carried on with the typing.... I typed all the time I was pregnant, I got a friend to cover me for a month, while I was in hospital and two weeks after ... and then I carried on and typed up until the baby was nearly one. And then ... we both had a letter saying that they were re-organizing, and they set up another office in [another town].'

Thus Maureen's spell of homeworking coincided with caring for a young baby, but the opportunity arose for reasons quite unconnected with this fact. Since her period of homeworking was followed by over six months when she did not seek paid work (she waited until she felt her child was old enough to go to a childminder, at 18 months), it seems likely that she would have withdrawn from the paid labour market when she had her baby had this coincidentally (and temporarily) convenient circumstance not arisen.

For most of the women, then, part-time employment or homeworking was, or had once been, a means of organizing their lives to enable them to undertake paid work and carry out the tasks of domestic labour. Often it had to be combined with other strategies — enlisting the support of friends or relatives, paying for childcare, or negotiating with husbands about how domestic responsibilities should be shared, for example. It is crucial that this part-time employment and homeworking strategy should be seen as the useful *partial* solution which many of my respondents found it to be, rather than as a panacea for all mothers who either need or wish to be employed.

Long hours of work

It was immediately evident from the details given in the interviews that some respondents had been unable to resolve the problem of having two main areas of responsibility, home and family, and job, by seeking part-time work or homework, by the sharing of domestic duties with husbands or children, or by seeking support from either their families or outsiders. Although such strategies enabled some to be 'working mothers' with little difficulty, others, although not necessarily denied access to the strategies, found themselves working very long hours in order to keep everything running smoothly. Because it is women with long weekly hours in paid employment who find domestic responsibilities such a difficult additional burden, I shall confine my discussion here to the forty women who were employed for at least 30 hours per week when interviewed.

Each respondent was asked to describe her daily routine on days when she went to work. By adding together her hours in paid employment and the hours she spent doing domestic duties and caring for children during the rest of the day, it was possible to calculate how many hours the women spent working each day. Including travelling to work time (40 minutes on average) the average was about 11 hours work each day. Almost a third worked 12 hours or more, with one woman working 14 hours — the longest working day.

What kinds of tasks were they performing? Most of the women rose early, some very early. Eighty per cent got up before 7.00 a.m., and almost half before 6.30 a.m. One woman frequently rose as early as 4.45 a.m., and eleven between 5.00 and 6.00 a.m. Only three rose after 7.30 a.m. Tasks done in the morning before leaving for 'work' typically included getting the family's breakfast, making beds, preparing sandwiches and flasks for husbands and/or children, dressing children, tidying up, washing up, putting washing machines on, or pegging washing out, and dusting. A small minority chose to leave home in the mornings without performing any such tasks, but in all of these cases their children were teenagers or older. Several women appeared to have almost a day's work to do before they left home in the morning.

> RUTH: 'I usually get up about 6.15, followed by the children if they hear me about. I will tidy through . . . I would get their breakfast, my husband's, tidy through the kitchen, take his breakfast up, fill his flask — which is about as far as I go as regards getting his dinner ready, then by the time that I have either washed or bathed the children . . . . I dress the 4-year-old, I then dress myself. I then take my husband to work (takes 15 minutes) . . . just generally finish picking up what the children have had, make sure they've cleaned their teeth, brush their hairs. We leave the house about 8.15. I take Jane to the childminder's.'

> CAROL: 'I get up, I get the breakfast, my breakfast and his breakfast, I wash up — oh, and I do his sandwiches and his flask — I clear away, wash up. Then I clear the fireplaces out, I hoover the lounge, the hall and the stairs . . . . If I have a very early start, like quarter to five, I will do either washing or ironing. Then I always call the girls at quarter past seven. I get their breakfast, then I'm up there making their beds, and I make our beds as well. Then I come down, I wash up. Then I go and get dressed . . . I take

the girls down to catch their bus on the way to work.'

About half of those who had a full hour's break at midday said that during this period they regularly did chores such as shopping, going to the bank, paying bills, and in a few cases visiting elderly relatives. Several women who lived near their place of employment went home to do chores, such as preparing the evening meal or cleaning up, which had not been done before leaving in the morning.

The working day by no means ended when they left their employment. Even in the minority of cases where women had other family members who cooked an evening meal, there were many chores waiting for them. These might typically include preparing the evening meal, serving it up, washing up, ironing, washing clothes, bathing children, preparing meals for the next day, cleaning, and shopping (usually once a week).

Despite their heavy workload, a few of the women (usually those with older children) found time to go to evening classes, sing in choirs, go dancing, or run Girl Guide companies or Cub packs. Some women stressed that they would work longer hours on evenings when their husbands were out. Two examples can illustrate how a mother who is employed full-time may spend her evening.

MAVIS (*employed 47 hours per week*):   '[I] leave work quarter to 5 ... collect Colin [aged 1] from childminder ... come in, change him, get him ready for bed, and cook my tea ... and then ironing, any tidying up that I haven't done ... I usually stop doing anything at 9 o'clock .... If I haven't done it, it doesn't get done.'

SHIRLEY (*employed 40 hours per week*):   'Come in at 6, by which time [my husband's] in and got the tea on the go, Brian [aged 2] is in .... Spend some time with Brian, get him ready for bed ... wash up, generally clear up ... probably put the hoover round, put Brian to bed, sit down (about 8 o'clock).'

Tina explained that she 'always' worked on evenings when her husband was not at home. This reflected a concern (which she shared with some of the other women) to get chores 'out of the way' while men were not around. For some this seemed to be part of a sense that it was 'offensive' to men to have women performing domestic tasks around them.

CAROL: 'I did my biggest wash Tuesday night, because he wasn't there, and I got that all dry yesterday ... I got it all finished before he came home .... I try and do it so that I'm not always working when the family are there, I try and work it so that if he is away on that particular day and I have got something to do the next day, I bring it forward, so that — I didn't want him to sort of come home . . . and me over the washing machine. And me not having time to listen to him.'

For most of the women, days 'off', whether at weekends or during the week, were days spent 'catching up' on household chores.

TINA: 'I usually do all my cleaning on my day off, I find that I can manage to get through the house. It's a full day's work.'

GAIL: 'The weekend is usually spent doing the jobs that you don't have time to do during the week.'

Not surprisingly, most of the women found that they tended to get tired. However, the majority did not regard this as a problem, and simply accepted it as a fact of life.

MAVIS: 'I do tend to get tired. I keep going till I finish, I sort of go to bed and flake out and that's it till the morning.'

CAROL: 'I do get tired, but I know that I mustn't stop until I've finished, because if I sit down as soon as I've cooked the meal, I have to really wrench myself to get back up again.'

Along with several others, Nancy responded to my questions about tiredness by indicating that this was a matter which caused her some anxiety. Interestingly, she was not at all sure whether she was right to worry about it or not.

NANCY: 'Well, funny you should say that . . . up till now, *no*, but the last six months, when I've had my periods, I seem to be tired all the time — and I feel old, you know? It's never hit me before — I suppose it's me age, it must be — but to be quite honest with you, I've thought about going up the doctor's with it . . . and then I've thought, well, perhaps I'm burning the candle at both ends, and don't know. Are you expected to be tired at my age — you know? . . . . I put it down to the fact that . . . you can't go home like your husband does and sit down and have a meal put in front of you, that's what I think . . . and that's why I haven't been nowhere . . . . The last six months, I am beginning to think . . . I feel like a zombie sometimes, and you think, "What's it all about?" — you don't seem to have time for the little things what matter.' (*Nancy is aged 38*)

One or two women seemed to be anxious about any tiredness only because they felt the need to conceal it from their husbands. This concern served to illustrate the fact that they could not expect additional help with domestic chores from their husbands, even if they revealed to them that they were overworked.

RUTH: 'I get the days when I know that I've worked hard. My husband might turn round and say I'm beginning to look tired — but then, once again, I've got to be a bit careful, because if I did start to look tired every night, then it would just be a case of "You pack up work", and that would be it.'

Thus many women adopted the strategy of themselves performing long daily hours of labour. This strategy was often combined with others, but in some cases it was overwhelmingly the most important one. Carol had a full-time job as a sales assistant, and was training to become a supervisor (a position which she has subsequently obtained). She receives little help from her husband and daughters, and has no other relatives who could provide her with regular support. She can afford few modern appliances in her home, and is unwilling to change her standards of household care. What option has she left but to perform herself the often onerous tasks of domestic labour, in the early mornings, in the evenings, and at weekends? Her own labour is the only factor over which she feels she can (legitimately) exercise control. Her case is more extreme than most others, but illustrates well the situation of many mothers who have full-time paid jobs.

Labour-saving domestic appliances and standards of household care

In the course of the interviews, details were collected about respondents' access to 'labour-saving domestic appliances', which (allegedly) lighten the burden of domestic duties.[5] *Table 18* shows the women's access to such domestic appliances and compares this with the ownership of these goods in the general population, as shown by the General Household Survey.

Whilst washing machines, vacuum cleaners, and refrigerators were seen by most women as basic essentials which were required in every home, some of the less commonly held items were seen as aids to working mothers which they wanted but were only able to afford because they were in paid employment.

MARGARET: 'I wouldn't have had them if I wasn't working —well, I would have had a washing machine, but I doubt very much whether we'd have had a dishwasher, because I wouldn't really have needed one, and we wouldn't have been able to afford one. I've had a dishwasher since I've been working full-time.'

Table 18   *Ownership of selected domestic appliances*

appliance	my respondents %	general household survey (1981) %
vacuum cleaner	98	94
refrigerator	100	93
deep freezer	76	49
washing machine	96	78
tumble drier	35	23
dishwasher	11	4

(*Source of GHS figures*: OPCS Monitor Ref. GHS/82/1 1st June 1982.)

This tendency amongst the respondents to purchase additional household items using their own wages may partly explain the discrepancy between my figures, and those produced from the General Household Survey.

A minority of the respondents disclosed that although they had certain of the appliances in their homes, they rarely used them. This was particularly true of automatic ovens (a number of women said they did not know how to work them, or did not trust their reliability), but was also sometimes a result of financial pressure.

> SUSAN: 'Frankly I've cut down on using my [automatic] washing machine in the last couple of years because of the electricity. I find electricity bills and gas bills a bit crucifying. I tend to soak a lot of my washing in Ariel in the bath, now, and in the summer I do hand washing — it's an economy I have made.'

Some of the women who lacked items which others regarded as basic essentials had found themselves in this position as a result of arrangements which had accompanied the breakdown of their marriages.

> CATHY: 'He wouldn't let me have [the washing machine] .... I had a tumble-drier and I had an automatic washing machine. And I had a fridge-freezer .... I know this is probably going to sound a bit far-fetched, but *I* know this is what happened. He promised the two eldest ones everything ... so that they would stay with him ... and he said that he wouldn't fight for the youngest one, if I agreed to be re-housed ... and I couldn't bear the thought of not having my little one ... so I just went along with everything he wanted ... and that was that, you know.'

Thus most, but not all, of the women interviewed were able to make use of modern domestic appliances. Many believed that possessing such items reduced their workload in the home. But there were some who, for one reason or another, had no access to even those items regarded as basic, and the domestic workload of these women, especially with regard to washing and cleaning, must have been heavy indeed.

Of course one strategy theoretically available to women who need to find a way of coping with the duties of a paid job and the tasks of domestic labour is the straightforward reduction of the latter; this might best be described as the strategy of lowering standards of household care. This has a certain 'common-sense' appeal, and is one which has been advocated by popular writers on 'coping with a double life' (e.g. Conran 1977). Its crucial weakness is that it neglects the ideological basis of ideas about acceptable standards of household care, and the function which these perform in a capitalist society whose members ('consumers') must constantly be reminded of the need to improve material conditions of life. Very frequently this 'improvement' involves additional work for those members of society (in this case women) who are assigned such tasks. Despite this pressure, which militates against any significant reduction in domestic labour, several of the women acknowledged that, since taking paid employment, they had adopted different standards of household care.

HEATHER: 'I think most women can cope with doing what housework they have to do, they perhaps have to let their standards drop a little, or not do things as often as they used to do them when they were at home all the time — it's picking out the priorities . . . like, my oven doesn't get cleaned as often, or the windows don't get cleaned as often — we can all live quite happily in that situation.'

LORNA: '[if I was at home] it would be much cleaner — and I wouldn't feel so guilty.'

Others, however, were quick to point out that having full-time employment did not mean that they took 'short-cuts' or neglected what they saw as 'their' responsibilities. Shirley's comments endorse my earlier remarks about the ideological basis of attitudes to domestic labour.

SHIRLEY: 'I'm not one of those working mums who dives in from work and chucks everything in the [washing] machine and hopes to Christ it's all right — the only thing I put in there is nappies, sheets, towels — and everything else I wash by hand.'

One woman emphasized the fact that there were always household tasks to be done, and that because of this, women would 'make time' (that is, would deny themselves the alternative activities in which they could engage) to do them.

> BRENDA: 'I think when you're out to work, you've only got a limited amount of time to do everything, so you're going to get through it anyway — no matter what labour-saving devices you've got, you've still got to get through it.'

The ambiguous nature of the women's attitudes to housework is consistent with the findings of other researchers (e.g. Gavron 1968; Oakley 1974b). Many women stressed that they did not enjoy doing household chores, and did no more than was strictly 'necessary', but at the same time they were mostly anxious to stress that their homes ran smoothly, and were not places where the comfort and convenience of husbands and children were put at risk. This ambiguity can only be understood when the social relations of household work are examined as part of the contradictory structures of a society which is both patriarchal and capitalistic.

SOME THEORETICAL IMPLICATIONS

In considering the theoretical implications of my analysis, I want to make some observations about the ambiguous nature of the contemporary family household. It seems clear that negotiations about the sexual division of labour, both within the household and in terms of income-generating activities, are not currently resolved without conflict between the sexes. These negotiations refer principally to the role of female labour — should it be exchanged for wages or not? — and its implications for the role of male labour in the household. In such negotiations women typically start from a position of relative powerlessness, men from a position of relative powerfulness. This is entirely to be expected in patriarchal families where marriage involves the state-sanctioned economic dependence of women on men.

I wish to argue, however, that a pure model of patriarchy is inadequate to explain the nature of intra-familial negotiations concerning how female labour is exercised. In particular, it fails to explain variation between different family households, and variation within the same households over time. I want to suggest that ambiguity over the issue of female labour can be partially understood by the incorporation of a model of the 'maximization of household economic interests' into the model of patriarchy. My contention is that within family households negotiations about female labour may be resolved either on the basis of tradition (patriarchy) or on the basis of rationality (maximization of economic interests), or both. Where one or the other is clearly dominant, negotiations will tend to consensus; where both models have equal or similar importance for household members in explaining their social world, negotiations will tend to conflict. The reaching of consensus, of course, does not necessarily imply that the spouses share an objectively equal situation. My point is illustrated in *Figure 1*.

Figure 1   Model of negotiations about female labour within family households

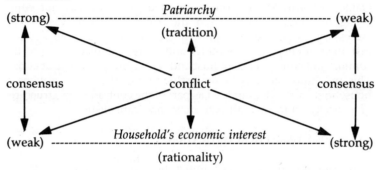

The following examples may demonstrate my argument. Heather works as a full-time supervisor in a large retail store. Her husband is a quantity surveyor. They have two children aged 13 and 10. Conflict within the household about Heather's full-time employment is apparently minimal:

> HEATHER: 'He was very pleased for me to come here. When I came here actually he was redundant, so that was my initial step in coming here. He was there to look after the children. I liked it so much that I wanted to come back, and my mother-in-law offered to help . . . . There has been the odd occasion when he's sort of laughed and said "Ooh, you know, I wish you were here to make me a cup of coffee when I pop in", but he knows how disinterested with life I was without a job, and . . . of course, we've got another full income coming in, which, I mean, helps us to enjoy a lot more in life.'

Here, I would suggest, the couple operate with a weak model of patriarchy and a strong model of the maximization of the household's economic interests. The family enjoys a relatively high standard of living, and the couple have a relatively egalitarian relationship.

By contrast, Christine, who works 28 hours per week as a clerical assistant, spoke of her husband's ambiguous attitude to her employment.

CHRISTINE: 'I don't think he likes me working — but I think he likes the money it brings in — that's about the top and bottom of it . . . he doesn't like the fact that you don't spend quite so much time doing the housework and, you know, making everything look fantastic. And although he says half-heartedly he'll help out with the children when they're on holiday and things like that, it always materializes in some way that he can't for some reason . . . and I think just basically he doesn't really like it.'

Here the situation is clearly one where conflict predominates. This is a household where both patriarchal values (Christine's husband would like a subservient wife performing domestic labour at home) and rational economic values (he appreciates the extra income his wife brings in) co-exist, although neither is overwhelmingly powerful. The result, I would argue, is semi-permanent conflict, and indeed, Christine made numerous references to the instability of her marriage.

My respondents do not include non-employed mothers, and because of this I use a hypothetical example of a family household operating with a strong model of patriarchy and a weak model of economic rationality. Such a family would include a father employed full-time and a non-employed mother who worked only on an unpaid basis in the home, even after her children were at school. This arrangement is unlikely to be in the household's economic interests, but would conform to a husband-dominant, wife-subordinate model consistent with patriarchy. I would contend that many such family households, apparently content with their lower standard of living and their 'traditional' arrange-ments, exist without extensive conflict.

It is important to bear in mind that the relative strength of the two models is likely to change over time within a single family household. Thus the household's interest in maximizing income may be paramount prior to the birth of children, and during this phase the young couple are likely to be in agreement about the importance of both spouses engaging in paid work. With the presence of young children this factor may decline, and there may be a resurgence of the patriarchal model in which women care for their children at home on a full-time basis. As children grow older and start school the position will again be subject to change. As already suggested, the conflict between couples which frequently precedes the wife taking paid employment is often reduced as the husband becomes aware of the advantages to the household (and perhaps principally to himself) of a second income. Patriarchy then recedes in the face of economic rationality. Of course many households are characterized by almost perpetual conflict over the sexual division of labour. Here there may either be a failure to reach one or other of the 'consensus' models I have suggested, or, most importantly, external factors (such as long-term unemployment or low male wages) may intervene, forcing the members of the family household to adapt in ways which they might otherwise find unacceptable (so for instance a wife might seek work only because the family cannot manage on the husband's low wages).

It seems possible that the conflict within the family household which is generated by the ideologies of patriarchy and capitalism may sometimes be sufficiently intense to provoke the breakdown of the marital relationship. This would certainly be one possible means of resolving the conflict. Whilst the precise elaboration of the process of conflict resolution in the household is beyond the scope of the present study (which did not collect systematic data about marital breakdown), it would appear to be a topic on which future research might usefully focus.

In the present context of changing labour market conditions, involving not only rising rates of unemployment but also changes in the structure of the labour market, it is as yet unclear whether the problems confronting capitalist societies will be attacked by a rejection of patriarchal ideology (a tactic used in the two world wars when women were called upon by the state to labour in industry, and nursery facilities were made available as an alternative to domestic childcare), or by a reinforcement of it (again, a tactic which has been used in the past to contend with unemployment). Historically, the ideologies of capitalism and patriarchy can be shown to have been both mutually competitive and mutually supportive. Clearly, the precise nature of the relation between the power of capital and the power of patriarchy requires further detailed elaboration: this, too, must be an urgent task for feminist analysis.

I will now consider briefly those strategies which involve accommodations between persons other than the two spouses, and used by single parents. It might be suggested that the various strategies available to women fall into two categories: a *private* category, including all those strategies which involve negotiations between individuals and within families, and a *public* category, where outside institutions such as the state and employers are involved. State and commercial childcare, and part-time employment, would then be seen as in the public category. It might indeed be argued that policy-makers and the state should concentrate exclusively on the latter, leaving personal and private arrangements to the individuals concerned. Many of my respondents said such things to me themselves.

However, I would like to suggest that to see the issue in this way is to pose a substantially false dichotomy. Although the 'private' strategies are indeed private in the sense that they are developed and put into effect within individual families and individual households, they are only so in this limited sense. It can equally be argued that they are not genuinely private because in every family where a mother wants or needs to take employment recourse must be made to such strategies.

This raises the issue of how far these 'private' strategies can or should be incorporated into public policy. As Novarra (1980) and others have demonstrated, the world of paid employment in advanced industrial societies remains oriented towards the male employee, for whom employment, rightly or wrongly, is taken to be a (if not the) central life interest. Although a few concessions have been made to women (part-time work and flexi-time are examples) it is still substantially true that if women wish to participate in the labour market, they must adapt to, and fit in with, the current requirements of most paid work, its routinization and standard organization of working time — requirements which are designed primarily to serve the interests of capital. In the general run of things, a woman who is a mother will have to make greater personal adjustments to fit in with these requirements than will most men, or indeed most childless women.

In 1984 women are faced not only with coping with the inconvenient way in which paid work is organized (and so relying, as I have indicated above, on a wide variety of alternative sources of primarily female labour to care for children) but also with seriously insufficient employment opportunities. In such a climate it is not realistic to expect campaigns for 24-hour state childcare, however broadly-based or well-conducted, to bear fruit. Many families are currently being forced into poverty, with all this means for women, because of the way labour and its rewards are organized. In any case, access to wage labour has never meant access to emancipation or equality for women, despite Engels' famous phrase — 'the first condition for the liberation of the wife is to bring the whole female sex back into public industry' (Engels 1972:137–38). I return to these points in the final chapter, which contains my concluding remarks and some observations about the study's implications for social policy.

CODA: LYNNE'S STORY

Lynne is 25 years old, has four children, and has been married since she was 19 to David, a self-employed carpenter and joiner. Her first child, Craig, aged 7, was born two years before her marriage (and is not David's child), and she has subsequently had twins, Darren and Mandy, now aged 4, and more recently another son, Jason, aged 1.

Despite her onerous family responsibilities, Lynne has spent only short periods of the nine years since she left school away from employment. When we met, she was working part-time in the evenings as a hospital domestic, but, as I describe below, she has undertaken a range of different jobs in the past. She has clear plans about her future in employment, and expects to be able to develop a career in nursing.

Lynne was born in Canada, but moved to England with her family soon after leaving school. Her mother is a trained nurse and her father a draughtsman. Because of the family's imminent emigration, Lynne took a part-time job serving take-away meals for the few months between leaving school and going abroad. On arrival in England, she found full-time work as a sales assistant in a large chain store. She recalled that 'it was ... quite a nice company to work for', but stayed in the job for only about seven months, as she became pregnant shortly after her arrival in England. The pregnancy was unplanned, but did not seriously disrupt Lynne's life as her family supported her, enabling her to cope with premature motherhood (she was just 17 years old when Craig was born). Her experience illustrates how, with a supportive family network, an unplanned teenage pregnancy can be accommodated with the minimum of drama. Lynne's recollections of her feelings at the time display none of the sense of panic or disaster which was evident in the accounts of some of the other women in this study who had had similar experiences.

'I was quite excited about it, you know — of course you are ... but you don't realize what the work entails.'

Lynne continued to live with her parents after the baby was born, and before Craig was a year old she found (with her mother's help) part-time employment as a nursing assistant in a local hospital.

'[I took the job] to help my parents ... my mother ... because she worked at the [hospital] ... she managed to get me a job there, part-time, and it helped of course with the costs of the baby and everything.'

The arrangements necessary to enable Lynne to leave Craig for this

30-hour a week job again involved securing the active support of her family: 'My mum and my sister worked it between them . . . and, shift-wise, I'd . . . do opposite shifts to my mum.' This strategy for employment worked well, but the strain on a 17-year-old of caring for a young baby, and also holding down a 30-hour a week job was considerable, and after about eight months Lynne found 'it got too much'. She gave up her work as a nursing assistant, and went instead to work in a local sweet factory, where she was able to work a shorter week (22 hours), and in the afternoons only. Again her mother and sister took over Craig's care while she was at work. Lynne found this second arrangement less exhausting, and continued in the job for almost a year, until her marriage, when she was 19, to David. She did not take to factory work, however, and recalled that, 'I didn't like that very much at all . . . it wasn't my thing.'

On marriage she left the job and was able to stay at home full-time with Craig, who was now about 2 years old. Her second pregnancy followed shortly, and the twins were born about a year after her marriage. Their birth substantially increased the burden of Lynne's domestic responsibilities, and so she remained out of paid employment for the first eighteen months of their lives. By this time, however, financial pressure was beginning to mount, and Lynne looked around for an evening job. She felt this was all she could manage as she had to work at a time when David would be at home to care for the children. The first such job she found was working in a snack bar for three hours each evening, as a catering assistant. The arrangements enabling her to take this job worked satisfactorily, but after three months the snack bar closed down. Lynne knew that she needed to find other work and now returned to hospital employment, again as a nursing assistant. She was able to obtain part-time work in the evenings, but this time the hours were longer (27 per week), and included weekend work — both Saturday and Sunday mornings. Lynne and David found it more difficult to incorporate this job, and the children's care, into their domestic arrangements. David again cared for the children when Lynne was out at work, but as Lynne explained:

> 'I wasn't getting home till about 9.30, and on the weekends when I was working my husband could have been working and earning more than me . . . it wasn't working out very well for either of us — I was getting too tired, and he was — you know — feeling that he could be earning more rather than me. . . . [Then] I gave it up . . . [because] he had to go to work in London. He went up to London because he was getting more money . . . and he wasn't getting home till later in the evening.'

These changed circumstances made it inevitable that Lynne would give up her job. Her reasons for holding it were purely instrumental ones, and thus once it began to be an obstacle preventing maximization of household income, her job had to go. Lynne did not abandon the idea of doing paid work, however:

> 'After that I decided to work nights in an agency as a nursing assistant . . . I did Friday and Saturday nights . . . and David looked after them . . . . The money was about the same — maybe a bit more . . . . [It was in] various hospitals in the area. Every week it was somewhere different.'

This night-work was an acceptable alternative to Lynne's previous job, as it did not conflict with David's opportunities for earning money, and he was available to care for the children while Lynne was at work. She continued working in this job for about a year, before giving it up because her fourth child, Jason, was due. She tried to go back to the work again after he was born, but found it too much of a strain:

> 'I did a few more nights after I had the baby, but I had a lot of trouble having him, and he was premature, so I didn't do any more nights, and didn't work any more for eighteen months from when I left until . . . I came back to . . . what I'm doing now.'

When interviewed, Lynne was working as a hospital domestic in the evenings. She had recently changed her contract of employment, from 10 hours per week to 15, and explained that she had moved on to the longer hours as she had been working overtime in any case. She thought she might continue to do some extra hours on top of her new contract, but 'It depends on whether I'm going to get taxed or not — if I get taxed too much I won't do it.' This comment further underlines Lynne's instrumental approach to her employment. She had been working as a hospital domestic for seven months when we met, and she intended to stay for some time:

> '[I'll stay] unless something better comes along — which I don't think it will at the moment — until I feel I can do my [nursing] training . . . which might be another five years.'

The considerable burden of Lynne's domestic responsibilities has been shared over the years by both her mother and sister, and by her husband, as a means of enabling Lynne to take up paid employment. Since her marriage, David has regularly taken responsibility for the children while Lynne has been out working, but, as her comments reveal, he has only played a limited part in performing duties at home.

> 'He washes up every evening . . . but . . . it would be a bit much to ask him to come home and do a load more . . . he's never really been very domesticated . . . . He would do things if I asked.'

Indeed, it is clear that David has tolerated Lynne's employment only because of the financial pressure on the family.

> 'He didn't like [me having a job] at first . . . but he doesn't mind now . . . . We've got used to it . . . you know, having to do it . . . . It's not so much in this job, but previous jobs, I should say — this job's not so bad. But, you know, he likes more or less everything to be done as he gets home . . . . but I have to do the baby, get him ready for bed, and that . . . it was previous jobs more than this, that he didn't really like.'

The couple's instrumental approach to employment (about which, of course, they have little choice, with a family of four children to provide for) means that they spend very little time together. David, who is self-employed, works 'every day — he's very busy', and this includes weekends. In the evenings, he arrives home from work just half an hour before Lynne has to leave for hers. As Lynne said, 'I usually manage to sit and eat my dinner with him . . . then by the time we've finished . . . it's time for me to come out to work.' She gets home from her job a little before 9.00 p.m., and will be up again next morning just after 7.00 a.m. At present her earnings are being saved in a building society, with the specific objective of buying the council house in which they now live. They live from week to week on David's earnings, and on the support which they get from the state in the form of Child Benefit. The couple have domestic appliances such as an automatic washing machine, refrigerator, and vacuum cleaner in their home, but live an essentially frugal life, as they spend next to nothing on entertainment, do not have family holidays, and do not run a car.

At present, both Lynne and David are reasonably happy with their arrangements, both at home, and for employment. They are maximizing their household income (the cost of childcare for three pre-school children would be prohibitive), and at the same time organizing domestic work in a traditional (patriarchal) way, such that Lynne takes prime responsibility for the children, and does all the housework, washing and cooking. Further, they currently have a common objective in view (buying their home), which helps to promote consensus between a couple who are able to spend very little time together. It seems possible, however, that the future may hold conflict for the couple, as well as a continuation of their very hard-working lifestyle. Tentatively, I want to suggest that Lynne's clear ambition to undertake nursing training — 'I will change my job . . . [when] I feel I can do my training' — indicates that she intends to seek satisfactions other than instrumental ones from employment. She wishes to develop a career for herself beyond the domestic sphere; to do this she may require David's more active support at home. His present unwillingness to undertake domestic tasks (if unchanged) would represent a serious obstacle to Lynne's plans; and her career aims may pose a threat to his view of their marital relationship. Lynne's is a case where much depends on the respective power of two competing ideological frameworks. It may be possible for the couple to avoid conflict if a rational and economic model is adopted, at the expense of a traditional and patriarchal one. But, if attempts are made to sustain both, then continuing consensus between Lynne and David appears unlikely. The conflict, if it were to emerge, would then be over the issue of Lynne's labour, and how it should appropriately be performed.

6 Conclusions

OBSERVATIONS ON THE THREE PORTRAITS

The individual respondents whose stories have been told at the end of the previous three chapters have been used to illustrate some of the subjective meanings which women attach to life and labour. This is an important aspect (although in no sense the 'whole story'), and it is important to consider seriously how individuals interpret their own lives and attempt to make sense of their social world.

For women like Barbara and Maureen, the social world is a fairly straightforward place, where, provided the rules are adhered to, life is a relatively uncomplicated affair. Barbara's life is centred unequivocally on her family. In her view it is her task as a married woman and a mother to put her family's needs first, and she does not regard these as in any sense a burden. Her labour is needed first and foremost in the home, and only when she has energy to spare, and reduced demands on her attention has it been appropriate, she feels, to seek to exchange her labour for wages. There is agreement within her family about these priorities, and consequently, very little conflict. Maureen has a very different outlook from Barbara, and derives considerably less satisfaction from the domestic sphere. She values material prosperity for her family, however, and is able to contribute to this through her own wage labour. She accords importance to her husband's career, but recognizes that although it is absorbing (of time and energy) for him, she cannot be involved in it. Her talents, she believes, do not lie primarily in the realm of home and family, and although she takes pride in the efficient organization of her home, she derives most satisfaction from her responsibilities in employment. She has marketable skills and abilities, and believes it is entirely appropriate that she should sell these in the labour market, and buy commercial childcare rather than remain at home with her children.

For Lynne, however, the social world contains more ambiguities and contradictions. She faces a complex world where decisions about her labour have never been straightforward, and where she must accommodate the onerous demands of her young family before taking decisions about her future. She is ambitious for a future in which, like her mother, she will have a rewarding and purposeful career, but in the meantime, she finds she must seek entry to the labour force on terms which are unfavourable to her, and which only reinforce her inability to earn as much per hour as her husband. Thus financial pressure forces Lynne and her husband into a pattern of labour which leaves them free to spend very little time together, an arrangement which they have chosen only because it is the only rational one available to them.

These three women have developed a range of different strategies for employment, and have followed a variety of patterns of labour. This variety gives some indication of the complexity of the range of factors which shape individual women's employment careers; and while in some cases the advantages which many women would gain from a breakdown of the traditional sexual division of labour (with its basis in patriarchal structures) are readily apparent, it should not be forgotten that some women perceive the rewards of childcare (i.e. of motherhood as currently constructed) as attractive and fulfilling. We need to note that motherhood (apart from the 'bearing' of children) is not a 'natural', but a socially-constructed state, and one which is reproduced through women nurturing from one generation to the next (Chodorow 1978). The high value which many women place on the mothering role can partly be explained by contrasting it with the non-nurturant and less expressive roles which are assigned to men in sexist societies. Barbara, for instance, would surely not exchange her experience of being at home with her sons full-time until they were all at school, with Maureen's quite different approach, in which motherhood (of young children) and full-time employment were successfully combined. Traditional arrangements in the home contain many pitfalls for women (not least the near-certainty that, because of divorce or widowhood, they will spend some of their lives without the support of the husband on whom they have become dependent), but in promoting social change which will alter these arrangements, it is crucial not to devalue childcare and the tasks which are assigned to women in the existing sexual division of labour. What must be confronted, however, is the assertion that 'the social organization of parenting produces sexual inequality, not simply role differentiation' (Chodorow 1978:214).

Thus proposals designed to promote social change must take account of the whole range of individuals' needs and wishes, and of how these are constructed. Not all women would welcome the opportunity to spend some of their years in paid work in part-time employment, for example, just as not all women wish to make use of the provision for maternity leave and subsequent re-instatement in their jobs. It is important to recognize that existing social arrangements restrict choice; the evidence from this study offers many illustrations of decisions about employment which are taken through force of circumstance. Whilst all women would benefit from the removal of those patriarchal and economic structures which currently render women relatively powerless, employment is not a panacea for women, and can be a trap. Rather, women require both more open access to employment, and a redistribution of society's rewards in their favour. These changes would enable them to make freer choices, and would help to eliminate their economic dependence on men.

It must be said, however, that recent economic developments and ideological shifts, in Britain as elsewhere in modern industrial capitalism, render such advances for women extremely unlikely in the foreseeable future. As modern capitalism wrestles with the intractable problems of unemployment and declining profitability, we can expect a renewed emphasis on patriarchal family ideology, which will again be presented as the solution to all our problems. We are already accustomed to hear the family invoked in protestations about declining moral standards, the breakdown of law and order, and juvenile offenders. The theme has already been taken up with regard to female employment, and its extension into policies of the state cannot be ruled out. It is hard, indeed, to see what benefit there will be for women in such a development. It will provide no assistance for the three women whose stories have been told at the end of the preceding three chapters, and we should note that even Barbara, who places most importance on the domestic sphere, and was content to spend seven years out of the labour market caring for her children at home, actively wants to remain in paid employment now that her children are growing up.

THE INTERRELATIONSHIP OF CAPITALISM AND PATRIARCHY

In discussing the conditions and experience of female labour, and in particular the arrangements under which women have been drawn into the labour force as semi-permanent wage-labourers, I have attempted in the study to reveal the nature of the uneasy tensions between the current demands of the labour market and the present ideological assumptions of western capitalism. In order to interpret the data, rather than simply to record it as a series of individual facts, a particular theoretical framework has been used. This framework, selected on the basis of a critical review of existing analyses of female labour, enables us to examine the evidence from the study in its historical and social structural context. Its purpose is to illuminate the complex relationship between capitalist relations of production and the sexual division of labour, with a view to developing a fuller understanding of the specific nature of female labour.

The first point to note in considering how female labour is exercised in a modern capitalist society dominated by patriarchal structures and values is that the structural features of that society have no simple effects. Rather, in a social system where women are subordinated to men and labour is subordinated to capital we can note a range of responses; these are illustrated by the different patterns of women's employment careers, as well as by the different meanings which individual women attach to their participation in wage and domestic labour. The choices available to individual women in relation to the use which they make of their labour-power are set within the narrow limits permitted by institutional arrangements. In the preceding chapters, I have noted the socialization, education, and training of girls, the sex-segregation of the labour force, inequality in wage rates according to sex, the socially constructed economic dependence of women on men, the role assigned to women within the family, and the overall subordinate status of women. The force of each of these factors for individuals will vary, with the result that individuals' experience of labour will also vary. Some women, for example, will escape economic dependence on men: in Chapter 3 I showed that for women living with children but without men, wage labour might take on a greater significance than is usual for married women who are mothers. This can result in a more or less total integration into the labour market, and the development of an employment career along the lines of what is currently the norm for men. In another example, a woman who was for some years unable to bear children came to lay considerable stress on her paid work, to the extent that when she eventually became a mother, she chose not to resign her job, but instead to accommodate the demands of children within her existing wage-work arrangements. Other women (although they were not found amongst my respondents) may succeed in escaping a 'girl's' education and training, and hence confinement to women's work and wages.

I have suggested that we can move towards an understanding of the nature of female labour if we recognize that there are currently two main ideological models with which individuals operate in their attempts to make sense of the social world. These ideological models are the products of the structural features already described. They can be summarized in the phrases 'economic rationality' (which is the guiding principal of capitalist activity) and 'patriarchal tradition' (which underpins the relations between the sexes, and hence the sexual division of labour). In certain historical contexts, these two ideological models have been complementary, to the extent that some theorists have felt it unnecessary to distinguish between them. Thus the subordination of women has sometimes mistakenly been taken to be a product of capitalist social relations. In the present study, an attempt has been made to examine the effects of the two models and their relationship to each other. In the post 1945 phase of British capitalism, the demand for female labour coincided with a successful stimulation of consumer appetites. Women who were drawn into the labour force came from families which responded to this stimulus by adopting rational economic values. Individually, they were able to interpret the resulting shift of some female energy from domestic to wage labour as part of a process of increasing material standards of living. The power of patriarchal ideology did not disappear however, and numerous empirical studies, my own included, demonstrate that women do not use their wages exclusively for personal consumption, but spend them on their families, especially their children. Further, we have seen in the present study that it is women who must be active in developing strategies which will enable them to take up paid work, and we can note one constant feature of such strategies, their failure to challenge the assumption of male dominance. Men can be, and are, incorporated into some of the strategies for employment, but not at the expense of *their* employment careers.

I have suggested above that the theoretical framework used in the present study consists of two key components: its explanatory power lies in the relationship between those two components, which is not constant, but varies both according to historical context and across the range of social experience. The structures of capitalism and patriarchy both have powerful effects. In previous stages it has been possible for capitalism to adapt itself to existing patriarchal social arrangements and values to its own advantage, but in recent decades there has been a shift towards increasing tension of both a structural and ideological nature. This tension results from a systematic (but limited) weakening of patriarchal power within the household, which can be explained in general terms by reference to three factors: a gradual (though limited) reduction in male-female wage differentials, and thus some increase in the importance of female earnings for maintaining household living standards; a lesser acceptance of women's confinement to the domestic sphere (explicable by reference to the extension of secondary education and the availability of employment for women); and western capitalism's smaller demand for (traditional) male labour (replaced by machinery and cheap third world labour) which reduces male power in the family household through rising levels of male unemployment. These developments within capitalism have not eliminated patriarchal power, but present a challenge to it; the resulting tension has become apparent in the ambiguous nature of relations within the family household, relations which are and have been expressed through greater or lesser conflict around the question of female labour. In the changing economic conditions of the 1980s (discussed below) it is not possible accurately to predict how the relationship between capitalist relations of production and a patriarchal sexual division of labour will develop, although we have some foundations on which to base speculation. We do, however, possess analytical tools which equip us to develop a theory of female labour, as I have tried to demonstrate.

A NOTE ON CHANGING ECONOMIC CONDITIONS

During the four years since work on the present study was begun, there have been some important developments in economic and social arrangements which affect women's labour. The period has witnessed a substantial increase in registered unemployment (both male and female), a rise in company liquidations and in numbers of redundancies, some changes in the law relating to women and employment, systematic Government attempts to reduce public expenditure, changes in regulations concerning eligibility for state benefits, and several explicit restatements of patriarchal family ideology by members of the Conservative Cabinet.

The changes in the labour market are, of course, not new developments, but represent the exacerbation of trends which have been emerging throughout the past decade. The numbers of registered unemployed in Great Britain had already reached 1.23 million in September 1979: over the past four years, this total has risen sharply — the unadjusted figure for September 1983 was 3.04 million. In September 1979 over 370,000 women were registered as unemployed: by September 1983 this figure had risen to 927,000. Almost all observers recognize that the official figures under-represent the real numbers of unemployed, especially unemployed women. What are the implications of high unemployment rates for women? First, we need to note the issue of youth unemployment. The women interviewed as part of the study first entered the labour force during the late 1950s and the 1960s. Many of them were able to change their jobs several times in their initial years of employment, often in search of more interesting work, better pay, or promotion. None had spent long periods out of work before bearing children. The experience of young women today is quite different. Many girls are out of work, or employed on various youth training schemes, at an age when the girls of their mothers' generation had no difficulty in obtaining work. This is bound to affect their future employment careers: if when still young, they leave the labour force to have children, they will have little in the way of work experience or skills with which to bargain when they re-enter it in five or ten years' time. For older women, the picture is similarly grave. As noted in Chapter 4, female unemployment rates have been rising faster than male, and although women's concentration in the service sector of the economy has so far provided some protection against unemployment, current technological developments threaten this area of their work as well. Recent work carried out at Sussex University suggests that the introduction of micro-electronic technology will result in fewer jobs for women in certain service occupations. In particular, the researchers expect the distributive trades and, probably, office work (where many of the new, technical jobs may go to men), to be affected in this way (SPRU Women and Technology Studies 1982). In an increasingly tight job market, we can also expect fewer voluntary job changes. This has important implications for the characteristics of variation and flexibility which were identified in the study, and if the situation persists it is probable that women (knowing that jobs are hard to come by) will begin to have a less varied experience of employment.

In relation to women's employment, we also need to recall that the gradual narrowing of differentials between women's and men's wages, which occurred between 1970 and 1977 and is usually attributed to the 1970 Equal Pay Act, was reversed in the late 1970s and in 1983 differentials were wider than they were in 1976. I have already acknowledged that arrangements whereby women receive lower wage rates than men are in conformity with patriarchal ideology. If women's hourly wage rates remain at their 1983 level (which seems likely unless the 1970 Equal Pay Act is amended), they will continue to represent structural constraints limiting women's opportunities for economic independence.

If we turn to changes in government policy, we can also observe attempts to re-establish a patriarchal sexual division of labour. The 1980 Employment Act imposed new conditions for women wishing to claim the right to re-instatement in their job following maternity leave, which had been introduced in the 1975 Employment Protection Act. In 1982 the Government announced new regulations concerning the eligibility for unemployment benefit of women who are mothers. These made it necessary for women to demonstrate to the satisfaction of officials that they had made childcare arrangements which left them genuinely free to take up employment. Other regulations, relating to non-contributory benefits, have not been changed, but appear to be more rigorously enforced. We may note the case involving a 63-year-old widow whose benefit was stopped by the Department of Health and Social Security when an elderly (male) family friend was found to be living at her home (*The Guardian* 4 October 1982).

The present Government is firmly committed to reducing levels of public expenditure. It has made efforts to do this by holding down wage levels and reducing employment in the public sector. This policy has had important effects on women, who are over-represented in this sector of the economy. An illustration is provided by the 1982 National Health Service dispute, in which employees, most of whom are women, resisted attempts to keep their annual wage increase below the inflation rate.

The commitment to reducing public spending also has other effects on women. One of the Government's objectives is, where possible, to shift the care of the elderly, sick, and disabled, and of young children away from the public sector (where its place has never been secure) and back into the community. Since it can be demonstrated that the vast majority of 'carers' are women, and that in many cases their 'caring' activities prevent them from seeking paid employment, we may take this policy as further evidence that patriarchal ideology is still exerting a powerful force. Other effects of Government policy — fewer nursery places, and cuts in the school meals' service — also put obstacles in the way of women who are attempting to develop strategies which will enable them to combine a paid job with responsibilities at home.

Finally, we need to pay attention to Government restatements of patriarchal ideology, and their implications for women's labour. The comments made publicly by Patrick Jenkin, when Secretary of State for Health and Social Security have achieved some notoriety:

'For a mother to feel that she can just go on as before, and that she can rely on other people to look after her children for her . . . I just don't think that that makes for a healthy society . . . . If the good Lord had intended us all having equal rights to go out to work and to behave equally, you know he really wouldn't have created man and woman.'

(BBC, *Man Alive*, 30 October 1979)

Ministers have also been heard to point out that high rates of unemployment have coincided with the increasing participation of women in the paid labour force. There is a continuous, implicit message that women's right to paid work is not of the same order as men's.

These developments, all of which tend to reinforce the sexual division of labour and to confine women's labour to a restricted sphere, are countered by certain other changes which cannot be ignored. High rates of unemployment amongst men could have the effect of increasing male participation in domestic labour: some evidence has been put forward to support this view (Pahl 1981) but we must await further research before we can be certain of how the sexual division of labour will be affected. There is also some suggestion that the trade unions are starting to take more serious issues concerning women at work. There has recently been interest in (and action on) sexual harassment at work, positive action for women workers, protection for part-time workers, and securing genuine equal pay. Whilst concrete achievements remain comparatively few, it is apparent that women's increasing share of trade union membership (estimated by Coote and Kellner (1980) at almost a third of all members in 1980) is beginning to draw more women into union activity, and to place issues which matter to women on the collective bargaining agenda. This suggests a fuller integration of women into the labour market.

Taken together, however, the economic and social changes of the past few years have tended to maintain the confinement of women's labour to a restricted sphere, rather than to open up new avenues of opportunity. Women workers will need to make all possible use of their varied experiences and flexible approach to work if they are not to lose their (limited) grasp on freer choices about how they will labour. This depressing picture of the recent past makes it all the more crucial for current and future social policy decisions to be informed by an adequate understanding of the factors which shape women's labour. I therefore conclude by considering the policy implications of my study, and making some suggestions for future research.

INDICATIONS FOR FUTURE RESEARCH

In the study it has been possible to trace the 'employment careers' of a small group of women who live and work in Kent. The research method employed has uncovered material about the women's patterns of labour, and how these are affected by changes and developments in their personal and family lives. However, because all the women in the study were aged between 25 and 45, no information was obtained about the final stage in a woman's potential employment career, the fifteen or so years before she reaches retirement. Women in the age-group 45 to 60 might fruitfully be studied in this way: amongst other matters, it would be interesting to investigate how the responsibility of caring for elderly parents (often assigned to middle-aged daughters in our society) affects the employment patterns of such women, and what impact taking on the role of grandmother has on women's working lives. In addition, larger-scale studies might be undertaken: these would provide an important test of the conclusions drawn from the present, small, study.

Another useful direction for future research might concern the impact of the current recession, and, in particular, of high rates of registered unemployment. Such studies would need to consider the effects of unemployment (both male and female) on domestic life, and in particular on the sexual division of domestic labour. In this context a study of domestic bargaining between spouses and of shifts in ideology about family life and patterns of labour would be important topics. For this purpose it would be especially useful to focus on two-parent families where the husband is long-term unemployed.[1] Women's experience of unemployment remains an under-researched area: the development of a fuller understanding of what unemployment means for women, and of the conditions in which it arises, would represent a significant contribution to both theoretical and empirical knowledge.

I have already discussed some of the theoretical issues surrounding the relationship between capitalism and patriarchy and suggested that the ideologies which underpin these two sets of social relations are not always compatible. On this basis, I have argued that (under present conditions) conflict over the issue of female labour is likely to arise in family households. However, it was not possible in the study to investigate the precise ways in which conflict over the question of women's labour is generated and resolved. Nor was it felt appropriate to attempt an analysis of the nature of the strains placed upon marital relationships by conflict over women's labour, and of the extent to which these strains can account for an accelerating divorce rate. Such enquiries would necessarily involve study of men as well as of women, and of both spouses' understandings of the issues at stake. Research on men was beyond the scope of the present study, but the subject of men, the family, and the sexual division of labour is an important one which would repay serious investigation. It seems likely that certain aspects of such work can most effectively be undertaken by male researchers, for reasons akin to those which mean that feminist research (on women) must normally be undertaken by women.

Lastly, in connection with some of the empirical findings of the present study, further research is needed if we are fully to understand why for some women deviance from normative patterns of personal and family relationships leads to progressive integration into the labour market, while for others it has a restrictive and disruptive effect upon employment careers. Systematic analysis of the patterns of wage and domestic labour of a larger group of such women might better enable us to understand the social factors which underlie this phenomenon.

POLICY IMPLICATIONS

I have argued above that the structural features and ideological components of patriarchal capitalism in post-1945 Britain have not had simple and straightforward effects for women, but have elicited a variety of responses. These can be observed by examining women's patterns of employment, and the range of meanings which they attach to both wage and domestic labour. This situation raises difficult questions for policy-makers, and for those, including feminists, who seek to influence social policy. For it is clear that different women seek to incorporate wage labour into their lives in different ways and for different reasons. To accommodate them all, a wide and unpredictable range of services — educational, training, childcare, domestic, income-support, etc. — is needed. For this reason, it is difficult both for feminists to co-ordinate campaigns and for policy-makers to plan for demand. The provision of a statutory right (for women in certain circumstances) to maternity leave and reinstatement in their jobs is a case in point. Those fighting to achieve such legislation often had to deal with opponents who argued from the assumption that, once the law was passed, all women would seek maternity leave, and would return to their jobs after about six months at home. In practice, of course, only about one in ten women employed during pregnancy returns to her former job following maternity leave (Daniel 1980) — though most

of these women return well before the thirty-three post-confine-
ment weeks which is their maximum legal entitlement. (Rowland
(1981) reports 41 per cent returning within twelve weeks, and 76
per cent within twenty-six weeks.) It is very evident that women's
needs and desires are best served by an extension of opportunities
and of choice.

The single most important feature of current social policy
inhibiting such choice is the economic dependence of women on
men. This persistent handicap offers benefits for women which
usually turn out to be illusory ('a meal-ticket for life'), and underlies
their lower rates of pay, restricted access to employment, and
assigned responsibility for domestic labour. It is also responsible
for the plight of lone mothers who, despite their growing numbers,
are still treated as an aberration, and required to face more
difficulties in combining wage and domestic labour than any other
group. The state's construction of mothers as dependants sanctions
male power (inside and outside the family household) and
encourages men to abandon areas of domestic responsibility. Men
are socialized into believing they need not service their own
requirements for food, clothing, and cleanliness, and that as parents
they need only 'assist' in the care and upbringing of their children.
However, if parents are to be free to make decisions about their
domestic arrangements on the basis of aptitude for the tasks
involved, rather than on the basis of gender, then all adults,
including women, must be treated as individuals and allowed to
escape a dependent status. The current situation is increasingly
anachronistic as higher proportions of women head households for
longer periods of their lives.

It is an inescapable conclusion of the present study that many
women continue to bear unplanned children, despite post-war
developments in contraceptive technology and widespread sex
education. This is especially true of first children, whose conception
may no longer prompt marriage or plans for immediate adoption
(illegitimacy rates have risen sharply in recent years), but who
nevertheless have a very powerful impact upon their mothers'
lives. The failure to plan for pregnancy and childbirth bears witness
to a persistent belief that children are an inevitable part of family
life; this being the case, it matters little (so the argument goes) when
they are born. Those involved in sex education and family planning
appear to have failed to impress upon young women that bearing
children will have profound effects upon their working lives. The
burden of domestic labour will increase dramatically (especially in
the early years), and may cause them to leave the paid labour force,
albeit temporarily. Where pregnancies are planned, women can

choose how best to accommodate motherhood into their employment careers: they can complete a period of training, consolidate on-the-job skills, ensure that they fulfil service requirements if they want re-instatement after maternity leave, and give some thought to how and in what capacity they will seek re-entry to employment. In some cases, a planned approach to parenthood will enable women markedly to improve their employment prospects in later life, and for this reason further steps should be taken to ensure that their education enables young women to make informed and enlightened decisions about choosing if and when to bear children. However, it must also be acknowledged that at the moment many women see no point in attempting to plan their lives, and quite justifiably. The opportunities available to them are restricted by limited training and vocational education, and their confinement to the 'women's' occupations; the work they do tends to be casual and temporary and they are badly paid and vulnerable to redundancy (especially as part-timers during a recession). For such women, planning for family and working life will make sense only if opportunities for women are extended and if choices become less restricted.

This last point is relevant both to my earlier remarks about the need for economic independence and to what I wish to say in conclusion concerning the current organization of paid work. Economic conditions in the 1980s are presently posing grave challenges to existing social policy surrounding paid employment. There is a serious shortfall of paid jobs, and even relatively well-qualified, skilled, and fit individuals are experiencing, or under threat of, unemployment. The evidence suggests that in such a climate, women's employment opportunities are contracting. Whilst it is not within the scope of the present study to propose solutions to the general problem of unemployment, it is pertinent to consider ways in which the burdens and rewards of labour might be more equitably distributed. The following example can illustrate the point.

One of the problems faced by couples with dependent children concerns the need to generate additional income (for the state's support for children, in the form of Child Benefit and Family Income Supplement remains meagre). Often, even today, it is more rational for the man to seek overtime or additional work than for the woman to undertake (further) paid employment. This places the man in a position where he is less able to participate in the tasks of domestic labour, the burden of which falls yet more firmly upon the woman. It must surely be an urgent task of social policy to seek adjustments to a situation in which large numbers of those in employment are over-burdened by overtime or additional hours, or are working privately for cash or barter, while upwards of three million persons appear on the official register of those urgently seeking work. British society has long been characterized by sharp inequalities in the distribution of its rewards — property, wealth, access to education, health-care, and leisure activities, etc. The existing system of wage labour has not proved especially effective in reducing these inequalities. In particular, the nature of their participation in paid work has done little to expand women's share of the available resources. A progressive social policy needs to recognize these past shortcomings, and to be directed towards a specific objective.

By allocating material rewards to those who perform one form of labour (wage labour and its offshoots) but not to its essential underpinning, domestic labour, patriarchal capitalist societies have succeeded in skewing the distribution of resources and social power to the detriment of women. The inadequacies of this system of allocating resources are currently being revealed to all as mass unemployment becomes a permanent feature of our society: for many millions must be supported from non-wage sources, without reference to any labour they may or may not perform. In such a situation, it is increasingly obvious that a radical alteration is required in both the social organization of labour, and the allocation of social and economic resources. As we have learned, few women (or indeed men) find it stimulating to work *only* within the isolated confines of the domestic household. The importance of paid work as a source of social contacts should not be dismissed. (The demand for 'wages for housework' has failed to recognize this, and strikes no chord in women's hearts as a result.) Almost all adults now wish to participate in wage labour and we must therefore move towards a distribution of the available employment which will encompass all who seek it. This may mean shorter hours, longer holidays, and earlier retirement, as many observers have noted. The corollary of this development is that all adults will need to take responsibility for their individual requirements and for the care of their dependants on a daily basis. Meanwhile young children and the old or sick should continue to be provided for by services of the state: nurseries, homes for the elderly and sick, etc. In promoting such a shift, we also need to recognize that wages (for paid work to which all have access) should not be a means of supporting whole families. This will enable us to move away from the idea of a 'family breadwinner' (who is usually male) which has been so detrimental to women's interests. In consequence, much more substantial support will be needed for dependent children, and for others too old or unfit to work, or indeed for those who choose not to participate in the paid labour force.

Policy-makers must soon take decisions which are forced upon them by the critical state of the British economy, and in particular by unacceptably high levels of unemployment. These will inevitably require fresh approaches, new initiatives, and radical changes, but they will have to be made. In negotiations about these changes there can be no certainty that women's interests will not once again be put aside. Clearly a forceful feminist lobby will be a crucial pre-requisite if policy is to be shifted in a direction more favourable to women. In putting forward their case, women will face the serried ranks of a capitalist class on the defensive, as well as the opposition of a deeply conservative labour movement (at least on the question of sex equality). The odds still appear to be stacked against them: but, as women show signs of a growing resistance to subordination, we may also have confidence that in the coming struggle for a more equitable redistribution of social and economic resources, they will no longer be willing to 'suffer and be still'.

Postscript

I should like to update what has been said in the text of *Women's Working Lives* by commenting briefly on relevant developments since going to press.

First, the Department of Employment and the Office of Population Censuses and Surveys has now published the report of their 1980 Women and Employment Survey (Martin, J. and Roberts, C. (1984) *Women and Employment: A Lifetime Perspective*, London: HMSO). This survey of over 5,000 women represents a welcome and significant addition to the information available to students of women's labour. It includes some work history data which readers may wish to compare with my own findings. The survey involved asking 'relatively few open questions', in a single interview, however, and thus could not produce the kind of detailed information which only a smaller, in-depth study can hope to obtain.

Second, the need for research on women's unemployment which I mentioned in Chapter 6 is now beginning to be met. Angela Coyle's study of redundant women in Yorkshire has now been published (Coyle, A. (1984) *Redundant Women*, London: The Women's Press), and Frances Evans is currently preparing a doctoral thesis concerned with women's unemployment at the University of Kent.

Lastly, I want to mention the Matrimonial and Family Proceedings Act 1984 which has recently received the royal assent. In the context of my remarks about the illusory benefits which women derive from the economic dependence upon men, it is necessary to note that this new legislation recommends the courts to make maintenance payments payable after the end of a marriage 'only for such a term as would . . . be sufficient to enable (the recipient) to adjust . . . to the termination of financial dependence upon the other party'.

Appendices

1 WOMEN AND EMPLOYMENT IN KENT, 1961–1977[1]

During the 1960s and 1970s the number of employees in employment in the county of Kent increased by approximately 54,000, reaching 508,392 in 1977. Almost all of this increase was the result of more women in employment.

There were also important shifts in the relative importance of the main industrial sectors. In the county as a whole, the *primary* sector's share of all employees in employment dropped from 9.4 per cent in 1961 to 4.6 per cent in 1977. The *construction* sector also lost a small part of its share in the county's employment, the percentage dropping from 6.6 to 5.7 per cent over the same period. The *manufacturing* sector witnessed a growth in its relative importance during the 1960s, but lost this during the 1970s: it accounted for 26.8 per cent of employees in employment in 1961, 30.3 per cent in 1971 and 26.7 per cent in 1977. The *service* sector contrasted with the other sectors, as would be expected from experience in Britain as a whole, showing a steady increase, from 57.0 per cent in 1961 to 63.0 per cent in 1977.

In Kent, women were markedly less well represented than men in both the *manufacturing* and *construction* sectors. In 1961, 18 per cent of female workers were employed in manufacturing, compared with 31.6 per cent of male workers; in 1976 the figures were 17.9 and 33.8 respectively. The construction sector employed a mere 0.7 per cent of female workers in 1961, and only 1.1 per cent in 1976. The comparable figures for men were 10.1 per cent and 9.6 per cent. The *primary* sector contained 9.2 per cent of all male workers and 9.8 per cent of all female workers in 1961, and by 1976 the percentages were 5.0 and 4.1 respectively. Throughout the period, the overwhelming majority of female workers were employed in the *service* sector. This contained 71.4 per cent of employed women in 1961 and 76.9 per cent in 1976. Although it was also the largest employer of male labour, men's concentration here was less marked than women's: 48.7 per cent in 1961 and 51.5 per cent in 1976.

More detailed figures (referring to the three Employment Office Areas, Canterbury, Maidstone, and Herne Bay/Whitstable) are available from the Annual Census of Employment, and these offer a picture of the relative importance of the various sectors in the areas from which respondents were drawn for the present study.

Absolute numbers of total female workers employed increased in all three areas between 1961 and 1976. In Canterbury the increase was 3,530 (37.4 per cent), in Herne Bay/Whitstable 1,060 (34.7 per cent) and in Maidstone 7,959 (34.5 per cent). These figures are all well above the percentage increase in females employed in Kent as a whole, which was 25.2.

The percentages of female workers employed in the *primary* sector fell markedly during the period, although Herne Bay/Whitstable in any case started in 1961 from a low base, with only 3.9 per cent (122) of its female workers so employed. This dropped to 0.95 per cent (40) in 1976. In Canterbury, female employment in this sector (as a percentage of all female employment) dropped from 15.7 per cent (1,478) to 4.4 per cent (576) and in Maidstone from 19.5 per cent (4,498) to 5.8 per cent (1,804).

The *construction* sector had little importance as an employer of female labour throughout the period, although in all three areas a slight percentage increase is recorded. In Canterbury, where this sector was most important as an employer of women, it employed 0.8 per cent (75) of the female workforce in 1961, and 1.2 per cent (151) in 1976. In Maidstone the corresponding figures were 0.4 per cent (97) and 1.1 per cent (337), and in Whitstable/Herne Bay 0.7 per cent (22) and 0.9 per cent (37).

The relative importance of the *manufacturing* sector for female employment presents a more varied picture if the three areas are compared. Only in Canterbury did the importance of the sector for women remain fairly constant: 7.3 per cent (693) of women in this area worked in the manufacturing sector in 1961, 8.2 per cent (960) in 1971, and 7.1 per cent in 1976 (928). In Herne Bay/Whitstable manufacturing industry became much more important for women's employment between 1961 and 1971, but this position was not fully maintained: 9.6 per cent (299) of the area's women workers were so employed in 1961, 30.5 per cent (1,114) in 1971 and 21.1 per cent (882) in 1976. In Maidstone, the period began with a relatively high concentration of women in this sector, 23.7 per cent (5,470) in 1961, but this percentage gradually declined, dropping to 21.8 per cent (5,905) in 1971 and 16.2 per cent (5,032) in 1976. It will be noted that the absolute number of women so employed was not subject to great variation.

In all three areas, the period began and ended with a high concentration of women workers in the *service* sector. In Canterbury and Maidstone this concentration became more marked as the period progressed, while in Herne Bay/Whitstable the percentage of women employed in this sector dropped between 1961 and 1971, but began to rise again between 1971 and 1976. *Table 19* gives the detailed figures, both for female and male employment.

Table 19   *Female and male employment in the service sector 1961–1976 (as a percentage of all female and all male employment)*

area	1961 female % (no.)	1961 male % (no.)	1971 female % (no.)	1971 male % (no.)	1976 female % (no.)	1976 male % (no.)
Kent	71.4 (119,282)	48.7 (140,075)	72.7 (135,431)	49.3 (140,948)	76.9 (160,897)	51.5 (149,670)
Canterbury	76.2 (7,186)	61.1 (8,008)	85.3 (9,922)	71.1 (10,308)	87.2 (11,307)	70.9 (11,147)
Herne Bay / Whitstable	85.7 (2,655)	60.6 (1,959)	66.3 (2,422)	49.0 (2,175)	77.0 (3,219)	48.4 (2,112)
Maidstone	56.4 (13,014)	43.8 (16,258)	69.0 (18,679)	48.3 (20,832)	76.9 (23,865)	57.5 (26,200)

Detailed figures about the occupations of employed women in Kent are not readily available for the whole of our period. However, the 1971 (10 per cent) Sample Census yields data for that one year which may be of interest. The percentages in *Table 20* have been calculated from the actual numbers made available to me by Kent County Council. I have included only those occupations in which substantial numbers of women were employed.

Some interesting features can be noted. In all four areas, these occupational groups contained substantial percentages both of all women employees and of married women employees. In the most extreme case, over one third of all employed women in Maidstone were engaged as clerical workers. It is clear that women in these areas of Kent were highly concentrated in a small number of occupations.

Comparison of the percentages for married women with those for all women reveals that there was a greater tendency for the former to be employed in sales occupations (in every case the figure for married women was higher than that for all women), and

Table 20   *Women's employment in selected areas of Kent, by marital status and selected occupational orders, 1971, in percentages*

occupational order	Maidstone		Canterbury		Herne Bay		Whitstable		
	f	mf	f	mf	f	mf	f	mf	*
XXI clerical workers	33.5	29.9	29.8	24.3	18.4	16.2	26.5	29.0	
XXII sales workers	13.4	13.7	17.3	18.4	24.2	25.3	11.0	13.3	
XXIII service, sports and recreation workers	22.8	26.6	25.0	27.3	26.7	30.5	29.8	29.0	
XXV professional, technical workers, artists	14.6	14.7	16.4	12.3	13.5	13.6	9.2	7.2	
sum	84.3	84.9	88.5	82.3	82.8	85.6	76.5	78.5	

* f = all females; mf = married females.

the same was generally true of 'service, sports and recreation workers', with the single exception of Whitstable. Conversely, there was a tendency for married women to be under-represented in clerical occupations (again with the exception of Whitstable). This under-representation of married women was also found in the fourth occupational order, 'professional, technical workers, artists', although Maidstone and Herne Bay both show very little variation between all women and married women.

This general picture is not at odds with the information obtained from individuals in the empirical study. For example, it was frequently the case that women who had worked in clerical occupations before marriage and raising children later turned to other types of work (for reasons which are discussed in Chapters 3 and 4).

As is well known, official data on women's unemployment paints a seriously inadequate picture of the true situation as regards the numbers of women seeking paid work. In 1981, the General Household Survey estimated that 41 per cent of unemployed married women, and 16 per cent of unemployed non-married women (compared with just 6 per cent of men) were not registered as unemployed. This means that large numbers of married women in particular are excluded from official statistics about both numbers of unemployed women, and rates of female unemployment. It should be noted that the 1981 situation represents the continuation of a marked trend towards registration by unemployed women: in 1975, 70 per cent, and in 1977 53 per cent of unemployed married women did not register. The phasing out of the option for married women to pay reduced National Insurance contributions (since April 1978) has no doubt been partly responsible for this change, as Sinfield (1981) has pointed out. The General Household Survey has also shown that many more women would seek work if good child care facilities were available. Indeed, the inadequacies of official data concerning women's unemployment are so severe as to make them virtually useless. This situation has been further exacerbated by recent changes in the method of compiling the figures which now exclude those not claiming benefit. In addition, unemployment rates, broken down by sex and age for local areas, are not publicly available except in specific contexts.[2]

In the face of this inadequate data, it has seemed inappropriate (not to say foolhardy) to attempt a discussion here of trends in women's unemployment in the local labour markets with which the present study is concerned. It is only considered reliable to suggest that in Britain as a whole the decades 1961-81 witnessed a shift from low rates of female unemployment in the 1960s to rapidly accelerating rates in the late 1970s and early 1980s. Others have concluded that:

'Many more women are now out of work and their unemployment is lasting longer... The rapid increase in the numbers of women out of work has been one of the most dramatic changes in unemployment during the last decade.'

(Sinfield 1981:83)

2   DATA COLLECTION DETAILS

Standard Form for Personal Details

PERSONAL DETAILS   (No.   )
1.   Name: ....
2.   Date of birth: ....
3.   Marital status: ....
      (Show Card: Married, widowed, single, divorced, separated)
4.   Have you been married more than once? ....
5.   How many children do you have? ....
6.   What are their ages? ....

7. Sex of children? ....
8. Do all of your children live at home with you? ....
9. Are all of these your natural children? (or are any of them adopted, fostered or your husband's children, for example)
....
10. How many people besides yourself and your children live in your home? ....

DATE OF INTERVIEW ....

Outline Interview Schedule

Can you tell me what your job is at present?
What duties does that involve?
How many hours a week do you normally work? Days each week?
Do you ever work extra hours?
When did you first start working for this employer?
Have you been working there continuously since that time?
Have you changed your job or been promoted while you've been there?
If no: Do you think there is any chance of that happening, if you wanted it?
All: How do you feel about that?
If yes (to promotion): Would you like to be promoted further?
Why is that?
How would you describe the pay you get in your job?
(SHOW CARD 1: excellent; good; fair; poor; very poor.)
How easy or difficult do you think it would be to find a similar job in this area with better pay?
(SHOW CARD 2: very easy; quite easy; quite hard; very hard; don't know.)
Apart from your pay, are there any other benefits which go with your job?
What do you particularly *like* about your job and working there?
What do you particularly *dislike* about your job and working there?
How long do you think you will go on working for your present employer?
If you left your job, for any reason, do you think it would be possible to find another job at the moment?
Confirm details of family living at home:
husband, children (if any old enough, have they left school, are they working, do they contribute to family income?),

grandparents (their role in the home: are they able to help with domestic duties — care of children, cooking, cleaning, etc., or do they add to mother's duties?), any others.

Do you have any other relatives who live at all near to you whom you see at all often?

Do any of your relatives need your help because they are ill or infirm or for any other reason? What kind of help? How much of your time does this take up?

Your parents:

Has your mother ever had a paid job?

What was her occupation?

Did she go out to work when you were a child?

What is/was your father's job?

How do you think your parents feel about you having a job at the moment?

Your husband (if any):

Does your husband have a job?

What is his occupation?

Has he always done that job?

How do you think your husband feels about you having this job?

Your marriage:

How old were you when you left school?

When did you get married?

How old were you when your (first) child was born?

(as appropriate, ask about dates of divorce, re-marriage, husband's death, etc.)

Leaving school, first job and subsequent jobs Confirm date of leaving school, and age at that time.

Did you obtain any qualifications at school? Details.

What happened to you when you first left school? (e.g. job, college, unemployed).

Did anyone help you or give you advice about what to do when you left school?

Could you describe your first job? — what you did, what the pay was like, what the people you worked with were like, etc.

Was there anything you particularly liked about that job?

Was there anything you particularly disliked about it?

How did you get the job — advert, job centre, school, parents, etc.?

How long did you stay in that job?

Why did you leave? Probe fully.

For all jobs up to first childbirth gain details of:

nature of work,
how job was obtained,
what liked/disliked about job,
length of time in job,
why left job.

First pregnancy Did you deliberately plan to start your
family at that time?
(*if yes*, why did you choose that time?
if no, how did you feel when you found you were pregnant?)
Did you think at all about how starting a family was going to affect
your working life in the future?
At that time, did you think you would return to employment
again?
When did you expect that to be?

Going back to work after a break for childrearing What
was the first job you did after your child was born?
When did you start that job?
When had you first started to think about coming out to work
again?
Why did you want to work again?
How did your family feel about it? (husband, parents, etc.)
What special arrangements did you have to make so that you would
be free to come out to work?
Did any of this prove to be a real problem?
To what extent does your husband share in the domestic duties
(both running the home and looking after the children)?
Could you give me some examples of the things he does at
home?
Ask about any subsequent pregnancies, etc.
Have you ever had to have time off work because of your
child(ren)? (illness, breakdown of childcare arrangements,
etc.)
How did you feel about doing that?
What was your employer's reaction? (check whether paid, took
holiday, given unpaid leave, etc.)
Did you consider making any other arrangements? (e.g. asking
friends or relatives to help, your husband staying home, etc.)
Make sure respondent has described all her employment
Ask if she has ever done any paid work at home

Use of earnings I don't want to ask you detailed questions
about money, but I would like you to tell me about the kind of

things you spend your earnings on — first of all.

Do you think of the money *you* earn as part of the family budget, or as your own independent income?

Which of these things do you spend your own earnings on?

(SHOW CARD 3: personal things for yourself (e.g. clothes, make-up, hobbies, etc.); things for your children (clothes, toys, treats, school things); family holidays; car; improving your home (furnishing, decorating, domestic apliances, etc.); the normal day-to-day running of your home (food bills, general household goods); entertainment; other items.)

If you didn't have your own earnings, which of those things, if any, would you have to spend less on or go without?

Using the card: could you tell me which group your own take-home pay comes into?

(SHOW CARD 4: weekly pay (after tax, etc., but not including overtime):

A. less than £12 per week; B. over £12 but less than £20 per week; C. over £20 but less than £28 per week; D. over £28 but less than £36 per week; E. over £36 but less than £44 per week; F. over £44 but less than £52 per week; G. over £52 but less than £60 per week; H. over £60 but less than £70 per week; I. over £70 but less than £80 per week; J. over £80 but less than £90 per week; K. over £90 but less than £100 per week; L. over £100 per week.)

Labour-saving devices   Some people think the availability of labour-saving devices has made it easier for women with families to go out to work — could you tell me which of the following things you have in your home?

washing machine — automatic; vacuum cleaner; refrigerator; freezer; spindrier; tumble drier; dishwasher; automatic oven (one which times itself); anything else which you think saves time or effort?

Do you think having these things is important in enabling you to cope with having both home and work responsibilities?

Typical day   I'd like you to describe to me a day's work and duties (choose a day when you go out to work) starting from when you get up, through the day until you either sit down and relax or go to bed at the end of the day.

Fatigue/illness   Do you think that being a working mother has any effect on your health? What about tiredness?

Attitudes Looking back over your life so far, and the way you have combined being a mother with also having a paid job, do you think this is something which you would like your own daughter to experience in the same way as you have?

If you would like anything to be different for her, what would it be?

Imagine that for some reason you become unemployed (it doesn't matter why) and you are looking for another job. Which of the following, if any, would you look for, and which would be the most important?

(SHOW CARD 5: 1. work which you have done before; 2. good pay and benefits; 3. suitable hours for your needs; 4. good holidays; 5. promotion prospects; 6. pleasant people to work with; 7. interesting and/or demanding work; 8. something quite different from anything you've done before; 9. a job where you could acquire new or different skills.)

Is there anything you would look for which isn't on the Card?

How far are you prepared to travel to work?

Unemployment Have you ever registered as unemployed when you have been looking for work?

Would you ever consider doing so?

Do you think you would gain any advantage by doing so?

Do you pay full NI contributions, or the special reduced rate for married women?

Career development Have you ever had to change your own plans for working in order to fit in with your husband's job/career?

If *yes*, how did you feel about that?

Would you be willing to do so (again)?

Statement *Either*

'More and more families nowadays seem to find it necessary to have both husband and wife earning in order to maintain an acceptable standard of living'

or

'It is increasingly difficult to maintain an acceptable standard of living if there is only one wage coming into the family.'

Do you think the statement is true or false?

Why do you think that should be the case?

How do you feel about it?

Choosing again If you could start again right from when you left school, and you had opportunities for training or education which perhaps you didn't have at the time, do you think you would still do the same, or is there anything else you would like to have done?

Dual responsibilities Do you think there are any ways in which life could be made easier for women who have responsibilities both at home for their families, and at work?

Trade unions Do you belong to a trade union?
Have you ever belonged to (any other) trade union?
(*if yes to either*:
Were you or are you at all involved in the union — for example, have you ever attended branch meetings, held any office in the union, or taken any kind of industrial action?
if no to either:
Has anyone ever approached you at work (in any of your jobs) and asked you to join a trade union?
Why did you choose not to join?
Are there any circumstances in which you think you would join a TU?
Does anyone else in your family belong to a TU?
Whether a TU member or not:
What purpose, if any, do you think the TU serves where you work?
What about any other companies in which you have worked?)

Equal Opportunities Legislation During the 1970s there were a number of changes in the law concerning the employment of women — the Equal Pay Act, the Sex Discrimination Act, and the Employment Protection Act, which introduced the clause about maternity leave rights. [Explain] Do you think any of these changes in the law have affected you personally? If yes, in what way?
Do you think they have affected other women?
Do you think it was a good or a bad idea to change the law in the way these acts did:
    The Equal Pay Act
    The Sex Discrimination Act
    Maternity leave
Why do you think that?

Would you be willing to be contacted again, if I wanted to check any details at home, or at work?

(*if yes*, obtain address and telephone number.)

Postal Questionnaire

NAME ....
EMPLOYER
in 1980/1 ....
in 1981/2 ....
OCCUPATION
in 1980/1 ....
in 1981/2 ....
HOURS WORKED PER WEEK (normal hours)
in 1980/1 ....
in 1981/2 ....
PERIODS OUT OF EMPLOYMENT
Have you had any periods away from work or out of work since you were interviewed in 1980? (Don't include holidays or your own temporary sickness.)

YES / NO (delete as applicable)

IF YES, please give details (e.g. how long, reasons, etc.)

....
....
MARITAL STATUS
in 1980/1 ....
in 1981/2 ....
PERSONS LIVING WITH YOU AT HOME
in 1980/1 ....
in 1981/2 ....
HOME
Have you moved house since you were interviewed in 1980/1?

YES / NO (delete as applicable)

IF YES, please give your new address and/or telephone number:

....

Thank you very much for your help. The information you have given above is needed for the concluding stages of the research. It will be treated as confidential.

Sample Chronology:

Respondent number 26

date	personal/family events	employment, etc.
Feb. 1942	born Surrey	(Saturdays: shop assistant in Woolworth's before leaving school)
July 1958	left school, went to college	(temp. in London during summer holidays)
Summer 1960	left college	1. typist for London insurance company
Mid 1961		2. secretary to one of the export managers in a London export-import company
1964	married	3. moved to Yorkshire with husband; worked as secretary in building firm (35 hrs pw)
August 1968	husband's employment involved move to Kent	left job 3 because of move; also, expecting first child (three months pregnant) claimed unemployment benefit for three months
May 1969	birth of first child	
May 1973	birth of second child	4. started doing typing at home for husband's company intermittently, holidays etc.
September 1974	first child started school	
1975/76	wanting to start a job, so started second child with childminder one day per week	
February 1976	second child with childminder, experiencing marital difficulties	5. took morning job sorting magazines and newspapers in wholesale newsagents
June/July 1976		gave up job 5 because not enjoying it
October/November 1976		6. secretarial work in small electronics company — at first 9.30–1.00, later from before 9 till 3.30
end July 1978	finding job 6 too much	left job

date	personal/family events	employment, etc.
end August 1978		7. started part-time job as secretary (local authority) on two-year project, 9.00–2.30 (25 hrs pw)
September 1978	second child started school	
end July 1980		end of project so job 7 finished
summer 1980		(temped for one week for employer 6)
September 1980		8. started clerical job — pricing and ordering goods in wholesale chemist's warehouse (28 hrs pw)

3 RESPONDENT'S JOB, AGE, AND FAMILY SITUATION AT TIME OF INTERVIEW

name	current job	age	no. of children*	marital status
Alice	hospital domestic	39	3	divorced (co-hab)
Alison	hospital domestic	29	1	divorced
Andrea	telecomms. officer	40	1	married
Angela	administrative clerk	36	1	married (2nd)
Anne	kitchen assistant	35	2	married
Annette	clerical assistant	27	**	single (co-hab)
Barbara	sales assistant	35	2	married
Beth	kitchen assistant	43	1	married
Brenda	catering assistant	38	2	married (2nd)
Carol	sales assistant	33	2	married
Caroline	deputy supervisor (sales)	33	2	married (2nd)
Cathy	domestic supervisor	34	3	divorced (twice)
Cheryl	sales assistant	36	2	married
Christine	pricing clerk	38	2	married
Clare	sales assistant	39	1	married
Dawn	sales assistant	41	3	married
Doreen	clerical officer	43	4 (1 died)	married

* all ages
** no natural children, cares for her co-habitant's two children.

name	current job	age	no. of children*	marital status
Elizabeth	n/a	30	2	married (2nd)
Frances	(student teacher)	32	2	separated
Gail	assistant manager (building society)	30	1	married (2nd)
Geraldine	computer clerk	35	1	married
Heather	supervisor (sales)	32	2	married
Helen	domestic supervisor	43	3	married
Hilary	hospital domestic	32	3	divorced
Jackie	secretary	28	2	divorced
Jane	hospital domestic	35	4 (1 died)	divorced
Jenny	supply teacher	27	2	married
June	caretaker & childminder	36	3 (1 died)	married (2nd)
Kate	hospital domestic	34	4	separated (3rd)
Linda	sales assistant	42	2	married
Lorna	supervisor (sales)	33	1	married
Louise	secretary & clerical assistant	28	1	married
Lucy	sales assistant	38	3	married
Lynne	hospital domestic	25	4	married
Margaret	sales assistant	34	1	married
Margery	sales assistant	29	1	married
Maria	hospital domestic	29	3 (1 died)	divorced
Marion	domestic supervisor	25	1	married
Mary	clerical assistant	39	2	married
Maureen	secretary	31	2	married
Mavis	food packer/butcher's assistant	28	1	single
Meryl	telecomms. officer	32	1	married (2nd)
Nancy	domestic supervisor	38	2	married
Olive	hospital domestic	43	3	married
Pat	hospital domestic	35	4	divorced (co-hab)
Paula	clerical officer	38	3 (1 died)	divorced
Penny	hospital domestic	42	2	divorced
Pru	hospital domestic	37	2	divorced (co-hab)
Rachel	word processor operator	41	1	married
Ruth	cost clerk	32	2	married

* all ages.

name	current job	age	no. of children*	marital status
Sally	clerical officer	34	2	married
Sandra	hospital domestic	38	3	married
Sara	clerical officer	37	3	married
Sheila	hospital domestic	39	2	married
Shirley	sales assistant	25	1	married
Susan	clerical officer	44	3	divorced (*twice*)
Teresa	deputy supervisor (sales)	44	2	married
Tessa	telephonist	32	2	married (*2nd*)
Tina	catering supervisor	41	3	married
Tracey	kitchen assistant	35	2	separated
Valerie	accounts supervisor	39	3	married
Wanda	driver & car-washer	28	2 (1 adopted)	married
Wendy	sales assistant	37	1	married (*2nd*)
Yvonne	hospital domestic	33	2	married

* all ages.

Notes

CHAPTER 1

1.   The nature of these tasks has varied historically. See e.g. Oakley (1981) who discusses this point in her chapter on 'Domestic Work'.

2.   Baines (1970) estimated that over half a million women and juveniles were employed in textile factories in the United Kingdom in 1856. Pinchbeck (1981) demonstrates that girls aged under 20 were strongly represented among female textile employees.

3.   Turner (1962) refers to the 'unfair . . . disproportion between the wages paid to male and female domestic servants' (p.28). His evidence is confirmed elsewhere by McBride (1976) ('male servants' wages were almost double those of females' (p.50)) and by Horn (1975) whose account includes a detailed appendix on 'Domestic Servant Wage Rates'.

4.   The omissions and inadequacies of official employment data are well known. Seasonal workers, part-timers paid 'cash-in-hand', and home-

workers are amongst the women who work for money whose labour goes officially unrecorded. It is also notable that part-time employees who hold two or more jobs simultaneously may be recorded more than once, thus distorting figures on economic activity. Hunt (1980) has drawn attention to many of the deficiencies in the data on women at work, and has noted that the 'masculine concept of employment' used in collecting statistics, and the 'non-collection of data' are both serious problems which lead to unreliability.

5.   Figures from Department of Employment. In both the cases given, the 1979 figure is slightly lower than the high point, the 1977 figure.

6.   Health Service statistics for 1979 showed 815,928 whole-time equivalents in England, 48,221 in Wales, and 123,230 in Scotland. Since many employees, especially women, work less than 'whole-time', the number of actual employees is in each case considerably larger. (Department of Health and Social Security 1982; Welsh Office 1980; Scottish Office 1983).

7.   Notably in agriculture, cottage industries, and to some extent in mines, where whole families would perform labour for one wage, legally the property of the husband.

CHAPTER 2

1.   This assumption was partly responsible for some of the theoretical inadequacy of this type of analysis. Alternative views of the pre-industrial family can be found in Anderson 1980; Laslett and Wall (eds) 1972; Mitterauer and Sieder 1982; Shorter 1977; and Stone 1979.

2.   There has recently been some revival of this concern, expressed for example in public statements by members of the 1979 and 1983 Conservative Governments.

3.   The present author shares many of the concerns of those writers whose studies are discussed here. Theoretical differences between their work and the present study are outlined later in the chapter.

4.   Edwards has noted that 'new research has argued persuasively for distinctions among not two but three labour market segments — the "secondary" labour market, the "subordinate primary" labour market and the "independent primary" labour market' (Edwards 1979:166). The distinction between a subordinated and independent primary market offers a useful analytical refinement to the theory. While jobs in both retain the features of relatively high wages, job security, and some kind of promotional 'ladder', 'subordinate primary jobs are distinguished from independent primary jobs in that their work tasks are repetitive, routinised, and subject to machine pacing' (Edwards 1979:172).

5.   See discussion of occupational segregation in Chapter 1.

6.   In his analysis of capitalist production, Marx identifies the relationship between the owners of capital and the owners of 'mere labour-power'. In order to subsist, the worker must sell labour-power to the capitalist, in exchange for which capital is paid in the form of wages. The capitalist's opportunity to accumulate profit rests on his or her ability to control the

labour process in such a way that surplus value is extracted from the worker. It is around the amount of this surplus value that struggle between workers and capitalists revolves. And while it is in the capitalist's interest to maximize the amount of actual labour each worker produces, since wages are paid for labour-power (not labour itself), it is in the worker's interest to minimize it. For Marx, there is a minimum level below which wages cannot fall unless they are supplemented by some other income. (A modern example might be the use of Family Income Supplement to offset low wages.) Equally, there is a maximum level above which profits cannot rise (Marx 1950). Thus struggle between wage-labourers and capitalists is not confined to bargaining over wages and working hours, but frequently centres upon control of the labour process itself. Braverman (1974) whose analysis of de-skilling has developed this concept, examines changes in the capitalist organization of the labour process and shows that, contrary to popular belief, technological advances in the workplace have not resulted in a general 'upgrading' of the working population. Rather, the modern capitalist economy relies upon a 'giant mass of workers', in offices, factories, the retail trade and the service occupations, who are 'relatively homogenous as to lack of developed skill, low pay, and interchangeability of person and function'. The present study provides illustrations of female workers who bear all these characteristics. In subsequent feminist work on sex and skill, Phillips and Taylor have demonstrated that 'skill is often an ideological category imposed on certain types of work by virtue of the sex and power of the workers who perform it' (1980:79), and have suggested that Braverman's analysis can profitably be extended by examination of tensions between male and female workers.

Marx's concept of productive and unproductive labour has also been identified as relevant to any analysis of female labour under capitalism. 'Productive labour' produces surplus value for capital. Clearly women engaged as wage-labourers in profit-making organizations produce surplus value, but what about unpaid domestic labour? If it is not 'productive' then domestic labourers cannot be subject to exploitation (through the extraction of surplus value) in the same way as wage-labourers.

Engels, for whom the economic and social position of women was more central, saw the wife in the monogamous family as the equivalent of the proletariat, and the husband as of the bourgeois. This analysis led him to draw the well-known conclusion that 'the first condition for the liberation of the wife is to bring the whole female sex back into public industry' (Engels 1972:137). However, as Delmar has noted, 'Engels's work does not contain any criticism of the sexual division of labour . . . . This failure . . . marks the break between Engels's analysis [and that of classical socialism] and the feminist perspective' (Delmar 1976:285).

Feminist analysis of social relations has a long history reaching back way beyond the present century. It has long been acknowledged that women as a group have been subject to the control, exploitation, and oppression of men as a group, both in the 'private' sphere of personal and family relations, and in the 'public' sphere of wider social and economic life. In recent decades, however, the radical feminists have developed and elaborated a theory of ideology, essentially a theory of patriarchy, which seeks to provide a more complete analysis of women's oppression than was previously attempted. Millett (1977) has pointed to the especially powerful *economic* hold which men have over women, the nature of which is to be found in men's control over female labour-power (a point also made by Hartmann). Because women labour in both capitalist and non-capitalist societies, and because women's productive (and reproductive) labour is subject to male control both in the private and the public spheres, the central focus for radical feminist analysis becomes the specific ways in which men oppress women, and in which they maintain and recreate their system of oppression. Thus capitalism is not the important object of analysis, since it is but another in a series of economic systems in which women's oppression takes place. For radical feminists, the point is to develop theoretical understanding which will enable women first to resist, and later to overcome, male oppression; this involves analysis of psychological processes just as much as of historical and material ones.

7.   Engels's expectation that sexual inequality would disappear as women were drawn into capitalist production as individual wage labourers, and radical feminism's attempt to explain all human history in terms of relations between the sexes are examples of such difficulties (given by Hartmann 1976).

8.   The word 'patriarchy' has been used extensively and often loosely in feminist writings. In my view it is most useful when used to refer to an ideology of male dominance and female subordination. Critical accounts of the term's use are available elsewhere (e.g. Rowbotham 1981) and I will not repeat those arguments here. Rowbotham, however, makes the critical observation that the term 'implies a structure which is fixed', and it is precisely to avoid this implication that I have referred here not to 'patriarchy' but to 'patriarchal capitalism'. Patriarchal structures and values — the material and ideological mechanisms whereby women are subordinated to men — are amongst the most salient features of modern capitalist societies such as Britain, and I use the term here to emphasize this fact.

9.   For Marx, a 'relatively redundant' or 'surplus' population is both a product and a necessary condition of capital accumulation. He explains:

'The characteristic course of modern industry . . . depends on the continuous formation, the greater or less absorption, and the reconstitution of the industrial reserve army. . . . Thus the whole movement of modern industry is characterised by the continuous transformation of part of the working population into unemployed or into half-timers.'
(Marx 1930:698-99)

Because developments in capitalist production enable employers to improve the effectiveness with which they can exploit individual labour-power, they are able to buy more labour-power by systematically replacing 'skilled workers by unskilled, mature labour-power by immature, men by women, grown-ups by young persons or children' (Marx 1930:702). In

Marx's view, it is the variation in the size of the industrial reserve army which regulates the movement of wages. Marx identifies three categories of surplus labour. The 'floating' category consists of workers in industrial centres who 'are sometimes repelled, and sometimes attracted in great numbers' (Marx 1930:708). The 'latent' category consists of a surplus agricultural population, which is forced by a decreasing demand for its agricultural labour to seek employment in the cities. Finally, the 'stagnant' surplus population is made up of workers who are only very irregularly in employment, and whose extreme poverty makes them especially vulnerable to exploitation.

10.   Braverman turns to Marx's categories of surplus population in explaining this phenomenon:

'These two opposing statistical movements of male and female workers are contradictory in form only. In essence they represent two sides of the same phenomenon, the increase in the relative mass of the industrial reserve army. Among male workers this takes the form of a sloughing off into the ranks of the so-called nonparticipants in the labor force, or in other words an increase of the "stagnant" portion. Among female workers it takes the form of a growing body of female labor which is drawn from the mass of women who previously did not work, and hence represents an enlargement of the "floating" and "stagnant" reserve army of labor by additional hundreds of thousands and even millions each year. As the available pool of unemployed labor is expanded among men by their relative *repulsion* from industry and trade, it is expanded even more among women by their increasing *attraction* into industry and trade.'

(Braverman 1974:391-92)

11.   See Kaluzynska (1980) and Molyneux (1979) for accounts of how the 'domestic labour debate' (as it has come to be known) has been developed and elaborated over the past decade.

12.   See Edholm, Harris, and Young (1977) for a detailed discussion of various analytical uses of the term 'reproduction'. Referring to the reproduction of the labour force, these authors note: 'human reproduction can obviously be subsumed for general theoretical purposes under the general notion of reproduction of the labour force, but for the specific analysis of women's situation, the two must be kept separate' (Edholm, Harris, and Young 1977:110-11).

13.   Hartmann (1979) has recently drawn attention to Dalla Costa's demand that wages should be paid for housework, arguing both that the demand raised women's consciousness about 'the importance of house-work', and that its basis in 'the claim that women at home not only provide essential services for capital by reproducing the labour force, but also create surplus value through that work' prompted the debate about the relationship between domestic labour and capital (Hartmann 1979:5).

14.   See Land (1980) for discussion of the family wage. Barrett and McIntosh (1980) have argued that 'the relegation of women to the home cannot be explained solely with reference to the "needs" of capital, but was

the object of struggle, and therefore choice, of the working class' (Barrett and McIntosh 1980:53).
15.   Allen (1982) discusses the persistence of women's waged work in the home in Britain.

CHAPTER 3

1.   Field's (1981) chapter on 'The Poor' includes sections on single-parent families and the low paid which discuss this point. Townsend contains sections on one-parent families (Townsend 1979:753-83) and on 'The Failure of Family Income Supplement' (Townsend 1979:633-34). In the chapter on 'The Incidence of Poverty', he notes: 'Women were at a disadvantage at most, but not all, ages. The proportion of women in poverty was higher than that of men at all ages except under 15, and on the margins of poverty, higher at all ages except 30-44' (Townsend 1979:285).
2.   Recent data on the phenomenon in Britain include Sedley and Benn (1982), Cairncross (1982b), Rendel (1982). In addition, the BBC broadcast a programme on sexual harassment in its '*File on 4*' series (28 July 1982), and ran a debate on the issue in its series '*You, the jury*' (Radio 4, 16 August 1982).
3.   The Employment Protection Act (1975) introduced six weeks' paid maternity leave for women employed for 16 or more hours per week who have been with their employer for at least two years, and a right to reinstatement in their jobs for up to twenty-nine weeks after confinement. This law came into force in June 1976. Before this, some trade unions had negotiated collective agreements with employers which provided for maternity leave and reinstatement.
4.   Louise married before the Sex Discrimination Act came into effect (29 December 1975). It was not possible to check her allegation that she was effectively dismissed on marriage to another employee, but this practice is known to have existed elsewhere and has been successfully challenged under the Act, in the case of *McLean v. Paris Travel Service Ltd* (Coussins 1976:65).
5.   At this time (1978) abortions could be performed legally up to twenty-eight weeks of pregnancy, under the Abortion Act (1967). If this account is correct, the difference between ten and sixteen weeks was significant, since the vast majority of abortions are carried out before the twelfth week of pregnancy (80 per cent in 1978).
6.   An attempt to analyse why the women described did not conform to normative expectations concerning personal relationships, or had particular health problems, was beyond the scope of the study. However, such characteristics do not occur randomly in the population, nor are they simply accidents of fate or a matter of luck, as shown by evidence from both the sociology of marriage and the family, and the sociology of health and illness.
7.   At the time (August 1980) a single parent with one child needed to be

in paid employment for at least 24 hours per week, and to have a total income of less than a prescribed level of £56 per week to be eligible for Family Income Supplement. The benefit was calculated at half the amount by which income fell short of the prescribed level, with a maximum payment of £13.60 (information supplied by Department of Health and Social Security).

8.   Hilary's view receives support in recent work on clinical depression in women (Brown and Harris 1978). The authors identify four factors indicating vulnerability to clinical depression: 'loss of mother before eleven, presence at home of three or more children under fourteen, absence of a confiding relationship, particularly with a husband, and lack of a full- or part-time job' (Brown and Harris 1978:235-36). At the time, all but the first of these applied to Hilary. Brown and Harris note: 'We were particularly interested in a few of the women who took up employment *after* the occurrence of a severe event, none of whom developed depression. One working class woman...commented that...it "gave me a great boost" and "greater self-esteem" ' (Brown and Harris 1978:236). As they suggest, see also Gavron (1968), Oakley (1974b), and Ginsberg (1976).

9.   See Freeman (1982:146–47) for discussion of 'unofficial bargains' between women workers and management.

CHAPTER 4

1.   Material from the author's article 'Variation and Flexibility: Key Characteristics of Female Labour' (*Sociology* **16** (3), August 1982) is reproduced here with permission.

2.   The headings were: clerical and secretarial, sales, domestic and catering, hairdressing, communications, factory (manual), childcare and au pair, nursing, agricultural, waitressing and bar work, delivery and driving, demonstrating, teaching, junior managerial, technical, market research, miscellaneous.

3.   As opposed to the definition normally used in government statistics, of over 30 hours per week.

4.   See, for example, Hurstfield (1980), Sedley (1980), Hope, Kennedy, and de Winter (1976), and Allen (1982).

5.   The figure given is for April 1980 onwards, as the store gave its employees a pay rise at that time. The comparable figure in January 1980 was £1.35.

6.   These figures refer to average gross hourly earnings excluding the effects of overtime, for employees aged 18 and over.

7.   Throughout the company, part-timers worked an average of approximately 18 hours per week, although there was substantial variation from this figure.

8.   Writers on part-time employment have recently stated that benefits can accrue to employers. Leicester (1982) notes that 'both foreseen and additional benefits accrue to firm and workers alike' when job-sharing is

introduced, and Robertson and Briggs (1979) maintain that part-time work 'has economic advantages for both employees and employers'. The Equal Opportunities Commission (1981b) documents 'Potential benefits for the employer' in its pamphlet on job-sharing, and points out in a footnote that studies of job-sharing in the USA document 'an increase in productivity' (Equal Opportunities Commission 1981b:34,n.26).

9.   Walker has observed: 'Between 1974 and 1980, male unemployment has roughly doubled, while the numbers of women registered as unemployed has increased fivefold. For example, between 1974 and 1978, in the manufacturing industry, men lost 5 per cent of their jobs and women 9 per cent. The worst affected were part-time workers. In electrical engineering, 38,000 jobs were lost, but 18,000 were part-time jobs held by women — a 40 per cent loss for female employees compared with 5 per cent for males' (Walker 1981:22-3).

10.   Much has been written about the likely impact of new technology on employment. See for example Bird (1980), Gershuny (1978), Jenkins and Sherman (1979) and SPRU Women and Technology Studies (1982).

11.   See Coote and Campbell (1982:84-7) for discussion of how 'The Tories seized the initiative in reconstructing the family in popular ideology' — followed in 1978 by the Labour Prime Minister, James Callaghan.

12.   I.e. no money changed hands.

13.   If Maureen had been with this employer for twenty-six weeks, she would almost certainly have been entitled to bring a case of unfair dismissal under the Employment Protection Act (1975). I am not sure whether she had been wrongly advised, or whether the figures she gave were incorrect — perhaps she had been in the job for only twenty-four weeks?

CHAPTER 5

1.   This was entirely as expected, since other researchers have been similarly unsuccessful in tracking down this (mythical?) species.

2.   Only about one in six of the women reported that they cared (or had cared) for elderly relatives on a regular basis. For most of these, the caring was either short-term (e.g. during an acute illness), periodic (e.g. having parents to stay two or three times a year), or involved only duties such as shopping and taking to hospital. Of the remainder, two-thirds reported that they had never had to care for relatives in any way, and one-third that they were occasionally called on for assistance on a temporary basis. This low incidence of caring can mainly be attributed to age: as most of the respondents were in their thirties, the majority of them did not have elderly or infirm parents or in-laws.

3.   Thirteen of the women were contacted through a childminding association and three through a day nursery.

4.   The term homeworking is used to describe all work done for money within the home.

5.   It is sometimes argued that although, for example, washing machines reduce the labour of washing clothes and linen, their widespread

distribution has coincided with the development of higher standards of cleanliness, so that overall, the labour of the task has not been reduced by the new product.

CHAPTER 6

1.   Work on these topics is known to be in progress in South Wales (Lydia Morris) and the Midlands (Colin Bell and Lorna McKee).

APPENDIX 1

1.   The statistics included in this section are taken from *Kent Structure Plan, 1st Annual Monitoring Report 1978 (KCC)* and from detailed figures made available to the author by the Planning Department (KCC) (Springfield) in May 1981, by kind permission of the County Planning Officer. See also note 4 to Chapter 1.

2.   E.g. the *Kent Structure Plan 1st Annual Monitoring Report* (1978) contains a table entitled 'Unemployment and Unfilled Vacancies by Sector, July 1977, by grouped Employment Exchange Areas (Males and Females)'.

References

Alexander, S. (1976) Women's Work in Nineteenth-Century London: A Study of the Years 1820-1850. In J. Mitchell and A. Oakley (eds) *The Rights and Wrongs of Women*. Harmondsworth, Middlx: Penguin Books.

Allen, S. (1982) Waged Labour in the Home: the Myth of the Separation of Home and Work for Women in Britain. In K. Hvidtfeldt, K. Jørgensen, and R. Nielsen (eds) *Strategies for Integrating Women into the Labour Market*. Denmark: Women's Research Centre in Social Science.

Amsden, A.H. (ed.) (1980) *The Economics of Women and Work*. Harmondsworth, Middlx: Penguin Books.

Anderson, M. (1980) The Relevance of Family History. In M. Anderson (ed.) *Sociology of the Family: Selected Readings* (2nd edn). Harmondsworth, Middlx: Penguin Books.

Aries, P. (1962) *Centuries of Childhood*. London: Jonathan Cape.

Bailyn, L. (1970) Career and Family Orientations of Husbands and Wives in Relation to Marital Happiness. *Human Relations* 23: 97-113.

Bain, G.S. and Price, R. (1972) Union Growth and Employment Trends in the United Kingdom 1964-1970. *British Journal of Industrial Relations* 10 (3): 366-81.

Baines, E. (1970) The Woollen Manufacture of England, with Special Reference to the Leeds Clothing District (first published 1875). In K.G. Ponting (ed.) *Baines's Account of the Woollen Manufacture of England*. Newton Abbot: David & Charles.

Barker, D.L. and Allen, S. (1976) *Dependence and Exploitation in Work and Marriage*. Harlow: Longman.

Barrett, M. (1980) *Women's Oppression Today: Problems in Marxist Feminist Analysis*. London: Verso.

Barrett, M. and McIntosh, M. (1980) The 'Family Wage': Some Problems for Socialists and Feminists. *Capital and Class* 11 (Summer): 51-72.

Barron, R.D. and Norris, G.M. (1976) Sexual Divisions and the Dual Labour Market. In D. Barker and S. Allen (eds) *Dependence and Exploitation in Work and Marriage*. Harlow: Longman.

Beechey, V. (1977) Some Notes on Female Wage Labour in Capitalist Production. *Capital and Class* **3**: 45-66.
—— (1978) Women and Production: A Critical Analysis of Some Sociological Theories of Women's Work. In A. Kuhn and A. Wolpe (eds) *Feminism and Materialism*. London: Routledge & Kegan Paul.
Benett, Y. and Carter, D. (1982) Knocking the Opportunity: How Girls end up in Jobs they don't Want. *Employment Gazette* **90** (4): 167–71.
Bird, E. (1980) *Information Technology in the Office: the Impact on Women's Jobs*. Manchester: Equal Opportunities Commission.
Blaxall, M. and Reagan, B. (eds) (1976) *Women and the Workplace: the Implications of Occupational Segregation*. Chicago and London: University of Chicago Press.
Blood, R.O. (1963) The Husband-Wife Relationship. In F.I. Nye and L.W. Hoffman (eds) *The Employed Mother in America*. Chicago: Rand McNally.
Booth, C. (1886) Occupations of the People of the United Kingdom, 1801-81. *Journal of the Statistical Society* **49**: 314-435.
Boston, S. (1980) *Women Workers and the Trade Union Movement*. London: Davis-Poynter.
Bowlby, J. (1951) *Maternal Care and Mental Health*. Geneva: World Health Organisation.
—— (1953) *Childcare and the Growth of Love*. Harmondsworth, Middlx: Penguin Books.
Braverman, H. (1974) *Labor and Monopoly Capital*. New York and London: Monthly Review Press.
Braybon, G. (1981) *Women Workers in the First World War: the British Experience*. London: Croom Helm.
Brown, G.W. and Harris, T. (1978) *Social Origins of Depression — a Study of Psychiatric Disorder in Women*. London: Tavistock Publications.
Bruegel, I. (1979) Women as a Reserve Army of Labour: a Note on Recent British Experience. *Feminist Review* **3**: 12-23.
Burghes, L. and Lister, R. (eds) (1981) *Unemployment: Who Pays the Price?* London: Child Poverty Action Group.
Cairncross, F. (1982a) The Hand that Rocks the Cradle Could Rule Industry. *The Guardian* 29 March: 10.
—— (1982b) Sexual Blackmail at Work. *The Guardian* 23 June: 10.
Cavendish, R. (1982) *Women on the Line*. London and Boston: Routledge & Kegan Paul.
Chaney, J. (1981) *Social Networks and Job Information: the Situation of Women who Return to Work*. London: Equal Opportunities Commission and Social Science Research Council.
Chiplin, B. and Sloane, P.J. (1976) *Sex Discrimination in the Labour Market*. London: Macmillan.
Chodorow, N. (1978) *The Reproduction of Mothering: Psychoanalysis and the Sociology of Gender*. Berkeley, Calif. and London: University of California Press.
Clark, A. (1920) *The Working Life of Women in the Seventeenth Century*. New York: Harcourt, Brace, & Howe.

Cole, G.D.H. (1948) *A Short History of the British Working Class Movement, 1787-1947*. London: George Allen & Unwin.

Collet, C. (1902) Women's Work. In C. Booth, *et al. Life and Labour of the People of London*, First Series, *Poverty* vol. 4, 'The Trades of East London Connected with Poverty'.

Conran, S. (1977) *Superwoman*. Harmondsworth, Middlx: Penguin Books.

Coote, A. (1979) *Equal at Work? Women in Men's Jobs*. Glasgow and London: Collins.

Coote, A. and Campbell, B. (1982) *Sweet Freedom: The Struggle for Women's Liberation*. London: Pan Books.

Coote, A. and Kellner, P. (1980) *Hear this, Brother: Women Workers and Union Power*. London: New Statesman.

Coussins, J. (1976) *The Equality Report*. London: National Council for Civil Liberties.

Daniel, W.W. (1980) Women's Experience of Maternity Rights Legislation. *Employment Gazette* **88** (5): 468-71.

Davies, R. (1975) *Women and Work*. London: Hutchinson.

Delmar, R. (1976) Looking again at Engels' 'Origin of the Family, Private Property and the State'. In J. Mitchell and A. Oakley (eds) *The Rights and Wrongs of Women*. Harmondsworth, Middlx: Penguin Books.

Department of Employment (1973-1980) *New Earnings Survey*. London: HMSO.

—— (1984) *Employment Gazette* **92** (1).

Department of Employment and Productivity (1971) *British Labour Statistics Historical Abstract 1886-1968*. London: HMSO.

Department of Health and Social Security (1982) *Health and Personal Social Services Statistics for England*. London: HMSO.

Derow, E.O. (1982) Childcare and Employment: Mothers' Perspectives. In K. Hvidtfeldt, K. Jørgensen, and R. Nielsen (eds) *Strategies for Integrating Women into the Labour Market*. Denmark: Women's Research Centre in Social Science.

Edholm, F., Harris, O., and Young, K. (1977) Conceptualising Women. *Critique of Anthropology* (Women's Issue) **3** (9-10): 101-30.

Edwards, R. (1979) *Contested Terrain: the Transformation of the Workplace in the Twentieth Century*. New York: Basic Books.

Edwards, R., Reich, M., and Gordon, D. (1975) *Labor Market Segmentation*. Lexington, Mass.: D.C. Heath.

Eisenstein, Z. (1979) *Capitalist Patriarchy and the Case for Socialist Feminism*. New York: Monthly Review Press.

Engels, F. (1972) *The Origin of the Family, Private Property and the State*. London: Lawrence & Wishart.

Epstein, C. (1971) Law Partners and Marital Partners. *Human Relations* **124** (6): 549-64.

Equal Opportunities Commission (1980) *Women and Government Statistics*. Research Bulletin No. 4. London: HMSO.

—— (1981a) *Fifth Annual Report/1980*. London: HMSO.

—— (1981b) *Job-sharing: Improving the Quality and Availability of Part-time Work*. Manchester: EOC.

Evans, M. and Ungerson, C. (eds) (1983) *Sexual Divisions: Patterns and Processes*. London: Tavistock Publications.

Field, F. (1981) *Inequality in Britain: Freedom, Welfare and the State*. London: Fontana.

Fonda, N. and Moss, P. (eds) (1976) *Mothers in Employment*. Brunel University.

Freeman, C. (1982) The Understanding Employer. In J. West (ed.) *Work, Women and the Labour Market*. London and Boston: Routledge & Kegan Paul.

Gardiner, J., Himmelweit, S., and Mackintosh, M. (1975) Women's Domestic Labour. *Bulletin of the Conference of Socialist Economists* **IV**/2 (11).

Gavron, H. (1968) *The Captive Wife*. Harmondsworth, Middlx: Penguin Books.

Gershuny, J. (1978) *After Industrial Society? The Emerging Self-Service Economy*. London: Macmillan.

Ginsberg, S. (1976) Women, Work and Conflict. In N. Fonda and P. Moss (eds) *Mothers in Employment*. Brunel University.

Goldberg, M. (1970) The Economic Exploitation of Women. *Review of Radical Political Economics* **2** (1): 35-46.

Hakim, C. (1978) Sexual Divisions within the Labour Force: Occupational Segregation. *Department of Employment Gazette* **86** (11): 1264-279.

—— (1979) *Occupational Segregation: A Comparative Study of the Degree and Pattern of the Differentiation between Men and Women's Work in Britain, the United States and Other Countries*. Research Paper No. 9. London: Department of Employment.

—— (1980) Homeworking: Some New Evidence. *Employment Gazette* **88** (10): 1105-1110.

—— (1981) Job Segregation: Trends in the 1970s. *Employment Gazette* **89** (12): 521-29.

Harloe, M. and Lebas, E. (eds) (1981) *City, Class and Capital*. London: Edward Arnold.

Hartmann, H. (1976) Capitalism, Patriarchy, and Job Segregation by Sex. In M. Blaxall and B. Reagan (eds) *Women and the Workplace: the Implications of Occupational Segregation*. Chicago and London: University of Chicago Press.

—— (1979a) Capitalism, Patriarchy, and Job Segregation by Sex. In Z. Eisenstein (ed.) *Capitalist Patriarchy and the Case for Socialist Feminism*. New York: Monthly Review Press.

—— (1979b) The Unhappy Marriage of Marxism and Feminism: Towards a more Progressive Union. *Capital and Class* **8**: 1-34.

—— (1981a) The Unhappy Marriage of Marxism and Feminism: Towards a more Progressive Union. In L. Sargent (ed.) *Women and Revolution: A Discussion of the Unhappy Marriage of Marxism and Feminism*. London: Pluto Press.

—— (1981b) The Family as the Locus of Gender, Class and Political Struggle: the Example of Housework. *Signs* **6** (3): 336-94.

Hedges, J.N. and Barnett, J.K. (1972) Working Women and the Division of

Household Tasks. *Monthly Labor Review* **95** (4).

Hoffman, L.W. (1963) Effects on the Children: Summary and Discussion. In F.I. Nye and L.W. Hoffman (eds) *The Employed Mother in America*. Chicago: Rand McNally.

Hope, E., Kennedy, M., and de Winter, A. (1976) Homeworkers in North London. In D.L. Barker and S. Allen (eds) *Dependence and Exploitation in Work and Marriage*. Harlow: Longman.

Horn, P. (1975) *The Rise and Fall of the Victorian Servant*. Dublin: Gill & Macmillan.

Hunt, A. (1975) *Management Attitudes and Practices Towards Women at Work*. London: Office of Population Censuses and Surveys, HMSO.

—— (1980) Some Gaps and Problems Arising from Government Statistics on Women at Work. In Equal Opportunities Commission *Research Bulletin No. 4: Women and Government Statistics*. London: HMSO.

Hurstfield, J. (1980) Part-time Pittance. *Low Pay Review* **1**: 1-15.

Hvidtfeldt, K., Jørgensen, K., and Nielsen, R. (eds) (1982) *Strategies for Integrating Women into the Labour Market*. Denmark: Women's Research Centre in Social Science.

Iglehart, A.P. (1979) *Married Women and Work, 1957 and 1976*. Lexington, Mass.: D.C. Heath & Co.

Jenkins, C. and Sherman, B. (1979) *The Collapse of Work*. London: Eyre Methuen.

Kaluzynska, E. (1980) Wiping the Floor with Theory — a Survey of Writings on Housework. *Feminist Review* **6**: 27-54.

Kent County Council (1978) *Kent Structure Plan, First Annual Monitoring Report*. Maidstone: Kent County Council.

Klein, V. (1965) *Britain's Married Women Workers*. London: Routledge & Kegan Paul.

Land, H. (1980) The Family Wage. *Feminist Review* **6**: 55-77.

Lasch, C. (1977) *Haven in a Heartless world: the Family Beseiged*. New York: Basic Books.

Laslett, P. and Wall, R. (eds) (1972) *Household and Family in Past Time*. Cambridge: Cambridge University Press.

Leicester, C. (1982) Towards a Fully Part-time Britain. *Personnel Management* **14** (6): 28-31.

Lewenhak, S. (1980) *Women and Work*. London: Fontana.

Lister, R. and Wilson, L. (1976) *The Unequal Breadwinner: A New Perspective on Women and Social Security*. London: National Council for Civil Liberties.

McBride, T.M. (1976) *The Domestic Revolution*. London: Croom Helm.

Mackie, L. and Pattullo, P. (1977) *Women and Work*. London: Tavistock Publications.

McNally, F. (1979) *Women for Hire: a Study of the Female Office Worker*. London: Macmillan.

McNay, M. and Pond, C. (1980) *Low Pay and Family Poverty*. London: Study Commission on the Family.

Mallier, T. and Rosser, M. (1979) The Changing Role of Women in the British Economy. *National Westminster Bank Quarterly Review* (November): 54-65.

Manley, P. and Sawbridge, D. (1980) Women at Work. *Lloyds Bank Review* **135**: 29-40.

Marx, K. (1930) *Capital*. London: Dent.

—— (1950) Wages, Prices, and Profit. In K. Marx and F. Engels *Selected Works*, vol. I. London: Lawrence & Wishart.

Millett, K. (1977) *Sexual Politics*. London: Virago.

Mitchell, J. and Oakley, A. (1976) *The Rights and Wrongs of Women*. Harmondsworth, Middlx: Penguin Books.

Mitterauer, M. and Sieder, R. (1982) *The European Family: Patriarchy to Partnership from the Middle Ages to the Present*, trans. K. Oosterveen and M. Hörzinger. Oxford: Basil Blackwell.

Molyneux, M. (1979) Beyond the Domestic Labour Debate. *New Left Review* **116**: 3-27.

Myrdal, A. and Klein, V. (1956) *Women's Two Roles*. London and Boston: Routledge & Kegan Paul.

Novarra, V. (1980) *Men's Work, Women's Work: the Ambivalence of Equality*. London: Marion Boyars.

Nye, F.I. and Hoffman, L.W. (eds) (1963) *The Employed Mother in America*. Chicago: Rand McNally.

Oakley, A. (1974a) *Housewife*. London: Allen Lane.

—— (1974b) *The Sociology of Housework*. London: Martin Robertson.

—— (1981) *Subject Women*. Oxford: Martin Robertson.

Office of Population Censuses and Surveys (1971) *Census of Population 1971*. London: HMSO.

—— (1982) *OPCS Monitor*. London: HMSO.

Oppenheimer, V.K. (1970) *The Female Labor Force in the United States*. Berkeley, Calif. and London: University of California Press.

Pahl, R.E. (1981) Employment, Work and the Domestic Division of Labour. In M. Harloe and E. Lebas (eds) *City, Class and Capital*. London: Edward Arnold.

Pelling, H. (1971) *A History of British Trade Unionism* (2nd edn). Harmondsworth, Middlx: Penguin Books.

Phillips, A. and Taylor (1980) Sex and Skill: Notes Towards a Feminist Economics. *Feminist Review* **6**: 78-88.

Pinchbeck, I. (1981) *Women Workers and the Industrial Revolution 1750-1850* (3rd edn). London: Virago.

Pollert, A. (1981) *Girls, Wives, Factory Lives*. London: Macmillan.

Poloma, N. (1972) Role Conflict and the Married Professional Woman. In C. Safilios-Rothschild (ed.) *Towards a Sociology of Women*. Lexington Mass.: Xerox College Publishing.

Ponting, K.G. (ed.) (1970) *Baines's Account of the Woollen Manufacture of England*. Newton Abbot: David & Charles.

Rapoport, R. and Rapoport, R. (1971) *Dual Career Families*. Harmondsworth, Middlx: Penguin Books.

—— (1976) *Dual Career Families Re-Examined*. London: Martin Robertson.

Rendel, M. (1978) Legislating for Equal Pay and Opportunity for Women in Britain. *Signs* **3** (4):897-908.

—— (1982) Sexist and Sexual Harassment in Education, Training and

Employment. In K. Hvidtfeldt, K. Jørgensen, and R. Nielsen (eds) *Strategies for Integrating Women into the Labour Market.* Denmark: Women's Research Centre in Social Science.

Richards, J. Radcliffe (1982) *The Sceptical Feminist.* Harmondsworth, Middlx: Penguin Books.

Robertson, J.A.S. and Briggs, J.M. (1979) Part-time Working in Great Britain. *Department of Employment Gazette* **87** (7): 671-77.

Rowbotham, S. (1973) *Hidden from History.* London: Pluto Press.

—— .(1981) The Trouble with 'Patriarchy'. In R. Samuel (ed.) People's History and Socialist Theory. History Workshop Series. London: Routledge & Kegan Paul.

Rowland, V. (1981) *The Impact of Current Maternity Legislation.* Unpublished research report, jointly funded by the Equal Opportunities Commission and the Social Science Research Council.

Rubery, J. (1980) Structured Labour Markets, Worker Organisation and Low Pay. In A.H. Amsden (ed.) *The Economics of Women and Work.* Harmondsworth, Middlx: Penguin Books.

Ryan, M. (1981) Lee Jeans: How One Factory Fought Back. *New Socialist* **2** (November/December): 24-5.

Safilios-Rothschild, C. (ed.) (1972) *Towards a Sociology of Women.* Lexington, Mass.: Xerox College Publishing.

Scottish Office Information Services Division (1983) *Scottish Health Statistics 1981.* Edinburgh: HMSO.

Secombe, H. (1974) The Housewife and her Labour under Capitalism. In M. Anderson (ed.) *Sociology of the Family: Selected Readings* (2nd edn). Harmondsworth, Middlx: Penguin Books.

Sedley, A. (1980) *Part-time Workers Need Full-time Rights.* London: National Council for Civil Liberties, Rights for Women Unit.

Sedley, A. and Benn, M. (1982) *Sexual Harassment at Work.* London: National Council for Civil Liberties, Rights for Women Unit.

Shaw, J. (1983) Models of Learning and Their Role in Producing Educational Inequality. In M. Evans and C. Ungerson (eds) *Sexual Divisions: Patterns and Processes.* London: Tavistock Publications.

Shorter, E. (1977) *The Making of the Modern Family.* London: Fontana.

Sinfield, A. (1981) *What Unemployment Means.* Oxford: Martin Robertson.

Snell, M. (1979) The Equal Pay and Sex Discrimination Acts: the Impact in the Workplace. *Feminist Review* **1**: 37–57.

Spender, D. (1982) *Invisible Women: the Schooling Scandal.* London: Writers and Readers.

SPRU Women and Technology Studies (1982) *Microelectronics and Women's Employment in Britain.* Science Policy Research Unit, University of Sussex.

Stageman, J. (1980) *Women and Trade Unions.* Hull: Industrial Studies Unit, Adult Education Department, University of Hull.

Stone, L. (1979) *The Family, Sex and Marriage in England 1500-1800.* Harmondsworth, Middlx: Penguin Books.

Stromsheim, G. (1982) Part-time work as a Labour-market Phenomenon. In K. Hvidtfeldt, K. Jørgensen, and R. Nielsen (eds) *Strategies for*

Integrating Women into the Labour Market. Denmark: Women's Research Centre in Social Science.

Thompson, E.P. (1968) *The Making of the English Working Class*. Harmondsworth, Middlx: Penguin Books.

Thompson, F. (1973) *Lark Rise to Candleford*. Harmondsworth, Middlx: Penguin Books.

Tilly, L.A. and Scott, J.W. (1978) *Women, Work and Family*. New York: Holt, Rinehart, & Winston.

Townsend, P. (1979) *Poverty in the United Kingdom: a Survey of Household Resources and Standards of Living*. Harmondsworth, Middlx: Penguin Books.

Trades Union Congress Women's Advisory Committee (1980) *Part-time Workers*. Report for 1979-1980, Supplementary Report 1, 50th TUC Women's Conference.

Turner, E.S. (1962) *What the Butler Saw: Two Hundred and Fifty Years of the Servant Problem*. London: Michael Joseph.

Vanek, J. (1980) Time Spent in Housework. In A.H. Amsden (ed.) *The Economics of Women and Work*. Harmondsworth, Middlx: Penguin Books.

Walker, A. (1981) The Level and Distribution of Unemployment. In L. Burghes and R. Lister (eds) *Unemployment: Who Pays the Price?* London: Child Poverty Action Group.

Wandor, M. (ed.) (1970) *The Body Politic*. London: Stage One.

Welsh Office (1980) *Health and Personal Social Services Statistics for Wales*. Cardiff: HMSO.

West, J. (ed.) (1982) *Work, Women and the Labour Market*. London and Boston: Routledge & Kegan Paul.

Westergaard, J. and Resler, H. (1976) *Class in a Capitalist Society*. Harmondsworth, Middlx: Penguin Books.

Williams, J., Twort, H., and Bachelli, A. (1972) Women and the Family. In M. Wandor (ed.) *The Body Politic*. London: Stage One.

Yeandle, S.M. (1982) Variation and Flexibility: Key Characteristics of Female Labour. *Sociology* **16** (3): 422-30.

Young, M. and Willmott, P. (1973) *The Symmetrical Family*. London and Boston: Routledge & Kegan Paul.

Yudkin, S. and Holme, A. (1963) *Working Mothers and their Children: a Study for the Council on Children's Welfare*. London: Michael Joseph.

Zellner, H. (1972) Discrimination against Women, Occupational Segregation and the Relative Wage. *American Economic Review* **62**: 157-60.

Name index

Subject index

Note: pseudonyms of respondents in the study appear in quotations